Anti–Communism and Popular Culture
in Mid-Century America

Anti-Communism and Popular Culture in Mid-Century America

Cyndy Hendershot

McFarland & Company, Inc., Publishers

Jefferson, North Carolina, and London

Library of Congress Cataloguing-in-Publication Data

Hendershot, Cynthia.
   Anti-communism and popular culture in mid-century America /
Cyndy Hendershot.
       p.   cm.
   Includes bibliographical references and index.

   ISBN-13: 978-0-7864-1440-6
   softcover: 50# alkaline paper ∞

   1. Anti-communist movements— United States— History — 20th
century.   2. Popular culture — United States— History — 20th century.
3. Mass media — Political aspects— United States— History — 20th
century.   4. Cold War — Social aspects— United States.   5. United
States— Civilization —1945–   6. United States— Politics and
government —1953–1961.   7. United States— Politics and government —
1961–1963.   I. Title.
   E743.5 .H425   2003
   306'.0973'09045 — dc21   2002153824

British Library cataloguing data are available

On the front cover: imagery ©2002 PhotoSpin; inset, a scene from *The
27th Day* (1957)

Manufactured in the United States of America

McFarland & Company, Inc., Publishers
   Box 611, Jefferson, North Carolina 28640
   www.mcfarlandpub.com

For Antony with love

Acknowledgments

Thanks to Arkansas State University and the National Endowment for the Humanities for grants that made this book possible. Thanks to Jerry Ball for letting me use his archive of films and locating for me many of the films discussed in this book. As always thanks to Miss D., and to Antony, to whom the book is dedicated.

A version of Chapter One appeared in *Popular Culture Review* 12.1. A version of Chapter Five appeared in *Science-Fiction Studies* 28. Part of Chapter Nine appeared in *Journal of the Southwest* 41.4. A version of Chapter Ten appeared in *Paradoxa* 16. A version of Chapter Twelve appeared in *Journal of American and Comparative Cultures* 23.4

Contents

Introduction

In an address made at the American Legion Convention in Las Vegas in 1962, FBI Director J. Edgar Hoover characterized the Communist world in the following terms: "The communist world is a world of walls, searchlights, and guards—a prison for the heart, mind and soul" (*On Communism* 152). Hoover succinctly captured the image of the Communist society as it appeared to the anti–Communists of the Cold War, which held that, as a heavily guarded prison, the Communist world traps humanity, and subjects it to torture and brainwashing. Hoover's writings and speeches manifested a wealth of anti–Communist imagery. In his pamphlet "A Statement on Communism," Hoover argued that America "must recognize the Communist effort for what it is—an effort to inject poison into the bloodstream of America, to confuse, obscure, and distort America's vision of itself" (Hoover, *On Communism* 153). Here, the Communist world is pictured as a venomous creature infecting America. In remarks made at a *New York Herald Tribune* forum, Hoover forged a link between Communism and organized crime when he said, "Democracy is totally alien in deed and thought to the tactics of ruthless racketeering dictators" (*On Communism* 154). Hoover's writings and speeches illustrate a powerful strain of countersubversive anti–Communism that was a distinguishing feature of the Cold War Western stance. While by no means the only variety of anti–Communism prevalent in American life at mid-century, such countersubversive sentiment was perhaps the type best suited to dramatic representation in film, television, novels, and other popular forms of entertainment.[1]

Anti-Communist sentiment was widespread in American life from

1

the late Forties through the mid–Sixties, and, as pervasive as the sentiment was, it is not surprising that a variety of people and causes found opportunity to use the sentiment for their own particular ideological reasons. John Haynes points out that "Because dislike of communism was deep and broad among Americans, all sorts of groups with other agendas attempted to tie their programs to the anti–Communist cause." Among notable examples were educators—and even the interstate highway system labeled itself as "'defense highways' to speed the transport of troops and supplies" (183). As Haynes is quick to point out, however, the pervasiveness of anti–Communist feeling did not mean that the hysteria often associated with anti–Communist America was by any means equally pervasive (189). As this study will point out, popular culture's use of anti–Communist sentiment does indicate a pervasiveness of anti–Communism as a theme in popular representation, but the theme was manifested in a variety of ways: as it appeared in popular culture, it was not straitjacketed—it was not bound rigidly by any kind of monolithic ideology. Thus while the rhetorical language typical of Hoover is one element that characterizes popular culture's use of anti–Communism, depending upon the work, the word "anti–Communism" may have a variety of associated meanings and functions, including countersubversive propaganda, plot device, and object of parody.

In an interview published in *The Pilot* in 1956, Hoover commented that "Communism is a many-faced monster endeavoring to gain the allegiance of our citizens" (*On Communism* 64). Anti-Communist sentiment as expressed in popular culture primarily reacted to, explored, and militated against two of these faces: the external Communist, usually Soviet, and the internal Communist — the traitorous member of the American Communist Party (CP). By finding additional evidence of Communist threats, both internal and external, and then reiterating them, popular culture added a paranoiac dimension to these threats, which were, of course, already vibrant in its consumers' minds. Thus, though some aspects of real-life anti–Communism were paranoiac while others were not, the fictional worlds created by popular culture actually thrived on presentations of a paranoiac view of the Communist threat.[2]

One interesting aspect of popular culture's incorporation of this threat is the degree to which its projection was fashioned so it was seen to overlap with other threats of deep concern to mid-century American culture. Thus, the monster of Communism tended to conceal or at least divert people's attention from other demons thought to be at work in American society. One fear that dominated many representations of the Communist threat was in the link that was frequently forged between

J. Edgar Hoover, Director of the FBI and architect of much Cold War anti–Communist rhetoric. (Courtesy of the Library of Congress, Prints and Photographs Division, USZ62 123128.)

Communism and Nazism — and Hoover's words were instrumental in initiating and crystallizing this link. In an address given before the American Legion Convention, Hoover stated that "Both communism and fascism are the antithesis of American belief in liberty and democracy" (*On*

Communism 151). In the same vein, a Cold War Upjohn commercial linked Communism and Fascism by showing shots of Hitler, Mussolini, Tojo, and Stalin together and in stark contrast to American scientists. The narrator commented that America is a healthy and prosperous nation "thanks in part to the men who weren't shouting or marching, but just working quietly at Upjohn, hoping in their way to change things" (qtd. in Curtin 46).[3] Similarly, in *The Naked Communist*, W. Cleon Skousen traced the roots of Communism and Fascism back to a common source: Friedrich Nietzsche. Skousen stated that "In putting down National Socialism and the Axis we had only conquered one form of materialism. Another form, equally strong, immediately rose to take its place" (349). Thus, anti–Communist fears were frequently meshed with lingering World War II–era anxieties about Fascist dictatorships.

Other fears that were interwoven with and sometimes overlapped by fears of Communism in both nonfictional discourse and popular representation include nuclear war, organized crime, and juvenile delinquency. Perhaps the most striking aspect of anti–Communist rhetoric is how often it became a vehicle for criticizing internal weaknesses within the United States itself. Constant media reminders that there actually was a fully functioning Communist Party in America, combined with media representation and vilification of visible traitors such as the Rosenbergs, helped fuel the fear that Communism would take hold of the minds of Americans because they were weak and ripe for it. In his pamphlet "A Statement on Communism," Hoover, for example, identified weaknesses within the American system as a reason for the appeal of Communism to many Americans: "Yes, America does have many problems—serious problems. But the answer is not, as the communists assert, a destruction of what we hold dear, our liberties, our freedoms, our concepts of law, but a cooperative spirit of understanding, tolerance and fair play" (*On Communism* 153). In this vein, in popular culture and especially in the science-fiction genre, the generally perceived existence of a Communist threat, provided an opportunity to examine problems endemic to American culture.

This study deals with the complexities of anti–Communism in popular representation from the late Forties to the mid–Sixties. It debunks the notion that anti–Communist propaganda was simplistic discourse. Even in the most obvious propaganda pieces, such as government-sponsored films like *Red Nightmare*, the presentation of the Communist threat was never a simple one. The presentation of the very complex relations interlinking the American public, the American system, and the Communist threat is, indeed, paramount in popular representations of the issue, whether the popular work deals with an intense fear of the Communist threat, whether anti–Communist discourse becomes the occasion for Americans to deal with other fears plaguing their society, or whatever other themes may be the primary occasion for the anti–Communist agenda.

The first section of this book, the first four chapters, deals with how various discourses endemic to American society became intertwined with anti–Communist views. Seduction, paranoia, subversion, and individualism were all used in defining the Communist threat and distinguishing the American democrat from the Communist. Works such as *One Lonely Night* and *Jet Pilot* use the discourse of sexual seduction to illustrate the dangers of Communism: wrapped in the alluring package of a beautiful woman, the Communist threat could turn anyone into a potential dupe of the Communists — even John Wayne.

In the second section of the book, chapters five through eight explore how specific popular genres utilized the Communist threat in a variety of ways to affirm and reinforce their existing generic characteristics. Thus, science fiction, in films such as *Red Planet Mars, Invasion U.S.A.*, and *The Beast from Yucca Flats*, utilized fear of Communism to explore themes dear to the genre, such as fears regarding the potential dangers of science and technology. Similarly, the crime genre continued to project a culture of underworld thugs, though often substituting fear of Communism for the fear of the underworld — and especially organized crime — and sometimes combining the two.

One of the most interesting popular-culture manifestations given an extra surge of energy by an infusion of anti–Communism was the movie serial, a genre in which anti–Communist sentiment was used almost entirely to provide plot-device innovations. Two good examples of this are *Government Agents vs. Phantom Legion* and *Canadian Mounties vs. Atomic Invaders*. Further, another genre, parody, illustrates how humorous treatments of Cold War politics could often contrive to ask the most serious questions about both Communism and capitalism, as in cartoons featuring Bullwinkle and Rocky, the television series *Get Smart*, and the film *One, Two, Three*.

The third section of the book, chapters nine through twelve, deals with ways in which popular representations of anti–Communism intersected with historical events perceived to be organically related to the threat. Thus, the threat of nuclear war and impending apocalypse found eloquent expression in the realm of popular culture in a variety of anti–Communist works, such as the TV drama *Atomic Attack*, the espionage film *Atomic City*, and the film noir *Kiss Me Deadly*. In addition, intersections between history and fiction were forged from accounts of the real-life careers of FBI informants Matt Cvetic and Herbert Philbrick, whose exploits illustrate how the history of anti–Communism was transformed into fictional narratives that were often more flattering to the spies involved than straight biographical or autobiographical representations would have been.

In other examples of such interactions, sociological concerns related to the business world of Fifties society were expressed in such best-selling nonfictional works such as *The Lonely Crowd* and *The Organization Man*. Occasional works of fiction also articulated the anti–Communist explorations of the business world — the prime bastion of capitalism — and the potential vulnerability of that bastion to Communist infiltration. Good examples of this genre are the films *The Woman on Pier 13* and *The Fearmakers*.

The final chapter of this book explores the gradual erosion of anti–Soviet sentiment that took place in the Sixties as China began to replace the Soviet Union as the most diabolical representation of Communist evil. *Fail-Safe, The Manchurian Candidate,* and government propaganda films and television series chart this transition.

Controversy surrounding the dimensions and potential effectiveness of Communism's Cold War–era threat to America still rages, the declassification process sometimes clarifying, sometimes clouding, the issue. However real the threat of Communist conspiracy was at mid-century, popular culture embraced this threat as a very effective ingredient for enhancing the impact of both entertainment and propaganda. The degree of anti–Communist sentiment thus grafted onto popular culture is best looked at in terms of a continuum. At one end of that continuum, government-sponsored propaganda films represented firm official commitment to keeping the anti–Communist cause alive and vibrant; at the other end, the movie serial used the Communist threat mainly to breathe new vitality into its customary cliffhanging escapades. Most of the works discussed in this book are representative of neither of the polar opposites in this continuum.

Popular culture was instrumental in keeping Americans continually terrified by the Communist threat; however, it was equally capable of making them laugh at the absurdity of Cold War politics. Thus, if the Jack Webb–narrated *Red Nightmare* sent chills down the spines of its original viewers, as they contemplated graphic impressions of a possible future America ruled by the Soviets, the misadventures of Maxwell Smart in *Get Smart* made the Cold War clash between Communist and Capitalist fun.

Examination of postwar popular representation of Communism and anti–Communism shows that the issue was not simple, but was clearly very complicated indeed. Such examination shows further that the fear of the Red Peril that dominated American culture in the Twentieth Century was manifested in the media by works of entertainment of a wide and very rich rhetorical variety.

1. The Seduction of Communism

Anti–Communist propaganda of the Fifties crossed genre boundaries and injected popular culture with a new range of plot devices. At a time when the United States felt its entire way of life in a state of siege, the enemy being Communism and its potential spread, portraits of the Red Menace moved out of the confines of army training films and into mainstream popular culture. In this chapter, I focus on two anti–Communist works, Mickey Spillane's detective novel *One Lonely Night* (1951) and Josef Von Sternberg's romantic spy thriller *Jet Pilot* (1957). Both works portray Communism as a threat fueled by seduction; they illustrate anti–Communist discourse working within the mode of sexual discourse.

One Lonely Night focuses on Mike Hammer's investigation of a woman's death, an investigation that leads him to Communist Party headquarters in New York. Hammer passes for an MVD ([Soviet] Ministry of Internal Affairs) man and gains access to the organization. Wealthy socialite Ethel Brighton, who works for the Party, seduces him. Meanwhile, Pat, Mike's policeman friend, after learning of Mike's infiltration of the Party, enlists him to help with an investigation involving Lee Deamer, a prominent politician. Deamer's reputation is threatened by his insane twin brother, Oscar, who has apparently died after being pushed under a train. Deamer then asks for Mike's help in retrieving stolen secret-weapons documents. Mike discovers the documents and is prepared to turn them over to Deamer. After attempts are made on Mike's life, he believes at first that Ethel has betrayed him. However, he goes on to learn that such is not the case. Prior to turning over the documents, Mike learns that his secretary and fiancée, Velda, has been kidnapped by Communist agents. Mike saves Velda, killing many Communists in the process. He then reveals the true identity of Lee Deamer. He is really Oscar Deamer, a Soviet agent posing as an anti–Communist politician. Mike kills Deamer and places a fragment of the stolen documents in his dead hand, so Deamer will be discovered after death to have been a martyr to the anti–Communist cause, thus thwarting Kremlin plans.

One Lonely Night engages the issue of sexual seduction, indicating that its sexuality is one of the powerful allures of Communism. Initially in the novel, Ethel Brighton represents a stereotype of the Communist woman, one who uses sexuality to corrupt men ideologically. In the scene in which Ethel seduces Mike, she removes the fur coat she is wearing and reveals her naked body underneath.[1] Mike comments: "My wallet fell out of the pocket and I didn't care. The sling on my gun rack wouldn't come loose and I broke it. She shouldn't have done it. Damn it, she shouldn't have done it! I wanted to ask her some more questions. Now I forgot what I wanted to ask her" (56). The scene appears to be one in which the Communist woman, using her sexual wiles, undermines the American man. Through seduction, Communism strips Americans of their senses and their ability to fight back. This motif of seduction is repeated in a scene later in the novel in which another woman, Linda Holbright, who works for the Communists, goes to Mike's apartment. She seduces Mike, and he suspects that she is after information: "If she was going to, she should have asked me then. Any woman should know when a man is nothing but a man and when he'll promise or tell anything. I knew all those things too and it didn't do me any good because I was still a man" (80).

Initially, then, *One Lonely Night* seems to construct the Communist woman as one who uses her sexuality to undermine American vigilance; yet, this isn't in fact what is actually going on. Mike assumes that Ethel has betrayed him by revealing his true identity to the Party; he believes Linda has come to his apartment to get information. In both cases he is wrong. Ethel has fallen in love with Mike and has given up her belief in Communism after they have made love. After being shot by a Communist Party hit man, she tells Mike, "After … I met you I saw … the truth" (118). She had gone to the FBI to expose the workings of the Party. Similarly, Linda has come to Mike's apartment to offer her virginity to him — and nothing more. Mike's assumption, that when Communism and an attractive woman are brought together the woman will seduce the man into adopting Communist evils, turns out to be incorrect and clouds his ability to effectively investigate the case.

Indeed, despite the charges of misogyny that are frequently leveled at Spillane's fiction, *One Lonely Night* paints a portrait of the Communist woman as victim rather than as evil seductress.[2] The image presented here of the woman Communist as misguided also found expression in Fifties sociological studies.

In his book *The Appeals of Communism*, Gabriel Almond suggests that the adoption of Communist politics amongst middle-class young people usually resulted from "rebelliousness and emotional instability" rather than from ideological commitment (214).[3] In particular, Almond focuses on case studies of young American women who had joined the Communist Party, concluding that most of these women were misguided. One woman, Frances, joined the party in order to become promiscuous and thus "show contempt for the ordinary laws of society" (291). Almond states that "the Communist doctrine of sex equality helped her to reject her femininity" (291). Similarly, *One Lonely Night* portrays Ethel and Linda as rebellious girls who, once they have found their femininity through sexual relations with Mike, reject the Party and its doctrines. Thus, the real seducer in the novel is not a woman, but an ideology that corrupts young women.

The novel's rejection of the association of femininity and Communism is further underscored in the character of Velda, the most fervent anti–Communist in the novel. Mike professes ignorance on the subject of Cold War politics, stating, "More about the trials and the cold war. Politics. I felt like an ignorant bastard for not knowing what it was all about" (110). By contrast, Velda is well informed about the Cold War and has a violent hatred for Communism. She tells Mike that they must fight the Communists together: "Yes. You ... and me. The bastards. The dirty, filthy red bastards!" (86). This prompts Mike to think, "The boys in the Kremlin should see her now and they'd know what they were getting into" (86).[4] Velda insists that Mike allow her to help in his investigation of the Communists, even threatening to turn the matter over to Pat and the police if he doesn't let her help (93). Indeed, Velda's character embodies virulent anti–Communism combined with feminine beauty. Velda is "so completely lovable and so completely deadly," but her deadliness is positive because it is directed at the enemy (101). Mike pays her his ultimate compliment after she kills a Communist agent: "I had to grin because the girl who was wearing my ring was so smart and I began to feel foolish around her. I did pretty good for myself. I picked a woman who could shoot a guy just like that and still think straight" (100). Interestingly, then, *One Lonely Night* very strongly counters Fifties stereotypes of the woman, and especially the seductive woman, as one who is susceptible to—and therefore aids—Communist infiltration.

However, in sharp contrast with the images of women projected by

One Lonely Night, a strong association between the feminine and Communism was a recurrent element of Fifties anti–Communist rhetoric. Elaine Tyler May maintains that women were often cited as potential security risks and blamed for "a weakening of the nation's moral fiber at a time when the country had to be strong" (157). As Michael Rogin argues, popular culture of the Fifties frequently associated Communism "with secret, maternal influence" (9), a view stemming from widespread awareness of Philip Wylie's concept of Momism.[5]

Wylie's notorious concept, first expressed in *Generation of Vipers* in 1942 and then expanded upon in a 1955 revision of the book, associated the feminine with the degenerative influence of Communism. Momism, as Wylie dramatically portrays it, will lead to national death: "The nation can no longer say it contains many great, free, dreaming men. We are deep in the predicted nightmare now and mom sits on its decaying throne" (196). Wylie blames a pervasive feminine influence for World War II, the Cold War, McCarthyism, and the arms race. However, as we have seen, *One Lonely Night* rejects the easy equation between feminine influence and Communist infiltration.

Interestingly, although *One Lonely Night* is staunchly anti–Communist and anti–McCarthyist, Wylie himself accused Spillane of abetting a potential Communist takeover.[6] In an article entitled "The Crime of Mickey Spillane," published in *Good Housekeeping* in 1955, Wylie lambastes Spillane's fiction. While blaming Spillane for the decline of American society was commonplace in the Fifties, Wylie projected a unique perspective on the issue.[7] He argues that Spillane's novels were causing a degeneration in American society resulting in Americans giving in to "a lawless impulse that humanity has been trying to master for thousands of years in the effort to maintain civilization" (207). Wylie argues that if all Americans began to act like Mike Hammer, "the Soviets could take us over without dropping a bomb" (207). This leads Wylie to conclude that "Mike Hammer is like an enemy agent, a real foe of us all" (209). Wylie's comments appear outrageous today, for *One Lonely Night* at least serves to affirm the ability of a lone individual to battle the Soviet enemy single-handedly. Mike Hammer's words and actions strongly encourage the reader to realize what all Americans needed to know: that the Soviets were stupid and weak, and the seductive power of Communism could easily be exposed as fraudulent.

Perceptions of the Soviet Union in the Fifties operated within a contradiction that, on the one hand, saw them as more intelligent than Americans, and, on the other, saw them as more primitive. The image of a backward, primitive Russia predominated in postwar perceptions of

Communism. As Ellen Schrecker argues, postwar spy hunts were predicated on the notion that only through the aid of stolen information could the Soviets compete in the nuclear arms race: "Otherwise, how was it possible for the Soviet Union, which was viewed as a backward, barbaric nation, to have built a bomb?" (*Age* 32). In an essay entitled "How You Can Fight Communism," James F. O'Neil portrays the Soviets as people who use progress as a mask to hide their barbaric totalitarian impulses: "Next the salesmen and peddlers themselves must be skillfully disguised, deodorized, and glamorized. Hence Communists always appear before the public as 'progressives'" (quoted in Schrecker, *Age* 110). For J. Edgar Hoover, Communism was a disease that threatened to degenerate freedom, democracy, religion, and the American Dream, exposure to it would result in devolution. In Hoover's view, Communism "reveals a condition akin to disease that spreads like an epidemic and like an epidemic a quarantine is necessary to keep it from infecting the Nation" ("Testimony" 119–120). This perception of Communism as infectious was one that spanned the political spectrum: it was not confined to any one party. Thus, for example, in a 1952 campaign speech, Adlai Stevenson commented that Communism was "a disease which may have killed more people in this world than cancer, tuberculosis, and heart disease combined" (qtd. in Sayre 201). According to Raymond B. Allen, Communists should not be allowed to teach in universities because their totalitarian beliefs threaten the evolution of American democracy: "Communism would substitute a doctrine of fear, of little faith, and would submerge the human spirit to the vicious ends of a crass materialism" (7).

In a mid–1950s study that evaluated Americans' attitudes toward Communism, Samuel Stouffer discerned a belief among the majority of the people surveyed that "the less educated and working-class people were more likely to be communists than the better-educated and white-collar people" (172). In addition to a belief in Communists as ignorant, Stouffer related that 1950s Americans believed Communists were morally corrupt. Respondents labeled them "queer people" and "warped personalities" (175). In Harry Horner's sci-fi film *Red Planet Mars* (1952), the Soviet Union is portrayed as a backward country. Scenes of Russian peasants living in one-room huts filled with straw served to reinforce stereotypes of Russians as primitive and hence Communism as a political system that was much lower on the social evolutionary scale than American democracy. In the logic of the film, Russian peasant equals Soviet citizen. A 1952 *Life* magazine article, "Iron Curtain Look is Here!" satirizes backward Soviet fashion, subtitling the article "U.S. envoy's wife finds Moscow modes high priced, wide shouldered, not very handsome" (qtd. in Barson n.p.). On every level, Soviet life is portrayed as inferior to American life — with regard, for example, to political systems, shelter, and women's clothing.

The realization that crass stupidity hides behind the specter of Communism is one that Mike Hammer comes to in *One Lonely Night*. When, once inside Party headquarters, Mike easily passes for one of the group, his image of Communists as wily, seductive people crumbles: "Read the papers. See what it says about the Red Menace. See how they play up their sneaking, conniving ways. They're supposed to be clever, bright as hell. They were dumb as horse manure as far as I was concerned" (35). Yet, it is Mike's ignorance of politics that allows him to perceive the stupidity of the Communists and not be manipulated by the smokescreen of political rhetoric. The fantasy of *One Lonely Night* is that a violent private detective can do what no government official can do: wipe out Communism with physical force. After Ethel is shot, Mike fantasizes a one-man attack on Moscow: "But some day, maybe, some day I'd stand on the steps of the Kremlin with a gun in my fist and I'd yell for them to come out and if they wouldn't I'd go in and get them and when I had them lined up against the wall I'd start shooting until all I had left was a row of corpses" (121). While Mike begins the novel tormented by a harsh judgment given to him by a judge for his vigilante ways, he ends the novel by realizing that his purpose in life is to stop the Communists: "I lived only to kill the scum and the lice that wanted to kill themselves. I lived to kill so that others could live. I lived to kill because my soul was a hardened thing that reveled in the thought of taking the blood of the bastards who made murder their business" (149).

One Lonely Night works to demythologize the seductive ability of Communism. By portraying sexy, Communist women as misguided girls and Soviet agents as stupid murderers, the novel suggests that only a fool would be duped by the seductions that Communism offers. *Jet Pilot*, another Fifties film, in a very different genre, shows us the other end of the spectrum: the wild mythologizing of the Soviets that was commonly a part of anti–Communist propaganda films.

Jet Pilot focuses on a Soviet pilot, Anna (Janet Leigh), who flies into American airspace in Alaska. The Air Force puts a U.S. pilot, Col. Jim Shannon (John Wayne), in charge of her hoping that he will be able to learn from her what air technology and equipment the Soviets possess. However, Jim falls in love with Anna, and when the U.S. government threatens to deport her, he marries her so they can stay together. Government officials then reveal to Shannon that Anna is a Soviet agent and has seduced a British officer in order to get information for her country. The U.S. government then enlists Shannon to gather information from the

Shannon (John Wayne) is seduced by the charms of Soviet pilot Anna (Janet Leigh) in Jet Pilot *(1957). (Courtesy of the Library of Congress, Prints and Photographs Division, USZ62 123128.)*

Soviet Union by taking Anna there. Anna and Shannon go to Russia, where Shannon spies. The Russians catch on to his status as spy, however, and begin giving him a memory-loss drug. When they threaten to completely erase his memory and turn him into a vegetable, Anna saves him, and they fly back together to the United States.

By contrast with *One Lonely Night*, through the character of Anna,

Jet Pilot highlights American susceptibility to the seduction of Communism. Shannon and his colleague Major Rexford are angry about the Russian plane invading American airspace, but when a red-lipped, beautiful blonde steps out of the aircraft, they begin acting like love-struck schoolboys. Anna elicits sympathy from Shannon by telling him that she has been forced to leave Russia to avoid her own execution: "I came here to prevent myself from getting shot." Yet, she remains loyal to the Soviet government, telling Shannon that she is "not angry enough to talk against my country." Immediately, Anna begins seducing Shannon. He tells her that she must be searched, and she starts to undress in front of him. Then he tells her to go into the bathroom. She comes out wrapped in a towel, stands in front of the fire, and dresses in front of both Shannon and Rexford. Shannon comments, "This might be some new form of Russian propaganda." Shannon easily falls under Anna's spell. As Murray Edelman notes, one means of constructing a political enemy involves attributing excess sexuality to the group, and especially to the women of the group. Edelmen notes that "The attribution of a unique measure of eroticism is blatantly political because it defines the group in terms that ignore individual characteristics and potentialities while highlighting a provocation to oppression" (84).

In addition to being seduced by her good looks, Shannon is drawn to Anna's ability as a pilot. When Shannon and Anna go on a flight together in separate jets, Anna can almost keep up with Shannon's expert flying. After Anna demonstrates her prowess as a pilot, Shannon begins to fall seriously in love with her, kissing her, and calling her a "silly Siberian cupcake." While the film portrays the Soviet woman as beautiful and skilled, the ultimate point of the film is to demonstrate that, however seductive Anna is as a woman, she cannot compete with the seductions of capitalist society.

Thus, when Shannon takes Anna to Palm Springs, she is overcome with the wonders of consumer society. Shannon takes Anna to buy a bathing suit, commenting as they look at a suit, "We both believe in uplifting the masses." Anna is flattered that Shannon thinks she looks great in a bathing suit. When Anna sees the suite they are staying in she runs from room to room, then jumps on the bed with a childlike glee. She cannot believe that the suite is for one couple only, commenting that four families could easily live in this suite, and that many such families do so in Russia. As Shannon and Anna rest from dancing, Anna proclaims love to be a "dangerous narcotic," but is completely overwhelmed by a plate of prime rib she sees in the restaurant, commenting, "How can the Russians compete with such propaganda?"

While Anna initially seems like an easy convert to capitalism, the film reveals her duplicitous nature when Shannon discovers that she is a double agent. Shannon must face his gullibility, admitting that Anna is a "Soviet Tootsie Roll that made a chump of me." Yet, when she decides to help Shannon escape from the Soviet Union and then go with him, she seems more motivated by a desire for the lifestyle the United States has to offer than by love for Shannon. While in Russia, she nostalgically remembers the beef in Palm Springs and obsesses about keeping a nightgown that Shannon had bought for her there. The last scene of the film underscores Anna's materialism as she tells Shannon that she came back to the United States for steak. Shannon asks her if there was any other reason, and she tells him that she also came back in order to be with him, but she quickly turns her attention to eating the steak. Anna delivers the final ideological statement in the film when she wishes she could make the Russian people realize "that steaks are better than all the guns in the world."[8]

Unlike *One Lonely Night, Jet Pilot* attributes a mythological power to the Soviets. Not only can Anna easily dupe an American colonel, but his romantic efforts do nothing to dissuade her from her commitment to Communism. Whereas Mike's lovemaking ability converts misguided Communist women, Shannon is ineffectual in changing Anna; only the material comforts of the United States have any impact on her. Moreover, whereas *One Lonely Night* concludes that the Soviets are stupid, *Jet Pilot* credits them with super-intelligence, not only through Anna's evident skills as an agent, but also in their use of the new experimental mind-erasing drug they have developed, and which the United States does not possess. Only Anna can save Shannon from destruction; he doesn't have the intelligence or strength to save himself, despite what we might expect from a character played by John Wayne. *Jet Pilot* suggests that American men cannot defeat the seductions of Communism; only American products can do that.

As these two works demonstrate, the discourse of sexual seduction commonly informed Cold War propaganda. By operating within familiar discourses, Cold War anti–Communist works could frame the threat in familiar terms. Although these familiar discourses could be alluring, as is the case with sexual discourse, they could also be frightening, intertwining existing American fears with images of the Red Menace. The next chapter takes up a terrifying discourse that became combined with anti–Communist sentiment — paranoia.

2. Paranoiac Discourse and Anti–Communism

One discourse through which anti–Communist popular culture artifacts are often viewed is paranoia.[1] It is a commonplace to associate post–World War II America with paranoiac fantasy. And while debate continues as to whether the American Communist conspiracy was more a real, tangible threat or a paranoiac fantasy, it is undeniable that paranoiac logic is an important structural element informing many anti–Communist works produced in the mid-century period.[2] In this chapter, I explore anti–Communist works that make salient use of paranoiac discourse in creating their particular nightmarish visions of the Red Menace.

One cogent example is *The Whip Hand* (1951), a film that tells the story of Matt Corbin, a reporter for a magazine called *American View*, who, while on a fishing trip, runs across a Communist conspiracy in the Upper Midwest. In the small village of Winnoga (a fictional place, perhaps intended to be set in Minnesota or Wisconsin), Matt finds that the seemingly friendly people are really Communist agents working to protect a secret laboratory where an ex–Nazi scientist named Wilhem Bucholtz is engaged in biological-weapons research for the Soviet Communists. With the help of two members of the town who are not part of the conspiracy, Matt contacts his editor, who calls in the FBI. The plot is uncovered and foiled.

In several ways, *The Whip Hand* operates within the logic of paranoia. Norman Cameron has theorized paranoia as being characterized by a pseudo-community of villains that is complemented by a pseudo-community of friends. Cameron states that "what he [the paranoiac] takes to

18

be a functional community is only a pseudo-community created by his own unskilled attempts at interpretation, anticipation, and validation of social behavior" ("Pseudo" 37). The paranoiac recognizes the pseudo-community of villains through a gradual epiphany. Cameron discusses the moment of clarification as the "final delusional reconstruction of reality" in which the paranoiac exclaims, "I suddenly realized what it was all about!" ("Revisited" 56).

In *The Whip Hand*, Matt gradually uncovers a pseudo-community of villains in Winnoga. Although he comes upon the secret compound immediately upon arriving in the area, he initially believes the townspeople's explanations that the high security there is merely the result of the eccentricity of Peterson, a wealthy man who wants his privacy. Dr. Keller tells Matt that "Every small town has its eccentrics." At first, Matt learns that the fishing town of Winnoga has lost its fish supply due to water contamination and fancifully imagines an article entitled "Winnoga, the town that ran out of fish." However, Matt soon begins to see that the people are behaving very suspiciously. When Keller leaves the movie theater, Matt comments to Keller's sister, Jenet, "Busy man, your brother, for such a small population." His suspicion is further fueled by the manner in which the townspeople try to force him to leave. Matt tells Jenet, "Everybody is sure anxious to bid me a goodbye."

After Matt sneaks into the compound and is shot at, the sinister implications of what is really going on in Winnoga begin to crystallize in his mind: "First, we have interrogation. Then, fear. A warning shot. And now censorship." Matt intimates to Jenet that she is living in a Communist-dominated town: "What are these characters trying to do, drop an Iron Curtain around Winnoga?" Thus, the initially harmless people in the village, Steve Loomis and his wife (the owners of the town's inn), Dr. Keller, Mabel Turner (a trapper's wife), and others all turn out to be active Communist agents working for the cause of using biological weapons in a war against the United States.

In *The Whip Hand*, the pseudo-community of villains is complemented by a small pseudo-community of friends. Jenet and Luther Adams, the proprietor of the town's general store, help Matt in his quest to uncover the sinister truth about Winnoga. Luther is the only original inhabitant still living in Winnoga. He tells Matt that he refused to sell out in 1945, when Loomis and the other conspirators took over the town. Luther, however, is frightened of revealing too much information to Matt. He tells him, "I'm 79, and that's no way to live to be 80." Luther, however, does help Matt get a message through to his editor. As a result, Keller injects Luther with a heart-acceleration drug and murders him. Jenet also serves as a member of the pseudo-community of friends. She has refused to acknowledge the existence of the conspiracy because she has not wanted to accept that her brother could be part of anything so monstrous. After Jenet has seen and accepted the truth about the conspiracy, she comments to Matt, "I can't believe my brother's a Communist."

Other elements of paranoiac discourse also structure the film. One aspect of such paranoiac discourse is its belief in imminent apocalyptic destruction. This belief results in the paranoiac experiencing messianic delusions.[3] Division of the world population into heroes and villains characterizes the paranoiac world view. The extreme black-and-white binary logic of paranoia often creates the threat of apocalyptic destruction.[4] Thus, the Communist conspiracy that Matt uncovers is not a run-of-the-mill threat, but one that potentially may destroy all life on earth. Thus, Matt's mission is a messianic one, one that intends to save the whole United States population from a horrible death. Bucholtz's plan is to release biological agents that will destroy all life in the United States. He tells the FBI agents who come to arrest him, "I am benefiting mankind by ridding the world of all the people that oppose Communists ... Communism will rule the world!" Thus, Bucholtz and all the conspirators in the town are willing to die from the same biological agents that are intended to destroy the rest of the United States. Bucholtz comments, "I shall die willingly, knowing my work has been accomplished."

By utilizing the discourse of paranoia, The Whip Hand creates a nightmarish view of the Communist threat, one that combines the lingering World War II fear of Nazis with the postwar fear of Communists, all within an apocalyptic vision of biological warfare.

Philip Wylie's suspense novel The Smuggled Atom Bomb (1951) also creates a paranoiac worldview on which to graft its plot.[5] The novel's protagonist, Allan Diffenduffer Bogan (Duff), is a graduate student in physics. To help pay for his education, he does housework for a family, the Yateses, whom he boards with. Duff becomes suspicious when, in the room of Harry Ellings, another boarder at the Yates home, he discovers a mysterious box that he believes may contain uranium. Duff contacts the FBI, and Slater Higgins is assigned to the case. While the FBI is secretly pursuing the case, Higgins makes Duff believe that he is imagining things with regard to Ellings. Duff's suspicions are further aroused when Ellings dies mysteriously. He later discovers a suicide capsule that Ellings has taken. Duff becomes more actively involved in the investigation when Eleanor Yates, the teenage daughter of the family he boards with, is kidnapped. Duff traces her to the Stantons, a Russian immigrant family working for the Communists. After Stanton tortures both Duff and Eleanor on board his yacht, Coast Guard planes begin circling the yacht, and it crashes. Duff and Eleanor survive the crash and take refuge on an island, but Stanton's yacht explodes like an atomic bomb, as a result of the fissioning of the uranium he has been carrying on board for espionage purposes.

As in *The Whip Hand*, *The Smuggled Atom Bomb* indicates how ordinary citizens can stumble onto insidious conspiracy plots. Duff finds himself in a position that is typical — and, indeed, characteristic — for protagonists in works of paranoia. Everyone — even the FBI — discounts his theories as delusionary. Eleanor laughs at him when he reveals to her his theory that Harry Ellings is a spy (14). Higgins tries to make Duff believe himself to be just another crackpot when he goes to Higgins' office to report the discovery of the box. Higgins says, "Stories and rumors of A-bomb spies come in here as thick as reports of flying saucers. And we waste our lives on 'em all" (20). Even though Duff is marginalized by everyone because of his belief that espionage is occurring in the very house where he lives, his suspicions about his fellow boarder impel him to continue his investigation.

Duff's paranoiac outlook comes from Cold War American society and his education in physics. Duff comments that many top physicists have noted that "atom bombs could be brought into harbors in tramp steamers. Or smuggled into the country in sections and assembled in secret and planted — like mines, like infernal machines — to be set off in the centers of cities" (30). Duff's fears here reflect the influence of the scientists' movement and their campaign of mass paranoia with regard to nuclear weapons. In Duff's mathematics class, the professor seems assured that the Soviets will use atomic bombs on the Untied States. Duff asks the professor how many atomic bombs the Soviets possess, and he replies, "If our present political misadventures continues, we will probably find out how many in the most pragmatic fashion. They will be dropped on us!" (37). Within this climate, Duff knows that his suspicions are not unfounded.

What bothers Duff the most about his discoveries is the fact that ordinary American citizens are working for the nuclear destruction of the United States. When Duff thinks of Ellings, he finds it hard to comprehend that Ellings could be an enemy agent: "He merely thought, for the thousandth time, that a simple, gentle, goodhearted, mousy guy like Ellings could never be associated with anything un–American" (49). Later in the novel, Higgins is horrified by the fact that ordinary Americans could become traitors. He expresses his disgust to Duff: "But finding out that people who do things you've been led to admire are just rotten, low, filthy enemies! Traitors! It makes a man sick! It scares a man!" (108). Awareness of the fact that a good citizen like Ellings could be traitor produces a sense of the uncanny, a feeling that Harry Stack Sullivan sees as common in the paranoiac experience. In Sullivan's view, the projection that occurs in paranoia is of the internal "not me," the internal other, onto an external source (361). The normal people of Duff's world become uncanny as he sees the potential for otherness in everyone around him. Duff expresses this with a familiar idea from paranoia — the mysterious "they." Duff thinks to himself after Eleanor's kidnapping: "'They' wouldn't mind killing a girl. 'They' perhaps, were working to kill millions of people. You couldn't even think, rationally, of what 'they' might be planning" (113).

As in *The Whip Hand*, the paranoiac world of Wylie's novel implicates ordinary Americans as collaborators in a Communist plot, but also like *The Whip Hand*, the work ultimately locates the otherness within a foreign element. While Americans help Bucholtz in his experiments, it is the Soviet government using Nazi science that makes the biological warfare threat tangible. Similarly, in *The Smuggled Atom Bomb*, it is the Russian immigrant who makes the espionage ring possible. Eleanor expresses contempt for the fact that Duff is dating Indigo Stanton, revealing to him Indigo's Russian heritage. Eleanor comments, "She wants to meet any person in pants! Being tall she likes tall ones, if available. White Russian, she was. Family came here to Miami during the revolution" (97). While Eleanor has contempt for Indigo because she is a loose woman, Duff begins to pick up on a connection between Indigo's father's business and the espionage plot. Thus, in the paranoiac view of the novel, any Russian is suspicious, even those who claim to be White Russians. When Stanton kidnaps Eleanor and Duff, he reveals himself to be the stereotypical cold, cruel Russian of the paranoiac Cold War imagination. Stanton tells them, "You and Miss Yates will also be destroyed ... This will be painful — as painful as certain trained men on board can make it — for you both" (130). In the paranoiac fantasy of *The Smuggled Atom Bomb*, the brutal Russian emerges as the power behind "them."

Another anti–Communist Hollywood film from the 1950s, *A Bullet for Joey* (1955), also uses paranoiac discourse in order to paint its portrait of Communist conspiracy. The film focuses on a Soviet-backed Communist conspiracy led by Eric Hartman, whose plan is to kidnap top nuclear scientist Dr. Carl Macklin and take him to the Soviet Union. To effect his plan, Hartman employs gangsters, led by Joe Victor, a Mafia leader who has taken refuge in Lisbon. After being given a false passport, and assembling the members of his gang, Victor travels to Montreal, where his group concocts an elaborate plot to kidnap the doctor, and succeeds, but is pursued by Inspector Raoul Leduc, who has begun to catch on to the conspiracy after piecing together evidence from seemingly unrelated crimes. After kidnapping the doctor and Leduc, Hartman sets sail with Victor and his gang, planning to kill everyone except the doctor along the way. Leduc fires a flare and gets the attention of the Coast Guard. Leduc also convinces Victor to have a conscience about the espionage he is involved in. Victor kills Hartman but in the same shoot-out is shot and killed himself. The authorities rescue Leduc and Macklin.

While it is typical for many anti–Communist films to link organized crime and Communist espionage, *A Bullet for Joey* works within a framework of conspiracy theory.[6] One facet of the paranoiac worldview that is that seemingly random events actually fit together if one only looks closely enough at them and uses the right interpretive tools. Carl Freedman, for example, views the paranoiac as having "an abnormally high investment in the hermeneutic practice" (16). The elaborate Communist/Mafia conspiracy in *A Bullet for Joey* relies upon Leduc being able to pull together seemingly unrelated strands in his investigations. The murders of a police constable, an organ grinder, and Macklin's secretary seem to be unrelated; yet, Leduc succeeds in linking the three murders, thus tracing the crimes back to Victor's Mafia hit squad. Further, Leduc is able to tie the crimes together as Communist espionage, even though Macklin can give him no information about the project he is working on.

The film contrasts Leduc's ability to tie random strands together in order to reveal the conspiracy with the ignorance of Victor and his henchmen, who seem to be operating in some pre–World War II world of gangster crimes. Leduc asks Victor if he knows who he and his gang members have been working for. Victor replies, "Who cares? I was doing a job." When Leduc hints at the implications of the Soviets being able to develop new weapons of mass destruction due to their possession of the fruits of Macklin's scientific knowledge, telling him that "All of humanity is in danger," Victor says, "All I want to save is my own neck." Victor's gang is the epitome of people duped by Communists, people working in and for a vast conspiracy without even recognizing it.

Another manner in which *A Bullet for Joey* utilizes a paranoiac framework is through use of the personal as a means of effecting conspiracy. Paranoia frequently has its origins in sexual problems: case studies reveal, indeed, that sexual anxiety is often a precondition for paranoia. Sandor Ferenczi's studies of paranoiac patients reveal an account of a man who believed in delusions that his wife drained his energy vampirically due to her sexual lasciviousness (159). In another case Ferenczi discusses, a woman is shown to have perceived in the newspapers accusations both of her own moral weaknesses and of her husband's infidelities.[7] Indeed, many paranoiac delusions begin with individual sexual suspicions and gradually evolve into complete paranoiac delusional systems. And indeed, two key characters in *A Bullet for Joey* do become victims of the conspiracy as a result of sexual weaknesses. Macklin's secretary, Yvone, is a mousy woman dominated by an older sister who will not let her wear make-up or go out with men. Victor chooses Jack Allen, a handsome member of his gang, to take her on dates in order to gain crucial information about Macklin. Yvone is flattered by the attention, but grows skeptical when Jack proposes marriage to her. Jack professes his true feelings for her and as a result learns the location of the testing ground for the new weapon that Macklin is working on. When Yvone discovers that she is part of a conspiracy and tries to run away, Jack runs her down with his car. Thus, the sexual come-on is merely part of the conspiracy. The film suggests that, as in paranoiac fantasy, in a Cold War scenario, even the most personal elements of one's life may well all refer back to "them" and their vast designs.

Macklin also becomes a victim of his own sexual desires. Victor's first impulse is to use a "dame" to kidnap Macklin, but Hartman disagrees, believing that Macklin is not interested in women. When Victor enlists Joyce Geary, his former girlfriend, Macklin is smitten with her. Macklin's desire for Joyce blinds him from seeing the danger that Yvone is in. He tells her sister that "There's been an epidemic of starry eyes in my office lately," and epidemic is exactly what *A Bullet for Joey* is telling the audience these sexual attractions are. Although Joyce is conscience-stricken over her role in the conspiracy, in a comment about Macklin, she says, "Poor Carl, for all his intelligence he couldn't see through me." Thus, as in the paranoiac view, every aspect of life, even the personal, is dangerous because it links up with a vast conspiracy. Both *The Whip Hand* and *A Bullet for Joey* also project the Soviet threat as having almost god-like dimensions, in view of its ability to create such elaborate espionage plans.

"It's All Done with Mirrors," an episode of the 1960s TV series *I Spy,* also uses paranoiac discourse to present the Soviet threat in an almost supernatural dimension.[8] In this episode, Kelly is kidnapped and taken to a private hospital where Dr. Karolyi, a Russian behaviorist scientist, brainwashes him for a night and a day, making him believe that he must kill Scott, because Scott is a traitor. Kelly is then released by Karolyi, who uses his own nurse and girlfriend, Vanessa, as a contact for Kelly. Kelly tries to kill Scott in a restaurant, and Washington agents inform Scott that Kelly has been brainwashed by Karolyi. The Washington agents want to kill Kelly rather than see him be used as a pawn of the Soviets, but Scott believes he can save him. Scott breaks the brainwashing. At the end of the episode, Karolyi defects to the United States to avoid being arrested.

Alexander Scott (Bill Cosby) and Kelly Robinson (Robert Culp) are a spy duo who battle the Communist threat in the Sixties TV series I Spy.

In this *Manchurian Candidate*–style episode, the Soviets are given vast, almost supernatural, powers in the realm of science. Karolyi is able to brainwash Kelly in a very brief period of time. Karolyi tries to make a success of this brainwashing by telling Kelly, "And finally you will obey me as if I were your own personal god." In the paranoiac world of the episode, the Soviet government is accorded immense powers. Clearly, the episode provides cogent support for the views of Richard Hofstaedter, who argued that post–World War II perceptions of history partook more of the mythological than the historical. In the Cold War world: "History is a conspiracy, set in motion by demonic forces of almost transcendent power, and what is needed to defeat it is not the usual methods of political give-and-take, but an all-out crusade" (29). Thus, in the Cold War period, Communism appeared to be not merely a historically specific political system, but the embodiment of a mythological evil, and in this paranoiac view, the postwar Soviet Union also became perceived as mythologically great and evil on a cosmic scale. I.F Stone commented that anti–Communism painted Communists as "some supernatural breed of men, led by diabolic masterminds in that distant Kremlin, engaged in a satanic conspiracy to take over the world and enslave all mankind" (69). Certainly Karolyi's plan is diabolical. Not only does he convince Kelly that his partner is a traitor to the United States, but also implants in him a false memory that Scott was responsible for a childhood car accident Kelly was involved in.

Further, the Washington agents assigned to the case believe in Karolyi as an evil genius. The agents do not even hesitate in their decision when they learn that Kelly has been brainwashed by Karolyi. One agent tells Scott immediately, "We'd rather have him dead than gone." They are quite certain that the Soviet-style brainwashing techniques cannot be counter-manded. Hanna M. Segal argues that in the paranoiac Cold War mental-ity "to hide our own aggressive desires, we have to project the evil onto an enemy — real or imaginary — he must appear to be an inhuman mon-ster" (39). This view appears to be the one the Washington agents adopt. Because they desire to possess Karolyi's brainwashing techniques so that they in turn can use them on Soviet agents, they attribute more success to him than is appropriate. This point is borne out at the end, when Karolyi defects, and Kelly and Scott cynically believe that the government will be happy to get him and even assign them to be his bodyguards.

Even though the Washington agents believe that Karolyi's methods are foolproof, Scott does not. He willingly risks his life to prove that the effects of the brainwashing techniques can be nullified. Scott volunteers to bring Kelly back "undamaged," and the Washington office gives him forty-eight hours to accomplish this task. Scott tells the Washington agents that "I'm betting that their conditioning isn't that deep." Scott is correct. He is able to use his three years of friendship and work with Kelly to break the brainwashing. He stands in front of Kelly and tells him to shoot. Kelly shoots at Scott six times, but does not even come close to hitting him. Scott tells Kelly, "I'm betting the whole stack on you."

Thus, while *The Whip Hand, The Smuggled Atom Bomb,* and *A Bul-let for Joey* completely endorse a paranoiac view of the Soviet threat, this episode of *I Spy* exposes that belief as false. Because the Washington agents are so primed to believe that the Soviets can accomplish anything, even permanent brainwashing in an extremely short period of time, they are willing to kill Kelly. Scott is able to show the agents that the Soviets do not really constitute a mythological threat, but are simply human beings whose practices have weaknesses.

Along with the paranoiac discourse that often informs mid-century American works of anti–Communism, a discourse of subversion is also pervasive. In the next chapter I focus on internal and external subversion in anti–Communist popular culture.

3. Internal and External Communism in Popular Film

The United States' concern over Communism in the late Forties and early Fifties focused both on the enemy within and the enemy without. In the late Forties, the U.S. citizens' concerns were directed to a series of cases that alerted them to the threat of internal espionage. The Korean War (1950–1953) was perceived by many, as Regin Schmidt notes, as one of the "ominous signs of Soviet expansionism" (365). Two films from 1949 — *Conspirator* and *The Red Menace* — seem to reflect the fortitude of Americans in the face of internal subversion, while *The Steel Helmet*, a 1951 film, lauds American bravery in the face of an insidious Communist threat in a foreign country. All three films work to reassure their audiences that, in spite of all the dangers, Americans generally are loyal and brave.

Postwar America became increasingly frightened by Communist espionage. A series of events in the late Forties and early Fifties heightened the public's awareness of the danger of Communist spies. In 1945, it was revealed that the journal *Amerasia* possessed classified documents on military coordinates in Asia. In 1948, the public's attention was strongly alerted to the threat of communist subversion by Whittaker Chambers, when he accused Alger Hiss, a former State Department official, of being a Soviet agent. In 1949, Klaus Fuchs, who had been a British member of the Manhattan Project, fell under investigation for passing secrets to the Soviets, and in 1950 he confessed his guilt in this regard to MI5. In August 1949, the Soviets tested their first atomic bomb, a success brought about in part as the result of the efforts of Americans working for the

Soviets.[1] These and later events, such as the conviction and execution of the Rosenbergs, galvanized Americans to an enhanced perception of the dangers of Soviet espionage and to the need to be aware that even Americans could be turned to serve the enemy.

One fear that was associated with the threat of Soviet espionage was that Americans were naïve and therefore gullible in the face of Communist propaganda. For many anti–Communists, the kind of American perceived to be at risk for conversion to Communism was the naïve and trusting one. J. Edgar Hoover, in testimony given before the House Un-American Activities Committee (HUAC), commented that he "would have no fears if more Americans possessed the zeal, the fervor, the persistence, and the industry to learn about this menace of Red fascism," and went on to express fear that liberals, progressives, ministers, school boards, and parents had been "hoodwinked and duped into joining hands with the Communists" ("Testimony" 119). Herbert Philbrick's best-selling account of his years as an FBI spy within the Communist party paints a similar portrait of the American convert to espionage as a naïve person. Philbrick traces his own involvement with the party back to an anti-war sentiment that caused him to visit an undercover communist recruiter's office: "When I walked out of Mrs. Mills's office that day, stacks of Youth Council literature mingled with direct-mail samples in my brief case, I stepped for the first time onto that long, treacherous tightrope of the nine years, the three lives. But I didn't know that then — I was elated" (9–10).[2] Recent revelations about spies like Ted Hall seem to affirm this view that idealistic, young Americans were susceptible to Communist propaganda. For example, in an interview with the BBC, Hall justified his act of espionage in the following idealistic manner: "There are certain things that I say which are perfectly accurate, factual, statements, and they just cannot seem to be absorbed. Antagonists persist in the view that if I did something of this sort, it was to help the Soviet Union. It wasn't. Any action of that sort was, was, well, pardon the grandiose term, but I cannot think of another, was to help the world" ("Ted Hall"). While there was a deep-seated fear in American society that its own people, and especially the young, were susceptible to Communism, some anti–Communist propaganda painted a countering view.

Conspirator (1949), for example, focuses on an eighteen-year-old American girl, Melinda Greyton, who travels to England to stay with some family friends, the Pennistones and their daughter Joyce. While at a military ball, Melinda meets a dashing major, Michael Currah. Melinda falls in love with him and soon marries him, but shortly thereafter becomes suspicious of his strange disappearances. At first she suspects that he is hav-

The conviction and execution of the Rosenbergs alerted Americans of the dangers of Soviet espionage and of how even Americans could be turned to serve the enemy. (Courtesy of the Library of Congress, Prints and Photographs Division, USZ62 117772.)

ing an affair, but quickly discovers that he is a Soviet agent, passing classified military information to his Soviet contact, Radek. Melinda demands that Michael resign his post. He consents to do this, but continues to work as an operative. When the Party discovers that Melinda knows of his spying, they decree that she must be killed and order that Michael be her assassin. He argues against this, but finally consents. When he fails to kill her, the Party threatens him with death. Meanwhile, Melinda has informed military intelligence of Michael's actions. When a detective from Scotland Yard comes to arrest Michael, he finds that Michael has killed himself.

Conspirator initially portrays Melinda as a naïve American who is susceptible to Michael's influence. At the military ball Melinda falls in love with Michael at first sight and after the ball tells Joyce, "I've never been so happy." As a teenage American girl being courted by a thirty-one-year-old British officer, Melinda forgives Michael for what seem, at first, merely strange aberrations in his character. On one of their first dates, Michael and Melinda go on a picnic together. Michael talks about his childhood in Ireland, and Melinda romanticizes that country, while Michael talks about its oppressed state: "It was cold, dingy, and poor."

In Conspirator *Communist agent Michael Currah (Robert Taylor) uses his charms to try to convert his young wife Melinda (Elizabeth Taylor) to Communism.*

When Michael and Melinda visit his aunt in Wales, Michael takes his nephews and nieces out hunting. Melinda and one of the children discover a rabbit caught in a steel trap. Melinda is horrified, but Michael tells her, "It was only a rabbit, Linda." Michael's callousness horrifies Melinda, but she dismisses it when he proposes to her and tells her, "When we're married, you'll begin to understand me."

While initially Melinda appears to be a naïve American who might be susceptible to Michael's Communist indoctrination techniques, once they are married, she reveals herself to be a patriotic American. After their marriage, she plans a dinner party for Michael's military colleagues. She expresses her admiration for a neighboring house that is much larger than theirs. Michael takes this expression of envy as an opportunity to attempt to indoctrinate Melinda into Communism. He tells her that "The society that made it [the house] possible is vanishing." Melinda rejects this idea: "Everybody likes to live as well as they can." When Melinda discovers proof of Michael's espionage in his wallet, she confronts him: "You're a traitor!" Michael again tries to use propaganda to convince her of his rightness: "I'm a loyal supporter of the greatest social experiment in the world." Even when Michael explains his early involvement in the party in Ireland, Melinda refuses to express sympathy for his political views: "I've made up my mind that you must resign your commission." Melinda's disgust for Communism and loyalty to the Allies is never questioned by the film. Even though she is a young, impressionable girl who has fallen in love with an older man, she knows right from wrong, and knows further that Michael's Communism is a danger to the state, a danger that she must expose. While the film lauds Melinda's anti–Communism, it also diagnoses Michael's Communism as a symptom of neurosis.

In *The Appeals of Communism*, Gabriel Almond argues that both American and British youth were susceptible to Communism largely as the result of personal neuroses: "On the other hand, in the United States and England, where the party has never taken deep root, where the trade unions are non-political or allied with the moderate left, affiliation with the Communist movement has generally been viewed as deviational and extremist" (251). Early in the film, Melinda borrows a hat from Joyce's mother in order to impress Michael. Joyce chides her, telling her that Michael doesn't have a mother complex. Melinda replies by saying that "practically every man" has a mother complex. Melinda is right. We learn that Michael's Communism was fostered in Ireland due to his mother's influence. When his father claimed custody of him, Michael continued to work for the Party so he could defy his father: "I'd learned to keep secrets. Important secrets." Hence, Michael's Communism is not related to any political motivation, but is tied up with his Oedipus complex. His Aunt Jessica believes that his Communist period has been a phase of youth. Jessica tells him that he needs to "love someone more than yourself." This prompts Michael's marriage to Melinda, but the film argues that the Party wants to keep Michael in an arrested state of development. They oppose the marriage. When Michael tells one of his Soviet contacts about his marriage, the man comments, "You have committed a serious breach of discipline."

Conspirator works, then, to affirm the moral fiber of the American, even when she is a teenage girl. Melinda may be naïve, but her ability to expose her husband when she discovers his espionage reassured audiences frightened by the recent revelations of espionage that Americans were able to recognize and resist Communist indoctrination. Further, it gave assurance that Communist spies were the products of personal and familial neuroses, boys who had not grown up and overcome their oedipal conflicts.

Another film from the same year also affirms American loyalty by portraying as confused dupes those Americans who become Party members.

The Red Menace is a documentary-style film that focuses on the inner workings of the American Communist Party. The film focuses on Bill Jones, a disgruntled World War II veteran who becomes involved with the Party after he loses all his money in a real-estate scam. While attending Party meetings, Bill falls in love with Nina Petrovka, an Eastern European refugee who teaches indoctrination classes. After witnessing several disloyal party members being murdered, Nina and Bill decide to flee from the Party. They drive to Texas, where they turn themselves in to a local sheriff. The sheriff assures them that they are not guilty of anything and that they can have a normal life now that they have left the Party.

The Red Menace consistently portrays American members of the Party as dupes. J. Edgar Hoover, in *Masters of Deceit*, defines a dupe as an "innocent victim, the individual who unknowingly is under communist thought control and does the work of the party" (86). Each of the American characters in the film is a dupe, but one who can be saved and taught to see the deceitful nature of the Communist Party. Mollie O'Flaherty is a Party member who is used to seduce new recruits. When Bill meets her at a bar run by the Party, she takes him back to her apartment and uses a combination of sex and propaganda to snare him into the Party. In between kissing Bill, Mollie preaches in favor of Communism: "The Party's been behind every decent cause in this country." Bill grows bored with her propaganda and replies, "So, it's all been just a come-on for the Party." Mollie responds, "Don't say that, Bill." When we see her the next morning, it is clear that she has slept with Bill in order to solidify his interest in the Party. While Mollie appears at first as a kind of Communist femme fatale, the film ultimately portrays her as a misguided Catholic girl. When Father O'Leary visits Mollie and her boyfriend, Party poet Henry Solomon, Mollie is moved by O'Leary's speech advocating patriotism toward the United States. Later, after the Party ostracizes Henry for writing a poem that suggests "Marx merely carried on the ideas of other men," forcing him to commit suicide, Mollie returns to the church. Father O'Leary greets her and tells her that she shouldn't hate the Communists, because "They're misguided. They need our prayers." Mollie then joins her mother in a church pew.

Other American characters in the film follow a similar pattern. Sam Wright, an African-American man who works at the Party newspaper, *The Toilers,* begins to doubt the Party when he is asked to write an article denouncing Henry, who has been his friend. Sam's father visits him at the newspaper office and criticizes the Party for making him write the article: "It's a pretty poor party, that's all I got to say." His father then tells him that the preacher at his church has denounced Communism by making an analogy between it and slavery: "There's more slaves in Communist countries than there are anyplace, anywhere." Sam's father convinces him to leave the Party. With both Sam and Mollie, then, religion plays a key role in redeeming the American misguided by Communist propaganda. And indeed, religious organizations typically played a central role in anti–Communist propaganda. As John Haynes points out in *Red Scare*, some post–World War II anti–Communists joined hatred of Communism with intense religious fervor; evangelical Protestants and Roman Catholics alike aligned Biblical prophecies of apocalypse with current events: "Stalin appeared to be the Antichrist ... [and] preachers shifted from describing communism as only one of the many sins of modern times to being a chief evil of the era" (90–91).

Other American Communists in the film are martyred for their ability to see through the scam of Communism. Henry Solomon, ultimately forced to commit suicide because of a "deviationist" poem he has written, denounces the Party once his eyes have been opened to its hypocrisy. Henry accuses the Party of being made up of "trained red seals." He further comments that most of the people he has met in the Party are "psychopathic misfits ... only people like that could accept the Party." Henry dies because of his vocal opposition to the Party. Made unemployable because the Party sends a copy of his Communist membership card to each place in which he finds work, he commits suicide rather than face the continuing persecution brought about by the Party. Another character, Anthony Reachi, contradicts Comrade Yvonne Kraus in a class she is teaching for the Party. Yvonne tells him, "We'll have our way if it means bloodshed and terror." Reachi continues to disagree with the basic tenets of Communism, resulting in Yvonne denouncing him a "Mussolini-spawned dago." Guards then take Reachi out and beat him to death. The headline of *The Toilers* the next day reads, "Anthony Reachi killed because he was a Communist."

Similarly, the protagonist of the film, Bill, falls into the Party's trap because he is caught in a web prepared for him and other ex-servicemen beforehand. James Burnham in *The Web of Subversion* (1954), an anti–Communist nonfiction work, describes the dual internal and external communist threat in the following terms: "The web of subversion is not primarily a domestic growth. It is the domestic extension of an international organism. The spinning of the web and the defense against it are campaigns in a vast and continuing struggle that will decide what kind of world mankind is to live in" (203). When Bill visits the bank to complain about the real-estate scam he has fallen victim to, a Communist agent is there, listening, ready to prey upon disgruntled servicemen. At the offices of *The Toilers*, the publisher of the paper and Earl Partridge, the Party leader, are amused by the predicament of the GI. Partridge says, "It's a shame about those poor boys," a statement that sends them into paroxysms of laughter. Partridge has no concern for Bill, but merely wants to trap him into joining the Party: "When we get him into the Party, he'll find out it's not so easy to get out." In an article entitled "Communism in the United States," Hoover comments, "The progress which all good citizens seek, such as old-age security, houses for veterans, and a host of others, is being adopted as window dressing by the Communists to conceal their true aims and entrap gullible followers" ("Testimony" 141).

The Red Menace reassures its audience that Americans are merely misguided fools when they join the Party, and that, therefore, redemption is possible for those who decide to reject it. Redemption was a key feature of anti–Communism in postwar America, with the friendly witnesses to HUAC given the opportunity to receive redemption with regard to their Communist pasts. The redemption and fame accorded such friendly witnesses as Whittaker Chambers and Herbert Philbrick illustrate this idea. By suggesting that American Communists could be redeemed from their sinful involvement with the party, *The Red Menace* also suggested hope. Those Americans, then, who had met the devil and come back to tell the tale were strong and loyal Americans indeed.

In the film, the contrast between the redeemable American and the corrupt foreigner is most clearly seen through the character Yvonne Kraus. Yvonne, whose real name is Greta Bloch, is an illegal German immigrant who has collaborated with the Party in order to kill the real Yvonne in Mexico so that she could steal her identity. Greta has no redeemable qualities. She readily urges the liquidation of anyone who questions the Party. She urges the persecution of Henry. She follows Nina and Bill to a restaurant to eavesdrop on their conversation, and later exposes both of them to Partridge. When immigration officers arrest her, exposing her assumed identity, Greta goes crazy, hallucinating the revolution. The officer orders her to be taken to the "psychopaths' ward." The unredeemable qualities of Greta hence indicate a lingering postwar suspicion of the German, not as Nazi this time, but as Communist. There is a strain in early Cold War anti–Communist works that perceives the German threat as a strong one still.[3]

Like *Conspirator*, *The Red Menace* ultimately reassures its audience that Americans can be trusted. If they are seduced by Communism, authority figures in the United States can save them from the threat involved. In the closing scenes of *The Red Menace*, the sheriff in Talbut, Texas, a man by the name of Uncle Sam, reassures Nina and Bill that they can become part of the community again: "You folks have been running away from yourselves ... You're no more wanted by the authorities than I am." Uncle Sam then urges them to marry and have children: "What you two want to do is get yourselves hitched, raise yourselves a couple of real American kids." While *Conspirator* and *The Red Menace* address the threat of internal communism, the year after the film came out, the United States came face to face with the threat of external communism.

The Korean War represented the first tangible sign in the postwar world of communism's sneaky and insidious nature. The war began with a surprise attack that took the American military unawares. David T. Fautua argues that "The Korean War opened the Pandora's box of the Cold War ... As if on cue, the neglect in Army preparedness led to an early drubbing by the North Koreans" (110). A confident United States that saw itself as the postwar superpower was shattered in 1949. This was also the year that the Communists took over in China, and the one in which the Soviet Union exploded an atomic bomb for the first time, doing so years earlier than the military had expected. And then, in Korea, the United States found itself unprepared to fight a conventional war, having put too much stock in nuclear weapons. Up to that point, two dominant views had prevailed in the U.S. with regard to the future of war. One view held that the threat of nuclear war would abolish warfare altogether. The scientists' movement of the late Forties best articulated this idea.[4] For example, in *One World or None*, Irving Langmuir states that "We may some day come to regard the atomic bomb as the discovery that made it possible for mankind to bring an end to all war" (52).

Another common reaction was that any new war would inevitably be a nuclear one. This view resulted in many commentators minimizing the uniqueness of nuclear weapons. Major Alexander P. de Seversky, in an article published in *The Reader's Digest* in 1946, minimizes the damage done to Hirsohima and Nagasaki:

> If dropped on New York or Chicago, one of those bombs would have done no more damage than a ten-ton blockbuster; and the results in Hiroshima and Nagasaki could have been achieved by about 200 B-29s loaded with incendiaries, except that fewer Japanese would have been killed. I do not "underrate" atom bombs or dispute their future potential. I merely conveyed my professional findings on the physical results of the two bombs — and they happened to be in startling contrast to the hysterically imaginative versions spread throughout the world [121].

Further, an observer of Test Able at Bikini in 1946 reacted in the following manner: "Is that all? I was just thinking that the next war's not going to be so bad after all" (qtd. in Lifton and Mitchell 84). This view of nuclear weapons as the inevitable next step in warfare led the U.S. military to drastically cut their conventional troops. Fautua comments on the unhappy realization on the part of the U.S. military that "since the war took place on the periphery and was being fought for limited political gains, America's atomic superiority proved unable to deter the invasion and useless to recoup the lost territory. Only ground forces could do that" (110). The Korean War illustrated to Americans their previous miscalculations regarding the new face of war, and the conflict also affirmed American fears of an inhuman and cruel Communist enemy.

First-hand accounts of the Korean War and military assessments of the enemy's tactics paint a portrait of an evil and indeed almost supernatural enemy. In an article published in *Air University Quarterly Review*, the Communist enemy in Korea is summed up in the following terms: "He has inexhaustible hordes of laborers, and the speed and general quality of their work in large measure counterbalances their lack of modern machines. His long, varied experience in limited and guerrilla warfare pays off in cunning, skills, and disciplines peculiarly suited to operations in rugged and primitive Korea" ("Communist Camouflage" 90). Thus the cunning and grit of the Communist soldier in Korea compensates for his technological primitiveness in comparison with the United States. In a 1951 book, *The Reds Take a City*, first-hand accounts from South Koreans concerning the invasion of Seoul paint a portrait of a cruel and ideologically committed enemy. Kun Ho Lee discusses the horrible mock-trials that resulted in mass executions: "First they started vigorously to 'liquidate the reactionaries.' The terrible 'liquidation,' I hate to remember it even. They announced the opening of the so-called 'People's Court.' In effect this organization massacred innocent people" (50). Lee also relates that precious metals and personal possessions were seized from individuals and shipped to Moscow. "Maybe these things were special presents to Stalin," Lee comments (62). Lee ends his article by demonizing the communists: "It is an eternal enemy of the human race. Look straight at the revealed evil of the Reds. There can be no compromise, no concession" (64). In another eyewitness account in the collection an observer discusses how children converted to Communism betrayed their parents. He mentions a daughter of a philosophy professor who "denounced her father and mother as friendly to America, and both parents were arrested" (Riley and Schramm, "Surveillance"134). The Korean War drew Americans' attention to the Soviet-Chinese-Korean effort that seemed to signal the drive towards the start of Communist world domination and possibly World War III.[5]

A film made during the Korean War reflects concerns about Communist subterfuge and vindicates American soldiers in Korea as brave. *The Steel Helmet* (1951) focuses on Sergeant Zack, a hardened solider who is the sole survivor of a massacre directed by the North Koreans against his infantry platoon. Zack joins up with Short-Round, a South Korean orphan boy, and Corporal Thompson, an African-American medic who is also the only survivor of his platoon. Zack is eventually persuaded by Short-Round to help a company of men led by Lieutenant Driscoll, an ineffectual leader, find refuge and establish a base of operations in an abandoned Buddhist temple. The men capture a North Korean in the temple. North Korean snipers descend on the temple, and Short-Round is killed, a fact that results in Zack killing the POW out of anger. North Korean troops surround the temple, and everyone in the company is killed except Thompson; Zack; Private Baldy, a man who lost his hair as a child due to scarlet fever; and Tanaka, a Japanese-American solider.

The film paints a portrait of the Communist enemy as inhumane and devious. As Short-Round and Zack walk across the countryside, they see what appear to be two women praying at a Buddhist shrine; suddenly these two "women" take out rifles and begin shooting at Short-Round and Zack. After Zack kills the "women," he rips off their clothing and discovers that they are really two North Korean soldiers. As one soldier dies, he asks for Zack's help. When Zack bends down over him, the dying soldier pulls out a knife and tries to stab him. Later, Zack forces a band of civilian refugees to be searched because, as he says, "I don't want to turn my back and have some old lady shoot my head off." The Communist soldiers are devious, posing as women and using civilians to engage in guerrilla-style warfare. Zack also continually emphasizes the Soviet connection to the war, discovering a rifle from a sniper marked "Made in Russia." Zack says that the landscape holds "rice paddies crawling with commies just waiting … to wash you down with fish eggs and vodka." When Thompson meets up with Zack, he has just escaped a POW camp. He tells Zack that "They hate our guts." Zack responds, "That's not what Joe Stalin says." Driscoll suspects Thompson of collaboration when he learns that he has escaped from a camp, commenting, "Regiment's been getting a lot of stories about stragglers." Driscoll's suspicion reflects a general suspicion of American POWs in Korea that plagued wartime and postwar accounts of the role Americans played in the war.

Indeed, both during the war and after it, American soldiers were suspected of collaboration with the Communists because of the re-education process that POWs in Communist camps were known to have been subjected to. While the number of Americans who were thus successfully indoctrinated was in reality small, negative versions of prisoners' behavior made for sensational news stories both during and after the war. As H.H. Wubben comments, one myth about American conduct in Korea maintained that "American prisoners of war in Chinese and North Korean hands were morally weak and uncommitted to traditional American ideals" (5). As Wubben notes, these accounts reflect an inability to consider that Korea represented the first time that American POWs had been subjected to ideological persuasion, and, more surprisingly, reflected an American public that was "so gullible as to believe that such a chimera as the enemy's self-proclaimed 'lenient policy,' was, in fact, lenient" (19). Eugene Kinkead's *In Every War But One* portrays the American soldiers as selfish cowards, a view emerging from military sources themselves. For example, Kinkead cites an unnamed officer who blames the American POWs for being undisciplined and disloyal: "But to speak a widely-known truth, a certain number of those men who have come into the army after the Second World War, and as far as that goes today, are completely without loyalty" (178).

Against this backdrop of American suspicion regarding American soldiers, *The Steel Helmet* works to solidify an image of the loyal American soldier in Korea. The film, which is dedicated to the U.S. Infantry, in several important scenes highlights the lack of susceptibility of Americans to Communist propaganda. When the men capture the North Korean, he begins a process of indoctrination, seizing on the men he believes are susceptible. The North Korean approaches Thompson first, asking him how he can fight for the United States when within American society his race is segregated from the others. Thompson rejects the POW's suggestions outright, stating, "There are some things you just can't rush, buster ... Why don't you get wise, buster?" The POW then approaches Tanaka, asking him how he can fight for the U.S. when he knows that his people were placed in concentration camps during World War II. The POW tries to establish commonality between himself and the Japanese-American, stating, "You've got the same kind of eyes I have." Tanaka, however, like Thompson, completely rejects the prisoner's approach, saying to him, "Major, you're getting sloppy for a con artist." In the film, the American soldiers are wise to the tricks of Communism, and cannot be converted. Further, when Zack kills the prisoner due to his rage over Short-Round's death, it is because the prisoner mocks the prayer to Buddha that Short-Round is wearing when he dies: "Please make Sergeant Zack like me." The prisoner is not only crude in his indoctrination methods, but he lacks any recognizable human emotions. Thus, *The Steel Helmet* reveals the treachery of the enemy in Korea and vindicates the American soldier as brave and strong in the face of both battle and indoctrination attempts on the part of the Communists.

As these examples illustrate, popular film of the late Forties and early Fifties instilled the threat of Communism into the audience while simultaneously reassuring them about the ability of Americans to stand up to this threat, whether internal or external. These films illustrate Hoover's optimism that once Americans were alerted to the threat of Communism, they would rally to the cause: "I feel that once public opinion is thoroughly aroused as it is today, the fight against communism is well on its way" ("Testimony" 119).

The discourse of American individualism informs these films, illustrating how Americans thinking for themselves will reject Communism. The discourse of individualism is also important to some anti–Communist works of popular culture that contrast the individual Russian with his political system.

4. The Individual Russian and the Communist System

One strain of anti–Communism that spans various forms of popular anti–Communist works is the notion that within the corrupt Soviet system there are individual Russians of worth, people who are able to see the limitations of the system in which they live and defy that system by breaking through those limitations. Within this scenario, these kinds of Soviet Communists are victims of a system that has forced them to become drones for the Party, hate the United States, and promote war. In such a situation, only strong individuals would be capable of defying the system. Hence, popular anti–Communist works that create lone Soviet heroes shape them as individualists, that is, as characters cast from an American mold.

The Communist machine as envisioned by Hoover was one that made it very difficult for individuality to even exist, much less flourish. As Hoover describes the situation, "Party schools, cadre training, and regimented discipline were needed to saturate the members in communism. Weaklings were purged, expelled and exiled to Siberia, or executed" (*Masters* 37). In the Stalinist Russia that Hoover describes, the system was evil and crushed individuals like insects. However, beginning in late Forties anti–Communist films, Russian heroes emerged; people capable of defying the system appeared. The trend to project an image of the good person in a bad system continued throughout popular representations of anti–Communism in the Fifties and Sixties.

One early example of this trend is *Guilty of Treason* (1949), which

Posters such as these indicate tense Allied hatred for the Soviet Communist system under Stalin. (Courtesy of the Library of Congress, Prints and Photographs division, USZ62 117876.)

focuses on events surrounding the imprisonment of Cardinal Mindszenty in Hungary.[1] According to Csaba Teglas in *Budapest Exit*, the case of Mindszenty is representative of the excesses of oppression that occurred in Hungary in its post–World War II transition to Communism: "One of the most famous of these trials was that of Cardinal József Mindszenty. The cardinal, an outspoken and unyielding person, had been persecuted and jailed previously by the fascists. Now the communists arrested him. Before his trial, he was forced to take mind-altering drugs and was severely tortured for weeks. The cardinal was sentenced to life imprisonment for 'treason'" (62–63).

The film weaves a fictional narrative set around the events leading up to the imprisonment of Mindszenty. In the film, American reporter Tom Kelly gives a lecture to the press corps entitled "Treason in Budapest 1949." As he gives his lecture, the film shows us a flashback of Tom's arrival in Budapest in 1948.[2] At a café in Budapest, he meets a Hungarian music teacher named Stephanie Varna. Stephanie is in love with Colonel Melnikov, a Soviet military man. Although they love each other deeply, they are driven apart by politics. After visiting Mindszenty at his farm, she becomes an active member of one of the Hungarian underground groups currently opposing Soviet domination of their society and also opposing the arrest of Mindszenty. As a result of her activism, Stephanie is arrested. However, through Melnikov's intervention, she is initially released, but, later, he is unable to save her. She is tortured to death, refusing to accuse either Mindszenty or Melnikov of treason. Melnikov, filled with remorse over Stephanie's death, goes to her apartment, into which he is followed by Soviet soldiers who push him out the window. Tom goes back to the United States to inform the world about the horrors that are occurring in Soviet-dominated Hungary.

Guilty of Treason is representative of the kind of extremely anti–Communist propaganda films that were made in the late Forties. At the beginning of the film, we see images of Soviet aggression — tanks, soldiers marching — while a Soviet narrator comments that the Soviet Union is the "greatest force for peace that the world has ever known." The narrator continues, commenting that "We are the friendliest nation in the world." The film abruptly stops, and we realize that we have been watching a Soviet propaganda film that Tom is showing to his audience at the press corps. The film portrays the Soviet system as one of extreme cruelty. When Tom arrives in Budapest, he is horrified by the Soviet headquarters there, which he labels a "house of terror ... and its masters were Russians." The Soviets are totally ruthless, using diabolical torture techniques in order to force confessions out of those who support Mindszenty.

Before her arrest, Stephanie comments, "Every day hundreds are arrested, and never heard from again." After Mindszenty is arrested, the Soviets torture him with sleep deprivation, starvation, and drugs. In addition to their brutal torture methods, the film also portrays the Soviet system as hypocritical. They oppose Mindszenty partly because he wants true Communism. For example, one Soviet official comments that Mindszenty has opposed the Soviet land redistribution plan "because it didn't give enough to every farmer."

Although *Guilty of Treason* is very typical of early post–World War II propaganda films in painting an extremely negative view of the Soviet system, its agenda calls for a very different view to be applied to individual Russians. *Guilty of Treason* argues that individual Russians, like Colonel Melnikov, are good people who are trapped in a bad system. This opposition between individuals and government is established in the film principally by Mindszenty. Both in a private conversation with Tom and Stephanie and in a public address, Mindszenty emphasizes that he does not hate the Russian people, but does hate their system. Mindszenty says that he does not condemn the Russian people, but "I do condemn the police state to which they are enslaved." At the end of the film, Tom speaks directly to the camera, stating that "some day, if we could ever get through to the Russian people, things might be different." The character of Melnikov illustrates the notion the film puts forth that individual Russians deserve the sympathy of America, whereas the opprobrious socio-political system of the Soviet Union in which they are enmeshed deserves only condemnation.

Melnikov is caught between his loyalty to the Communist Party and his love for Stephanie. Melnikov believes that the Soviet system will allow him the personal happiness he seeks in marrying Stephanie. Early in the film, he tells her, "I'm sure if he saw you, Stalin himself would insist upon kissing the bride." While Stephanie recognizes that politics will inevitably interfere with their love affair, Melnikov denies this: "We belong to each other. Politics can't change that." Yet, in fact, politics not only destroys their love for each other, but it destroys both their lives as well. Melnikov finds himself powerless to help Stephanie, telling Tom, "There is nothing I can do. It is not my department." Ultimately, his guilt over Stephanie's death causes his own death, as he is discovered in her apartment and killed by Soviet soldiers.

Through the portrayal of his anti–Nazism, the film also emphasizes Melnikov's sympathetic status as a good man caught up in a bad system. When Tom first visits the Budapest café where he meets Stephanie, he hears a Nazi song being played. Melnikov stops the band, telling them, "Let

Nazi music stay dead with the Nazis." During a Christmas Eve meeting with Stephanie and Tom, Melnikov tells them that his whole family was killed by Nazis. Tom sees Melnikov's suffering as indication of the common ground shared by the Russians and the Americans, commenting, "We won that battle together." Melnikov laments the fact that former allies are now enemies, stating, "There are difficulties between countries that do not exist between individuals." Melnikov's disillusionment with the Soviet system comes from that system's willingness to align itself with Nazi elements in Budapest. Thus, Melnikov is horrified by Commissar Belov's suggestion that Mindszenty be accused of anti–Semitism in order to discredit him: Melnikov labels this a Nazi tactic. Later, he learns from Stephanie that the Soviets have been using a Nazi gang to attack their enemies. Tom is severely beaten by a gang that leaves a note by his body that reads, "Heil Hitler. Heil Stalin." Melnikov discovers that the Soviet system does not allow for his personal happiness and additionally easily aligns itself with the Nazis, who destroyed his entire family. His disillusionment with the Soviet system indicates his sympathetic status in the film.

Guilty of Treason is an important example in early anti–Communist films of a clear distinction made between individual Russians and the Soviet system. Throughout the Fifties and Sixties, this trend was manifested in a variety of different genres that incorporated anti–Communist ideology.

One cogent example is *The 27th Day*, a science-fiction novel written by John Mantley and published in 1956. It was made into a film of the same name in 1957. *The 27th Day* tells the story of five people abducted by aliens and given capsules that possess the ability to annihilate most of human life on earth. The aliens tell the abductees that if they can survive for twenty-seven days without using the weapons, the aliens will leave; otherwise, they will colonize Earth. The aliens then return the humans to Earth. Su Tan, a Chinese abductee, immediately kills herself, and her capsules evaporate. Eve Wingate, a British abductee, throws her capsules in the ocean. Jonathan Clark, an American journalist, goes into hiding with Wingate. Professor Klaus Bechner, a German scientist, travels to the U.S. and, after collapsing from malnutrition, allows the U.S. government to have his capsules. Ivan Godofsky, a Russian military private, finally gives his capsules to the Leader after being severely tortured. The Leader decides to use the threat of the capsules to blackmail the U.S. and force them to leave Europe. The U.S. complies. Then, prior to a projected Soviet launching of the capsules on North America, two things happen. First, Ivan kills the Leader before he can destroy human life in North America. Second, Bechner discovers how to reverse the capsules so that they destroy only evil people, yet make other people capable of living in harmony with each other. In the new world created by the capsules, the leaders invite the aliens to share the Earth with them.

From the beginning of *The 27th Day*, the Communist threat is perceived as the dangerous one because it involves using the capsules to end human life. In both the novel and the film version of the story, when Ivan is abducted, he is the only abductee to react violently. He fires his rifle at the alien, but it has no effect. Although Su Tan is also from a Communist country, she does not pose a threat, because she is a victim of Communist oppression: when the alien takes her away, Su Tan has just been raped by "Communist hirelings" (11). The German, American, and British abductees immediately forge a bond through their shared knowledge of the English language. When they decide to form a pact through which they agree not to turn the power of the capsules over to their respective governments, it is Ivan who poses the problem. Jonathan questions whether he can be trusted: " How do we know the Russian wouldn't agree to the plan and then give the bomb to the Central Committee as soon as he got back on earth?" (26). Ivan's agreement to the pact illustrates a central point of *The 27th Day*: that although individuals within Communist countries can be honorable, the system is so corrupt that individuals subjected to it are easily crushed. Su Tan's suicide eliminates the possibility of Chinese Communists using the capsules: Su Tan is horrified by living in a China "that now groveled in misery and famine beneath the heel of evil and ruthless men" (40). Su Tan's only possibility of escaping the corrupt Communist system, *The 27th Day* tells us, is through suicide. Ivan's problems, however, are not so easily solved.

The work portrays Su Tan as a victim of the evil Communist system; it portrays Ivan in a similar manner. He is the one abductee who must undergo mental and physical torture due to the pact he has made not to reveal the truth about the capsules. Although Ivan has been brainwashed by the Soviet system into believing that he should turn the capsules over to the Soviet government, he is affected by the aliens' idea that "it has never been the people themselves that cause a war, but their leaders" (22). This belief, that people in Cold War society are more astute than their leaders, causes Ivan to decide to keep the pact he has made with the other abductees. Problems arise not because Ivan is an untrustworthy individual but because in the 1963 setting of the novel a revival of Stalinism has swept the Soviet Union up under the dictatorial control of the Leader: "In one bloody night he had stepped from relative obscurity in the secret police into the footsteps of Stalin" (52). The Leader turns Ivan over to Gregor, a secret police official who runs a hospital specializing in the use of drugs

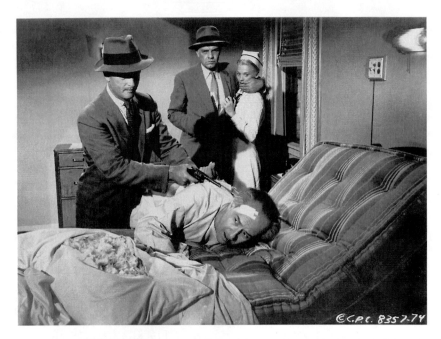

In this scene from The 27th Day, *Professor Klaus Bechner, who has been hospitalized, is threatened by American Communist agents.*

for torture purposes. Gregor is unsuccessful, however, in obtaining a confession from Ivan soon enough for the impatient Leader: this results in Gregor being executed.

Although Ivan has concern for the human race and is able to survive massive amounts of barbaric torture to keep the capsules from the Leader, the Leader himself is concerned only with power for its own sake. When Ivan breaks under torture and gives the Leader the capsules, the Leader is heady with power: "He had forgotten everything except that he was now, as of this particular earth-shaking moment, the most powerful man in the history of the world" (126). The inevitability of the Leader using the capsules once he possesses them conforms to Cold War American perceptions of the Soviet Union as a security dilemma. As Robert Jervis argues, this perception was based on each side of the bipolarity being "deeply fearful that the other side was aggressive or would become so in the future" (38). In the world of *The 27th Day* the Allies are justified in fearing aggressive action by the Soviets because a policy of initiating such aggressive action is exactly what the Leader adopts.

Although Ivan breaks under the extreme torture brought upon him at the instigation of the Leader, he ultimately proves himself to be an individual of conscience. Like Melnikov in *Guilty of Treason,* he is able to see beyond the system into which he has been indoctrinated. After revealing the truth about the capsules to the Leader, Ivan is given luxury as a reward. However, he is suspicious of any rewards that the Soviet system might decide to give him: "He was not stupid. He realized that, regardless of the honors which had been heaped upon him, he was being treated with the utmost courtesy because the bombs were only lethal as long as he remained alive" (153). When it comes to the moment when Ivan must launch the capsules on North America, he cannot do it. He shoots the Leader and is then himself killed by the Leader's henchmen. *The 27th Day* argues that individual Russians, such as Ivan, are men of conscience and peace; it is only ruthless leaders and the Soviet system that Americans must fear.

The 27th Day, both film and book, contrasts the Soviet system with the American system. Although the Americans also want knowledge of the capsules, they refuse to go to the lengths that the Soviets do in order to get the abductees to reveal the truth to them. Whereas the Leader is a man who rails at his underlings, "I intend that we shall use this weapon to rule the world!" (132) by contrast, the American president is a man of conscience who prematurely ages due to the stresses placed upon him: "The youthful buoyancy of his gait was gone. Dark circles were under his eyes and deep lines of care were etched into his face. Since the advent of the Aliens, the President had become an old man" (139). Thus, the fact that Jonathan is a man of conscience and desires peace is not surprising in the world of *The 27th Day.* The American system encourages good behavior.

By contrast, Ivan's heroic act to save North America from destruction is extraordinary. The Russian individual who has the strength to act against the Communist system is given mythic dimensions. Thus, Ivan is able to overcome the brainwashing that has always been an overwhelmingly powerful force in his life in the Soviet Union. The Leader and the media that he controls create and project a dominant image of the United States as an aggressive enemy. Although the Allies have made no threats to use their capsules, the Leader tells Ivan that "the great courage and spirit of our people are being humbled before the imperialistic warmongers of the West. They threaten us with total destruction if we do not accede to their demands" (124). As Jervis argues, under Stalin, the creation of evil capitalistic enemies was a necessity: "Foreign enemies were necessary to justify his own role as supreme leader and the Communist Party's control of all spheres of life" (47). The fact that Ivan can defy the Leader's propaganda and believe that the United States and its allies do not want war and destruction speaks to his heroic status in the work.

An episode of the Sixties TV series *I Spy* also portrays the individual Russian who can defy the Soviet system in heroic terms. In "A Day Called 4 Jaguar," American secret agents Kelly and Scott are on vacation in Mexico. When Kelly's girlfriend, Felicitas, is trapped under a Jeep after a road accident, she is saved by a bearded, blond, blue-eyed giant she believes to be the legendary Aztec god Quetzalcoatl. Asking Washington for help, Kelly and Scott begin an investigation. Washington sends an agent who identifies the giant as Dimitri, a Russian colonel who disappeared during a good-will tour in Mexico. Scott and Kelly set out to convince Dimitri to defect to the United States. Meanwhile, the Soviets have sent an agent, Nicolai, who poses as a Texan, to either kill Dimitri or bring him back to the Soviet Union. Scott, Kelly, and Nicolai all descend on Dimitri's secret compound. Nicolai convinces Dimitri to go back to the Soviet Union and then attempts to kill Scott and Kelly. Dimitri opposes this, and Nicolai shoots him. Nicolai is then burnt alive by the Aztec Indians, and Scott and Kelly escape.

Like *Guilty of Treason* and *The 27th Day*, this episode of *I Spy* opposes the corrupt Soviet system to an idealistic individual Russian. In the episode, the Soviet system is cynical and brutal. Thus, for example, Nicolai's contact condemns him because Nicolai has an ideological commitment to bring Dimitri back to the Soviet Union. The contact comments that "zealots are a bore." The Soviets view Dimitri purely as a commodity that they need to retrieve. While the Americans also want Dimitri as a commodity, Kelly displays sympathy for his desire to be off of the Cold War merry-go-round. Dimitri expresses his disillusionment with the Soviet system by stating, "They started to use me. Your country does it, too." Kelly tells Dimitri that he is "one who will not circle the track ... I've had the same sensation myself." Kelly agrees to leave Dimitri in peace and never reveal where is hiding.

By contrast, the Soviet system will not allow Dimitri to find happiness with the Aztec people. Further, Nikolai makes Dimitri feel suspicious of Kelly and Scott so that he will not sympathize with them as individual humans, but, rather, see them as cogs within the American system. He tells Dimitri that Kelly and Scott are lying when they expose him for trying to murder them and Felicitas, commenting, "It's what they call American ingenuity." Nicolai cynically plays on his and Dimitri's past as childhood friends in order to convince him to return to the Soviet Union. Dimitri is truly shocked when he sees Nicolai's true nature, revealed when he insists on killing Kelly and Scott. When Dimitri stops Nicolai from killing the American agents, Nicolai labels Dimitri as a fool. "Yes, I am a fool," he responds as he sacrifices himself so that Scott and Kelly will not be killed.

Like Melnikov and Ivan, Dimitri plays the role of the good Russian killed by the Soviet system. While Melnikov dies because of his personal feelings for Stephanie, and Ivan dies to save all of North America, Dimitri's sacrifice is particularly extraordinary: he dies to save two American agents simply because he has come to see them as human beings, not as pawns in the Cold War conflict. The idea of the sympathetic Russian who can see beyond the strictures of the Soviet system is an element present in anti–Communist films from a wide variety of genres. As we have seen, espionage films, science-fiction films, and television spy series are powerful examples of this trend.

This particular element is also present in *The Russians Are Coming! The Russians Are Coming!* (1966), a Cold-War comedy, which recounts the events surrounding a Soviet submarine that runs aground on Gloucester Island. The Russian naval men go on-shore seeking a boat to help them get started on their way home. They steal a car from the Whittaker family and go to West Village to locate a boat. Meanwhile, the village goes berserk with rumors about the Russians and forms a vigilante group. The Russians eventually get their submarine back in running order, but by this time the chaos has led to two results. First, the Russian captain has decided to fire the submarine's guns on West Village because he wrongly believes that some of his men have been taken hostage there. The joint efforts of Soviets and Americans in saving a small boy who is dangling from a church steeple smoothes over this conflict, and the captain no longer threatens to fire. However, Fendal Hawkins, a World War II veteran, has called the U.S. military about the presence of the Russians, and everyone fears that the Russian submarine will be sunk. The people of West Village provide an escort for the submarine, which results in the Air Force refusing to fire on the submarine. The Russians go back home.

The Russians Are Coming paints a portrait of Cold War conflicts within which both sides of the bipolarity are frightened of each other. By focusing on individuals and not the actions of the government, the film highlights prejudices that both sides of the Cold War conflict felt about each other. The first sequences of the film focus on the action aboard the Russian submarine. The sailors speak in Russian and there is no translation provided for the audience. The Russians' thrill and apprehension when first stepping on American soil is evident. In fact, it is pure curiosity about the enemy that causes the Russians to run aground in the first place. Alexei Kolchin, one of the sailors from the submarine, reveals to the Whittaker family that the captain of the vessel merely wanted to get a closer look at the United States and, as a result, miscalculated how close he was to land. As the sailors look over the Whittaker car in its garage, one sailor is fascinated to find a Coca-Cola bottle.

Yet, at the same time, the Russians are very frightened of the United States' government and its power. Alexei tells the Whittakers that he fears "U.S. of American air machine guns" that will surely kill him and the other sailors. When Walt Whittaker asks Lieutenant Rozanov if there are parachuters on the island, Rozanov is horrified. He asks, "There are parachuters on island?" clearly afraid that Walt is referring to American parachuters. Rozanov trains several of the sailors to pass as Americans by dressing in American clothes and repeating "Emergency. Everybody to get from street." When the men encounter a small boy, they are clearly horrified that they have to speak to him. The Russian stereotypes about the United States are shown in the film as largely ludicrous.

Similarly, the American stereotypes about the Russians are deflated. In the Whittaker household, there is only one rabid anti–Communist. This is Peter, a fourth grader with a deep hatred for the Russians. Peter reports to his parents that the Russians are "creeping" outside the Whittaker house, but they refuse to listen to him. When Rozanov and Alexei come to the door pretending to be Norwegian members of NATO, Peter prods his father, "Ask them if they're Russian." When they tie up the Whittaker family in order to find out where there are available boats, Peter yells, "Don't tell them anything! We'll be traitors!" Peter laments the fact that Walt gives the Russians the information they are seeking, "I'll bet I'm the only guy in the 4th grade whose father is a famous traitor." The film vocalizes extreme anti–Communist sentiment through characters who are children or fools. What Peter is unable to do in the film, make a distinction between the government of the Soviet Union and the behavior of the individual Russians who are stranded and frightened on Gloucester Island, other characters in the film succeed in doing.

The clearest indication of a distinction between Soviet Communism and individual Russians is manifested in the character of Alexei and his love for Allison Palmer, a young woman who lives in the village. From the beginning, Alexei despises the force that the sailors must use on the Americans. When Rozanov leaves Alexei in charge of guarding the Whittaker family, he points his rifle at Annie, the three-year-old Whittaker daughter. Alexei is horrified by the fact that he has pointed a gun at a small child. He tells the family, "I am most sincerously sorry for incident with little girl." After Walt wrests the gun from Alexei's control, Alexei hides in a field. Later, he goes back to the house to find Allison babysitting Annie. Allison is frightened at first by his gun, but he offers to give it to her, and she tells him, "I'm not frightened." She then cleans his head wound and gives him food. Allison seems fascinated by Alexei, asking him, "Can I call you Alexei? I never met anyone called Alexei before." As

Alexei and Allison walk on a beach, Alexei tells her that "Many are saying Americans are bad people ... So always mistrust American ... I wish not to hate anybody." Allison readily agrees with him: "It doesn't make sense to hate people." When Allison kisses Alexei, he is amazed and asks, "This mean the same as in Soviet Socialists Republic?" The romance between Allison and Alexei indicates a clear separation between individuals and governments. The fact that Allison and Alexei can fall in love indicates that individual citizens are different from their governments, and, most explicitly, that, contrary to all the usual indications, a Russian man can be peace-loving and kind. At the end of the film, when Alexei is about to leave for home, he tells Allison that he will see her again: "We somehow have a long life of peaceful coexistence."

The Russians Are Coming, like the works previously discussed, uses one individual Russian in order to illustrate the differences between the Communist government and individual Russians. In Adlai Stevenson's account of his travels in Russia, *Friends and Enemies: What I Learned in Russia* (1958), Stevenson admires the perceptiveness of individual Russians to see beyond the anti-American propaganda they have been inundated with for years. Stevenson comments that "The Communist leaders may fear and even hate us. If they do, it is wonderfully concealed and the average Russian's naturally friendly attitude seems to have survived decades of anti-American propaganda" (40). It is this aspect of the kind, open-minded Russian that the anti–Communist works discussed in this chapter all perceive.

Curiously, in all the works discussed above, a handsome, young Russian, who is in most cases blond, serves as the vehicle for this observation. In this form of Cold War aesthetics, handsome young Russian men are capable of seeing beyond the bondage of the Soviet system and often dying as martyrs because of the revelations they have experienced.

Because of the prevalence of anti–Communist sentiment in Fifties and Sixties America, that sentiment came to intertwine not just with different discourses, but also with very specific popular culture genres. The next section of the book explores selected genres that incorporated anti–Communist plots into their conventions.

5. Anti–Communism and Ambivalence in Science Fiction

It is a commonplace idea that many popular U.S. science-fiction films released during the early Fifties and Sixties portray Communism as a monstrous threat. In Susan Sontag's landmark article about Fifties science fiction (sf) films, "The Imagination of Disaster," she argues that "[s]cience fiction films are not about science. They are about disaster" (213). While Sontag's focus is primarily on the ways in which Fifties sf films engage the issue of nuclear war, the imagination of disaster applied to the American Fifties in general, disaster resulting from dehumanization, juvenile delinquency, the Bomb, radiation contamination, and, of course, internal and external Communism. Fear of Communism as a monstrous force that would bring about the end of the world was a common rhetorical feature of Fifties America. Anti-Communist sentiment often meshed well with the monstrous imagery of sf and horror, but while we often tend to view the anti–Communist sentiment of science-fiction films from the American Fifties as a simple black-and-white one, ambivalence was in fact a key factor in the genre's treatment of anti–Communism.

In this chapter I focus on three B sf films from the height of the Cold War. My purpose is to demonstrate that B sf films engaged complicated issues related to Cold War society. Examination of these films helps illustrate that representation of the Red Scare was fraught with emotional ambivalence. My chapter follows in the footsteps of sf critics who have seen Fifties sf films as engaging important social issues. Sontag's perception that Fifties sf films represent a combination of naïve artistic presentation with "the most profound dilemmas of the contemporary situation" has influenced later critics (224). The notion of the centrality of sf to expression of concerns over Cold War America is an idea taken up by later critics of the genre. Peter Biskind's classic study of Fifties films, *Seeing Is Believing*, makes a powerful argument that sf films more than any other type of film best expressed emotional feelings about Cold War America: "It was sci-fi, more than any other genre, that caught the hysteria behind the picture window" (103). In his study of American sf, *American Science Fiction and the Cold War*, David Seed argues that Cold War sf engaged the most serious issues of the period such as "nuclear war, the rise of totalitarianism and fears of invasion" (11). Seed further argues that his research proves "the fine responsiveness of fiction and film to a whole range of social, technological, and political changes taking place during the Cold War" (11). By focusing on obscure B sf films, this chapter seeks to demonstrate the pervasiveness in American society of reflections of the Communist threat. I have chosen these three films because they are unique in being sf films from the period that deal directly with the Communist threat.[1] I compare the three B films under discussion here—*Red Planet Mars* (1952), *Invasion USA* (1952), and *The Beast of Yucca Flats* (1961)— alongside nonfictional works dealing with the threat of Communism in order to demonstrate ways in which these films do not paint simple portraits of Red-Scare hysteria but, rather, display ambivalence by blaming both a foreign threat and American weakness for social disaster.

Hyperbolic anti–Communist propaganda of the Cold War period meshed well with the exaggerated metaphors—giant insects, prehistoric creatures—of these sf/horror films[2] Paul Boyer, discussing the postwar period, argues that "science fiction is best understood as a commentary upon contemporary issues" (258). Rob Latham, discussing *Invaders from Mars*, agrees that sf "taps into our collective dreams and nightmares, condensing complex historical development into memorable images and suggestive metaphors" (206). By engaging the social issue of anti–Communism on a metaphorical level, these films provided interesting and varied reactions to the threat.

In one familiar strain of postwar rhetoric, Communism is a literally demonic force. J. Edgar Hoover's *Masters of Deceit*, presented as a dispassionate history of the development of the Communist Party, nonetheless demonizes the Soviets: "events ... have taught Americans that the communist is not an angel of mercy, ministering to the weak, oppressed, and wounded, but a menacing demon spattered with blood and wielding a hammer and a sickle of iron" (95). In an article published in *Christianity Today*, Hoover comments that "The spiritual firepower of the Christian

Church — based on the love of God — is sufficient to destroy all the Soviet man-made missiles and rockets and extirpate this twentieth-century aberration" (*On Communism* 92).

One cliché of anti–Communist rhetoric is that the Communist's evil stems from his or her alien qualities—lack of normal human feelings.[3] Hoover discusses a Party member who "dreamed up the idea that bodies of deceased comrades should be sold for medical experimentation," so that the Party could gain profit both from the bodies themselves and from the money that would have otherwise been spent on funerals (*Masters* 146). Harry and Bonaro Overstreet see monstrosity in the Communist Party's desire for war: "We think of war as an abnormal interruption of peace.... We think of it, in short, as *terminable*—and therefore want to get it over and done with. The Communists, however, think of it as simply one phase of an *interminable* struggle" (81). The Overstreets also describe the process by which an ordinary person becomes a Communist as a monstrous transformation: "The party member is deliberately turned into an emotional alien within the larger non–Communist society which he inhabits; for only thus can he be brought to desire its overthrow" (262). Herbert Philbrick's best-selling account of his years as an FBI operative in the American Communist Party recounts his horror at the lack of "normal human" qualities among Party members.[4] Philbrick feared that he might himself undergo the same monstrous transformation: "I had to submit myself to the constant hammerings of communism ... Wouldn't it be a fine thing, I often thought, if the evil I was trying to fight consumed me instead?" (86–87).

Other writers, while certainly not pro–Communist, resisted the impulse to demonize. Fred Schwartz's *You Can Trust the Communists (...to do Exactly as They Say!)* emphasizes the scientific prowess of the Soviets, noting that the American military is ill-equipped to deal with brainwashing because "the Communist assault on the human mind is historically unique and alarming in its effectiveness" (129). "The way to defeat it [brainwashing] is to defeat the program of Communist expansion. When the door closes behind you in the brainwashing chamber, it will be too late" (144).

Another strain in anti–Communist discourse may be seen in Richard Crossman's compilation *The God that Failed*. Arthur Koestler's account of his years as a Communist (included in *The God That Failed*) describes his decision to join the Party as a religious conversion: "Nothing henceforth can disturb the convert's inner peace and serenity — except the occasional fear of losing faith again, losing thereby what alone makes life worth living, and falling back into the outer darkness, where there is wailing and gnashing of teeth. This may explain how Communists, with eyes to see and brains to think with, can still act in subjective *bona fides*, anno Domini 1949" (23). In another memoir in the same collection, Ignazio Silone characterizes the day he left the Party as one "of deep mourning" (113).

In some accounts, atheistic Communism is contrasted with the Christian United States.[4] Hoover says of Lenin that "At the age of sixteen, as he later said, Lenin ceased to believe in God. It is reported that he tore the cross from his neck, threw the sacred relic to the ground, and spat upon it" (*Masters* 24). Joel Kovel argues that according to one extreme anti–Communist Cold War mythos, Communism was fulfilling "the role of the beast of the apocalypse" (116). As Haynes points out, religious opposition to Lenin emerged due to his regime's executions of approximately twenty thousand priests, monks, nuns, and religious laymen in the early 1920s (89). By the Fifties, a perception of the Soviet state as rigidly atheist persisted, despite the fact that Stalin had loosened restrictions on religious worship and had solicited and gained the aid of the Russian Orthodox Church during World War II. Yet, other views of the Soviet Union were also present in nonfiction works.

Irving R. Levine's *Main Street, U.S.S.R.* was a best-seller that portrayed the Soviet Union not as a demonic or atheistic land but as a place where real people lived real lives. Levine, the first accredited American journalist in Moscow, pointed out that the successes of the Soviet system stemmed from a strong education system — stronger, he said, than that of the U.S. He praised the seriousness of Soviet students, which he saw as the foundation of success in the space race:

> Every opportunity is taken … to impress upon young people the need for a serious attitude in studies and also in free-time pursuits. This may partly explain why Soviet youngsters spend so many free hours poring over chessboards instead of chatting on the telephone. The Soviet attitude of earnestness, seen in recreation as well as in study, has its roots in the Soviet classroom [162].

So some writers during the Fifties emphasized that it was not demonic forces that gave the Soviet Union its successes, but hard work and discipline. In fact, anti–Communism in this period encompassed a plurality of discourses. Richard Gid Powers argues that "[f]or many Americans, McCarthy made ludicrous the notion that Anti-Communism could be based on sound morality or a realistic view of the world. In the mouth of McCarthy, the truths of anti–Communism would turn into evil, malicious lies" (235). And for many Americans not directly involved in politics, Communism remained a peripheral issue. As Haynes notes, throughout the late Forties and Fifties, Americans were more concerned with "preventing war, inflation, government spending, taxes, relations with the Soviet Union, nuclear war, housing, and union-management turmoil" than with the threat posed by either internal or external Communists (188).

The variety of representations of Communism in B-films suggests that extreme anti–Communist rhetoric and McCarthyism did not reflect what most Americans believed or cared about. The three films under discussion here waver between focusing on the threat of Communism and alluding to other domestic problems as more pressing. Hence, the variety of responses to Communism in nonfictional works of the Cold War created ambivalence in fictional representations of the threat. Thus, if nonfictional bestsellers seemed to provide cohesive views of Communism — whether they encompassed the demonic force of Hoover's work or the humanized Communist of Levine's work — fictional representation brought together these varying views and created an ambivalent portrait of the threat. Paul Brians, for example, has argued that fictional depictions of the Soviet Union typically included the notion of the "complicity of Americans in their own conquest" (320). The films under discussion here focus on such complicity, hence complicating a simple view of the Soviets as evil enemy.

In *Red Planet Mars*, U.S. scientist Chris Cronyn attempts to contact inhabitants of Mars by means of technology developed by Franz Calder, a Nazi scientist. While Cronyn is making his attempts, Calder in South America is also working on establishing contact with Mars — in his case doing so for the potential benefit of the Soviet Union. Cronyn begins picking up messages from Mars that detail the Martians' utopian existence and feature their long average life span and lack of any need for either fossil fuels or high-intensity agricultural activities. When the texts of these messages are released to the world, the result is the abrupt collapse of the economies of both the United States and Europe. In reaction to this calamity, the U.S. government and military decide to release the texts of no more Martian messages — though they reverse this policy when a further Martian message received by Cronyn's equipment seems to verify the existence of God. When this message and successive ones also with a religious content are released, a worldwide religious revival takes place that results in the overthrow of the Soviet Union and the other countries of the Soviet Bloc.

At this point, Calder travels from South America to the United States to confront Cronyn. He tells Cronyn and his wife, Linda, that the messages they have been receiving haven't really been coming from Mars at all — that they have, in fact, been faked by Calder himself as part of his plan to destroy both the democratic and Communist worlds. Linda refuses to believe him. And, indeed, while the three people are locked in a confrontation, a further message starts to come through on the equipment. Calder's reaction to this is to fire his gun at the machine, an act that results in a massive explosion that kills both Calder and the Cronyns. The President subsequently reveals that the incoming message, though never completed, clearly had a religious content. This film displays a tension between hatred for the Soviet Union and fear of American internal weakness.

Red Planet Mars, for instance, engages with the issue of atheism and Communism, portraying it as a false religion, but it does so in a complicated manner. Initially, a contrast between belief and unbelief is established in the film through conversations between scientist Chris Cronyn and his wife, Linda. While Chris propounds an uncomplicated view of scientific development as positive, Linda questions the value of science, arguing that "we've lived on the edge of a volcano all our lives" and that "science has made the volcano that we are sitting on." Chris sees scientific developments as positive, but Linda is not convinced that there is any wisdom in contacting Mars.

Linda is a bastion of religious belief. We see her tucking her son Roger into a bed situated beneath a reproduction of a Raphael painting of the Virgin and Child. When Admiral Bill Carey is assigned to the Cronyns' laboratory to facilitate communication with Mars, Linda voices her suspicions about the project: "We dare to fly in the face of Providence and bring it [Mars] closer to us." When the Cronyn transmitter makes its initial contact with Mars, Linda prays, "Dear Lord, don't make us sorry." The film most clearly highlights Linda's function as the spokesperson for faith when she urges the President to allow religious messages from Mars to be broadcast across America. Chris rejects these messages as unscientific, but the President agrees with Linda. And in the film her insistence on releasing these messages brings about the fall of Communism.

Linda also represents the liberated American woman, contrasting with the shackled women of the Soviet Union. As Joanne Meyerowitz argues, Cold War rhetoric, in an attempt "to distinguish the autonomous individuals of the free world from the suppressed masses under communism," promoted women's achievements (1465). She comments, too, that in women's publications such as The Ladies Home Journal, "authors often used the Cold War to promote women's political participation. One such approach contrasted the free society of the United States with Soviet oppression, including oppression of women" (1469).

While U.S. society during the 1950s certainly encouraged women to be content with domestic roles, in B films the ideal woman often is presented as combining the domestic with outside activity. Linda Cronyn's involvement in the creation and use of an interplanetary transmitter reflects a vision of the American woman as scientifically capable[5] — a vision not that unusual in films of the 1950s.

Pat Medford in *Them!* (1954), for example, participates with male colleagues in the search for giant ants in the New Mexico desert. Dr. Iris Ryan in *The Angry Red Planet* (1959) uses her scientific expertise to save Colonel Thomas O'Bannion when he is infected by a Martian amoeba. In *The Beast from 20,000 Fathoms* (1953), Leigh Hunter is a scientist who contributes her emotional support and her knowledge of paleontology to Thomas Nesbitt as they search for a prehistoric beast; and in *Revenge of the Creature* (1955), Helen Dobson, who is working for a master's degree in Ichthyology, is like Leigh in understanding the crisis better than her male counterparts: she is portrayed as combining scientific knowledge with emotional understanding.[6]

In *Red Planet Mars*, when Linda and Chris Cronyn visit an astronomer working on a top-secret project, he tells them that "they've [government operatives have] classified the sky": it is, then, significant that Linda has a security clearance to attend the meeting and take an active part. Furthermore, even when the military becomes involved in the project through the activities of Admiral Carey, Linda is kept informed about all conversations between Chris and the Admiral and openly voices her opinions. In the scene mentioned earlier, in which she convinces the President to release the religious messages from Mars, it is again clear that she has access to top-secret information. The film portrays a Soviet woman as stuck in the menial position of telephone operator but Linda, its representative American woman, is a full-fledged professional colleague as well as a wife and mother. Her scientific knowledge, combined with her religious belief, makes her a formidable adversary of the Communist threat as defined in the rhetoric of the 1950s — a threat, indeed, that in the film she almost single-handedly defeats, although it costs her her life. Yet the martyrdom of Linda and Chris at the hands of Franz Calder indicates one further interesting aspect of the film.

Even though *Red Planet Mars* is anti–Communist, the true embodiment of evil in the film is not a Communist but a Nazi. Anti-Communist propaganda frequently made analogies between Communists and Nazis. Hoover, for instance, focuses readers' attention upon exterminations committed by the Soviets, comparing them to those of the Nazis; he maintains that the United States holds values directly opposed to genocide:

> A belief, which has matured to a firm conviction, that in the final analysis love is the greatest force on earth and is far more enduring than hatred; this forbids our accepting the Communist division of mankind that by arbitrary standards singles out those fit only for liquidation [*Masters* 299].

This forging of a close association between the Communists and the Nazis made for an easy transition in public perceptions between the enemy forces of World War II and the ideologies perceived as menaces during the postwar period. William Pietz argues that American fear of totalitarianism in the Cold War period represented a view of the enemy state through the prisms of "traditional Oriental despotism plus modern police technology" (58). Pietz argues that both Nazi totalitarianism and Communist totalitarianism were conflated together and used rhetorically to save the West from charges of brutality (70). Thus, the desire on the part of the American government to distinguish itself from totalitarianism made the conflation between Nazi and Soviet both possible and desirable.

What is curious about *Red Planet Mars* is that its Nazi threat is projected as more powerful than Communism. Calder's plan to create general chaos dupes both the United States and the Soviet Union. Calder mocks his Soviet contact, Arjenian, telling him that he is not threatened by the Soviet Union's pressure to put him in prison or dispose of him if he fails in his attempts to contact Mars. Furthermore, Calder views Cronyn's use of his (Calder's) hydrogen valve to establish contact with the Martians as "stealing." While the Soviet leaders embrace the chaos Calder creates in the West, declaring that "we will build our new world on the ruins of the West," their world too is easily toppled by Calder — through the creation of the religious messages. These messages seemingly confirm the existence of God and cause political uprisings in the Soviet Union and Soviet Bloc countries. Calder frequently quotes from *Paradise Lost*, identifying himself with Satan: he tells the Cronyns that Lucifer is his hero. Thus, in *Red Planet Mars*, underneath the Communist threat lurks the more dangerous threat of an unrepentant Nazi intent on creating general anarchy as a means of avenging Hitler's defeat. The Soviet threat is easily dispelled by American faith in God, but the Nazi threat is enigmatic because it embraces both belief and evil, in that the Nazi system incorporated Christian faith into its political ideology.

Invasion USA, another anti–Communist film from the early Fifties, also makes an association between the Nazi and the Soviet threat in order to frame the evil of Communism in familiar World War II terms. The film tells the story of a group of people at a Manhattan bar who are hypnotized by a fortuneteller called Mr. Ohman into experiencing a group vision of a potential future. In the scenario that Ohman creates and we the audience share, we see that American selfishness and lack of support for a strong military have allowed the Soviet Union to invade the United States by way of Alaska. By disguising themselves as American soldiers, the Soviets succeed in A-bombing most major American cities. After the bombing, they effect a full-scale invasion, taking over Congress and New York City and setting up a Communist government for the United States. After Ohman reveals to the customers that they have seen only a vision of what might happen to the United States in the future, they decide to work with the military to prevent such an invasion.

Like *Red Planet Mars*, this film projects Nazi and Soviet as merged into one frightening enemy. For example, though there is a strong implication that the invaders in the film are Soviet, they wear clothing that strikingly resembles SS uniforms and the invaders' accents are hard to identify exactly: they might be German; they might be Russian. In fact, the invading force is typically referred to as simply "the enemy," or indicated simply by pronouns. One U.S. general asks, "Is he going to use his A-bomb?" While there are clear associations between the film's "enemy" and the Soviet Union, especially in a scene near the end of the film in which a woman's apartment is invaded by enemy troops and they drink her liquor and attempt to rape her (reinforcing stereotypes of the savage Russian), the shadowy nature of the threat allows the film to address the hostile forces in World War II as well as the Cold War, in much the same way as occurs in *Red Planet Mars*. However, a key difference between the two films lies in how in *Red Planet Mars* the Nazi is the power behind the crisis, and is a power that is stronger than the Red Menace, whereas in *Invasion USA* Nazi and Communist represent the same, merged totalitarian threat.

Of course, at the time the movie was released, the only really viable enemy for the U.S. — the only one thought capable of making good on a threat of military force — was the Soviet Union. But the kind of aggressiveness displayed by the enemy in staging a surprise invasion of the United States suggests Nazi and Japanese aggression before and during World War II, while at the same time reminding the audience that this same aggression is encouraged by Communist Party doctrine. As Philbrick relates of his experience in the American Communist Party, the overthrow of the capitalist state was the keynote of the policy of the Communist Party under Lenin and Stalin: "The Communist seeks by every means to create a split in our society, to provoke class and racial hatreds and intense conflict. All capitalist governments, the Communist is taught, inevitably become states of fascist oppression, thus creating the demands for a violent revolution as the only possible cure" (284). In *Invasion USA*, the United States retaliates only after being invaded and suffering immense material damage and loss of life. The President describes the enemy as "forces of evil, forces that will never rest until they've conquered the world." The enemy is thus ambiguous, displaying the aggressiveness of more than one "enemy" nation.

In *Invasion USA*, military officials puzzle over the Soviet plan of invasion as something unfathomable, and, within the confines of the film, as Russian forces take over the United States government, Soviet strategy is represented as undefeatable. This unbeatable quality is something echoed by the Overstreets: "A strange new force has entered our world, the strangest and most enigmatic in all history. Equipped with a formula and a strategy, and starting in one of the most backward countries of Europe, it has, in a brief forty years, taken control of one-third of the world's people and one-fourth of the world's territory" (ix). While *Invasion USA* attributes defeat of the United States by the Soviet Union to the mysterious evil of Communism, it also points a finger at weaknesses within the United States itself.

Fear of American decadence informed sociology in the Fifties: the film conveys a powerful sense of this decadence through the characters' selfishness and greed, qualities that have set up conditions that make the country ripe for invasion. In its portrayal of U.S. decline, the film echoes social critics such as Lewis Mumford and Philip Wylie. Joanne Meyerowitz notes that one typical target for criticism during the 1950s was the woman of leisure. Misogynists such as Wylie (who, as we have seen, wrote of the cultural decline produced by "Momism") and even such women's magazines as *Ladies Home Journal* were alike in their denunciation of the parasitic woman. Meyerowitz notes that "The flip side of this emphasis on hard work was a condemnation of idleness and frivolity. Articles opposed meaningful work to activities coded as the trivial pursuits of the woman of leisure: bridge playing, aimless shopping, and 'summers on the Riviera'" (1461). In *Invasion USA*, Carla Sanford represents the woman of leisure who is a signifier of the decay of American culture. She spends most of her time at a bar and dresses in extravagant evening clothes. She openly flirts with newscaster Vince Potter when she first meets him. She tells Vince that during World War II she worked briefly in a factory but quit because the work was ruining her hands. After the invasion, Carla reflects that "a month ago I wanted a mink stole. I thought it was important." Carla's decadence, however, like that of the other characters, is "cured" by the invasion: after waking from the vision of invasion produced in her mind by the hypnotist Ohman, she vows to do volunteer work at a blood bank.

Another American internal weakness the film emphasizes is conformity. Sociologists during the Fifties feared that the United States was becoming a country of automatons. Adam Wolfson argues that "what most
disturbed Fifties social critics was the bogey of conformity. They believed
that the American people were becoming ever more alike." While this fear
found expression in mainstream culture in such works as *The Man in the
Gray Flannel Suit*, it also informs sf/horror films. The most influential sociological study of the decade was David Riesman's *The Lonely Crowd*
(1950). Along with his two collaborators, Reuel Denny and Nathan Glazer,
Riesman sought to define a change taking place in the American personality: the inner-directed man was in decline in postwar America. An emer-
gent personality type known as the "other-directed" man was gradually
supplanting him (19). As guides for his behavior, the other-directed man
looked not to traditions instilled early in life but to friends and the mass
media (22). Consequently, "the goals toward which the other-directed
person strives shift with that guidance: it is only the process of striving
itself and the process of paying close attention to the signals from others
that remain unaltered throughout life" (22). This other-directed man was
an object of horror for many Americans of the day.

William Whyte's *The Organization Man* (1956), like *The Lonely
Crowd*, is a work of popular sociology. Whyte laments the encroaching
ability of organizations to take over every aspect of a man's life. He comments that "group-relations advocates have been saying, it is the whole
man The Organization wants and not just a part of him. Is the man well
adjusted? Will he remain well-adjusted? A test of potential merit could not
tell this; needed was a test of potential *loyalty*" (172). Such studies find the
internal problems of U.S. culture more worrisome than the specter of
enemy invaders or hostile ideologies. Thus, in *Invasion USA*, it is the characters' desire not become involved in social issues, to fit in rather than
speak out, that allows the enemy to take over American society so easily.

Other characters in *Invasion USA* encode different levels of American weakness. Carla's uncle, George Sylvester, a tractor manufacturer, opposes the military's request that he build tanks rather than tractors. When
Vince asks him if he will support a universal draft, George replies, "Draft
factories! That's Communism!" George is ultimately forced to turn his factory over to the enemy troops, who are planning to make tanks to achieve
domination over the U.S. And some other characters also show Americans
as self-serving. Ed Mulfory is a rancher who complains about taxes, making a toast, "Down with taxes!" Congressman Harraway also opposes tax-
ation and the universal draft. As the vision continues to unfold, Mulfory
is killed when Boulder Dam is bombed, and Harraway is shot during the

invasion of Washington. *Invasion USA* condemns American weakness as a major factor in the success of the Communist invasion. Thus, while the evil of Communism informs the film through the shadowy enemy forces with their enigmatic and cruel ways, Americans are asked to consider their own weaknesses as well.

The same kind of ambiguity marks *The Beast of Yucca Flats*. This film focuses on Russian-born scientist Joseph Javorsky, who has decided to defect to the United States and take with him information he possesses about a proposed Soviet moon mission. However, KGB agents follow him and chase him onto the missile range at Yucca Flats, where Javorsky is exposed to an A-bomb explosion that transforms him into a being akin to a prehistoric beast. Thus transformed, he kills two people and attempts to kill more. The local police finally track down Javorsky and kill him. The film reflects transmutations in the Cold War that were occurring in the late Fifties and early Sixties.

The late Fifties and early Sixties witnessed occasional periods of thaw in U.S. and Soviet relations, interspersed with periods of reintensified animosity. In one such period of thaw, Nikita Khrushchev became in 1959 the first Soviet premier to visit the United States. Khrushchev's journey included trips to Disneyland and a visit with the cast of *Can-Can*, including Frank Sinatra and Shirley MacLaine. Yet soon afterwards, the 1960 U-2 incident involving the shooting down of a CIA spy-plane over Soviet territory strained relations between the superpowers, when Khrushchev exposed the CIA cover-up of the mission by revealing that the U.S. pilot, Francis Gary Powers, had been captured and that espionage equipment had been recovered from his plane. In 1961, at the beginning of John F. Kennedy's presidency, the erection of the Berlin Wall further intensified U.S. anti–Communist sentiment and was one factor leading to Kennedy's famous 1963 "Ich Bin ein Berliner" speech, in which he lambasted Communism:

> There are many people in the world who really don't understand, or say they don't, what is the great issue between free world and the Communist world. Let them come to Berlin. There are some who say that Communism is the wave of the future. Let them come to Berlin. And there are some who say in Europe and elsewhere we can work with the Communists. Let them come to Berlin. And there are even a few who say that it is true that Communism is an evil system, but it permits us to make economic progress. Lass sie nach Berlin kommen. Let them come to Berlin.

These events, which heated up the Cold War, reached boiling point during the Cuban Missile Crisis in 1962.

In *The Beast of Yucca Flats*, a mixture of attitudes toward the Communist is evident. The film introduces Javorsky in a sympathetic light: he is a defector whose wife and child have been killed in Hungary, reflecting concerns over the oppression in Soviet Bloc countries, specifically the harsh Soviet crushing of the Hungarian Revolution in 1956. The brutal torture and execution of the revolution's leader, Imre Nagy, in 1958 was still fresh in the minds of the American public as an example of Soviet brutality. Javorsky has come to the United States to give the American government information about the Soviet moon project. Javorsky (played by wrestler Tor Johnson), with his heavy-set body and bald head, is strongly reminiscent of the physical appearance of Premier Khrushchev himself. In my interpretation of this film, Javorsky's transformation into the beast that terrorizes Yucca Flats speaks to American ambivalence about U.S.–Soviet relations. While the blame for the transformation of Javorsky falls on the KGB agents who chase him into a missile range, the film raises suspicion that Communists—even, indeed, defectors who come to the U.S. with apparently good intentions—cannot be trusted, because a beast lurks within them.[7]

One constant of anti–Communist rhetoric is the notion that the Soviet Communists are backward brutes. In the B film, Javorsky's metamorphosis from "noted scientist" to "prehistoric beast" suggests such a suspicion lingered during the early Sixties—a belief among Americans that if one scratched the surface of the Communist, one would find a beast underneath. Javorsky's caveman-like behavior suggests a state of devolution. He hides in a cave, shakes a stick at his victims, strangles a man dead, and makes the dead man's widow unconscious so that he can rape her in his cave. The film's narrator describes Javorsky as "a prehistoric beast in the nuclear age. Kill. Kill just to be killing." While Javorsky must undergo a monstrous transformation in order to become a killer, this description brings to mind the war-mongering of the Soviet Communists as they are portrayed in *Red Planet Mars* and *Invasion USA*.

The Beast of Yucca Flats, however, also suggests that American technology has had a hand in producing the Red Beast. The narrator condemns the atomic bomb, stating, "Touch a button. Things happen. A scientist becomes a beast." Later, the narrator shows open sympathy for Javorsky: "Shock waves of an A-bomb. A once humble, powerful man, reduced to nothing." The film implies that the American creation of nuclear weapons has had a hand, if not in creating, then at least in perpetuating, the beast of Soviet Communism. Thus, a central concern of the film is how atmospheric testing is destroying the United States from within. The narrator tells us how the wildlife has been driven off the testing range, and the last image in the film is of a rabbit approaching the dying body of Javorsky, suggesting an odd sympathy between him and the animals that are being contaminated by radiation.

Thus, although the film demonizes the bestiality within the Soviet man, it also points to monstrous U.S. policy in continuing atmospheric testing. Lewis Mumford, in *In the Name of Sanity*, expresses his fear that postwar paranoia in the U.S. will result in Nazi-like experimentation on citizens, leading to "the worst sadism" disguised as "responsible scientific experimentation with live subjects" (30).[8] He foresees a future in which "radioactive water has become the ideal medium of mass extermination" (68): in fact, one plan toyed with at Los Alamos involved using radioactive food to poison the Japanese population (Dowling 140). Mumford portrays the United States as an evil, manipulative power that through radioactive contamination "will ultimately exterminate life in every form" (86). He urges his audience to face the "real" enemy — "an enemy we have yet to confront accusingly in the mirror — ourselves" (109). Released three years before the atmospheric-test ban signed between the Soviet Union and the United States, the film seems just as concerned as Mumford with the danger we pose to ourselves.

In an article from 1961, Urie Bronfenbrenner pointed out the dangers of the American creation of a "Soviet bogeyman" (56). Bronfenbrenner warns of a mirror-image effect in U.S.–Soviet relations, an effect that the author believes deflects attention from the real dangers of Communism to the democratic world: "So long as we remain victims of the reassuring belief that the Soviet Union can acquire adherents only by force, we are likely to underestimate the positive appeal, especially to economically backward countries, of Communism not only as an ideology but as a technology that seems to work" (53). Films such as *The Beast of Yucca Flats* demonstrate that even by the early Sixties, American films were still finding comfort in metaphors involving almost supernatural power as an embodiment of the threat of Communism.[9] Yet in this film, as in the others, the threat of Communism is made stronger by other forces, either external (such as the lingering Nazi threat) or internal (contemporary U.S. decadence).

Anti-Communist propaganda found a home in Cold War sf/horror films. Examination of these films helps make clear that the American Fifties was not a time of complete and utter irrationality with regard to Communism and its threats. As Haynes points out, only three percent of the public in 1949 cited Communism as "the most serious issue facing the nation" (188). These films indicate then, by reflecting attitudes that the audience would not find objectionable, that hysteria over Communism has largely been a myth projected onto the Fifties. Thus, the low-budget sf/horror films discussed here ultimately fear Nazism, nuclear testing, or American weakness as much as Communism. Historical incidents such as the treatment of American POWs in Korea after the war, in which authorities and the public pointed the finger at Americans for the supposedly collaborative and weak behavior of the prisoners, indicates that Americans as often as not blamed their own society rather than the Soviet Union for its problems.[10] The films discussed here display concern with savagery in the U.S. itself, especially in the forms of rapid technological development and social decline. Thus, the patriotic, self-serving view one often expects to find in propaganda films is largely absent. While these films invoke the threat of a dangerous Soviet enemy, they also suggest that internal conflicts in the United States allow that threat to flourish. All three films suggest that sometimes anti–Communist sentiment did not so much reflect the dangers posed by the Soviet enemy as hold up a mirror to U.S. flaws and weaknesses.

Yet, the science-fiction genre was not the only popular genre of the Cold War to embrace anti–Communism as a topic. Crime fiction and film found the anti–Communist threat an easy one to incorporate into its world.

6. Criminals and Communists in Fifties Popular Culture

One manner in which anti–Communist culture of the Cold War demonized the Soviet threat was through portrayal of the Communist as evolutionarily lower than the criminal class. Anti-Communist films and novels of the Cold War portrayed a view of the corruptness of Communism by contrasting it with other criminal elements that were hated by U.S. society. Three examples of anti–Communist propaganda from the early Fifties use this technique to demonize the Communist threat. The film noir *Pickup on South Street* (1953) and the thriller *Big Jim McClain* (1952) use a contrast between the Communist criminal and the underworld criminal to point out the particular savagery of the Communist. James Wakefield Burke's pulp novel *The Big Rape* (1953) contrasts the behavior of Germans in postwar Berlin with the despicable behavior of the Russian invaders.

In the late Forties and early Fifties, the United States experienced a crime scare. The man who popularized and best represented the government's fight against organized crime was Estes Kefauver, a Tennessee Senator who became in 1950 the chairman of a new Special Committee on crime investigation popularly referred to as the Kefauver Committee. Kefauver's iconic status as a crusader against crime was solidified when the televised 1951 hearings on organized crime became one of the first important media events on television. As David Halberstam notes, during the televised hearings, "Estes Kefauver came off as a sort of Southern Jimmy Stewart, the lone citizen-politician who gets tired of the abuse of the

government and goes off on his own to do something about it" (191).
William Howard Moore notes in his study of the committee that both the
popular press and crime commissions illustrated "the old American pro-
clivity to view organized crime as something set apart from the economic
and social realities of American life" (41). Further, Moore perceives a direct connection between the postwar crime scare and the Red Scare that
gained momentum in the early Fifties: "The search for criminal conspir-
acies, moreover, paralleled the effort to ferret out communism and Communist sympathizers at home as the nation experienced frustration and
disappointment abroad" (41).

Kefauver's best-selling book *Crime in America* (1951) paints a picture
of organized crime as a degenerative force in American life. He predicts
a decline in American society that will bring about the end of American
political domination: "Nevertheless, it is a fearful thing to contemplate
how close America has come to the saturation point of criminal and political corruption which may destroy our strength as a nation" (17). Kefauver points to other "once mighty nations of other continents" that have
fallen due to criminal corruption (17). Kefauver offers only a slight chance
of the U.S. avoiding internal catastrophe due to the crime epidemic: "The
big question — and I put it bluntly — is this: has criminal and political corruption ... reached the point where America, too, must follow the down-
ward path of others? I say that we are dangerously close to that ruination
point — if not right on it" (18). The immediate and degenerative force of
underworld crime linked it with Communist degeneration in the minds
of Kefauver and others.

Kefauver, in a foreword to a book entitled *Barbarians in Our Midst:
A History of Chicago Crime and Politics*, demonizes the underworld criminal along the same lines the Communist was demonized, stating, "In the
midst of a world-wide struggle against a ruthless external enemy, law-
abiding Americans must devote some of their energy to a struggle against
a ruthless internal enemy" (ix). For Kefauver, the underworld criminal,
like the Communist, is corrupt as people are in the "Orient," and is reminiscent of man in the "Stone Age" (ix). Kefauver suggests that both Communists and underworld criminals represent a degenerative threat that
must be battled: "But we meet the communist threat with energy and res-
olution and so we keep in control, if we cannot stifle, this conspiratorial
underground movement" (x). Yet, while Kefauver's work suggests that
both underworld criminal and Communist are equally barbaric, two
anti–Communist films refute this view, using the underworld as a contrast
in order to highlight the extreme brutality of the Communist.[1]

Pickup on South Street tells the story of a pickpocket, Skip McCoy, who inadvertently steals top-secret microfilm from the purse of a woman, Candy, who is working unwittingly as a courier for her Soviet spy lover, Joey. The police confront Skip and ask him to turn over the film in exchange for a clean record. Skip, however, decides to try to make a profit by negotiating with the spies. Moe, an elderly woman who makes money by pedaling information about criminals, sells Skip's address to Candy. She tries to negotiate with Skip, but is shocked when he accuses her of being a Communist. Candy is horrified by the fact that she has been working for a Communist spy. Candy reveals this unwittingly to Moe. Joey subsequently kills Moe when she refuses to give him Skip's address. Candy visits Skip and steals the microfilm. She takes it to the police, but they ask her to deliver it to Joey, so they can arrest him when he turns it over to his contact. Joey discovers that a piece of the film is missing. This causes him to beat and shoot Candy, resulting in her being seriously wounded and hospitalized. This action angers Skip, who destroys the missing piece of the film, then follows Joey to his meeting with his contact. Skip breaks up the exchange between Joey and the contact and then pursues and savagely beats Joey. The police clear Skip of all charges, and he becomes romantically involved with Candy.

One way *Pickup on South Street* contrasts the criminals with the spies is through its portrayal of the underworld criminals as dupes of the Communists. Candy fits into this category. Because Joey has helped her give up her job as a prostitute by supporting her financially, Candy acts as courier for him, believing his story that he is a businessman working on a patent for a chemical formula. When, armed with five hundred dollars that Joey has given her, Candy innocently goes to negotiate with Skip for the film, she is shocked when he says to her, "So, you're a Red, who cares? Your money is as good as anybody else's." Candy is taken aback by Skip's accusation, and when he tells her, "I'll do business with a Red, but I don't have to believe one," she hits him in the face. While Candy is a former prostitute, she is horrified by the fact that she has been working as a courier for the Communists. Candy progresses from a politically naïve woman into a citizen who risks her own life in order to stop the Communists from getting the microfilm.[2] Thus, when Candy takes the film to the police and is asked by Zara to work as an agent — "You want to help us fight Communism, don't you?"— she doesn't hesitate. Even though she is severely beaten and even shot, she doesn't regret her part in the fight against Communism.[3]

The same element of self-sacrifice in the face of a Communist threat is seen in the character of Moe. While Moe sells the police and Candy information regarding Skip's whereabouts, she refuses to cooperate with

Communist agents. When Candy begs Moe not to sell Joey information about Skip, Moe replies, indignant, "What do you think I am, an informer?" She then confronts Skip, asking him, "What's the matter with you playing footsie with the Commies? ... I never figured you for a lout." Moe's death scene, in which she refuses to give Joey information, telling him simply that she doesn't like Communists, is one of the most emotionally moving scenes in the film.[4] *Pickup on South Street* hence portrays the female criminal as more morally solid and more patriotic than the male criminal.

Oddly, it is the underworld woman who has the strength to break the stereotype of the American woman as one susceptible to the seductions of Communism.[5] Candy and Moe, though outcasts, with their clear hatred of Communism, counter the stereotype of the woman who is susceptible to and the insidious agent of Communism. Though both are grifters, neither wants the dirty money that a Communist agent offers.

Skip's conversion to anti–Communist is more complicated. Once Skip examines the microfilm at the New York Public Library, he becomes aware of its value. Even if he dislikes the Communists, he is willing to make a profit by negotiating with them. Skip wants "a big score," even if it means operating as a knowing and willing traitor. Only the self-sacrifices made by Moe and Candy convince him that he must give up his score in order to protect his country's secrets. When Skip visits Candy in the hospital after Joey has beaten and shot her, Skip asks her why she has taken the microfilm. She tells him, "I'd rather have a live pickpocket than a dead traitor." When Skip realizes that Moe has died and Candy has risked death in order to protect him, he becomes angry and decides to destroy the microfilm and stop Joey from making his exchange.

In fact, it is Skip's brutality that allows for the contrast between the underworld thug, who is tough, but not without a conscience, and the Communist spy, who has no concern for human life whatsoever. In the film, the emergence of Joey as more brutal than Skip is predicated on the treatment of Candy. When Candy breaks into Skip's shack in order to look for the microfilm, he hits her, then playfully revives her with beer. Later, after she hits him, he hits her back. Skip's beatings of Candy are not serious, but Joey's beating of Candy is brutal for her and almost fatal. Joel Kovel notes that a central feature of Hoover's anti–Communist rhetoric was the notion that the security state "was all that stood between civilization and the fathomless barbarism of Communism" (133). *Pickup on South Street* illustrates this concept vividly, as the lowest elements of American society still possess the morals and strength to defeat the barbarism of Communism.

Big Jim McClain, another anti–Communist film from the same period, uses a contrast between underworld criminals and Communist spies in order to bring out the more degraded nature of the latter. The film focuses on the attempts of two HUAC investigators, Jim McClain and Mal Baxter, to discover a Communist spy ring in Hawaii that has infiltrated the dockworkers' labor union. The goal of the Communist conspiracy is to seize control of Hawaiian shipping and other communications. McClain and Baxter discover that Ed White, one of the labor union leaders who is posing as an anti–Communist, is in fact part of the core cell of spies. They follow him and discover who the other members are. Baxter, however, is kidnapped by the spies and dies when he has an allergic reaction to an injection of sodium pentathol. With the help of Dan Liu, the Honolulu chief of police, McClain finds the spies' meeting place. He breaks in on their reorganization meeting, beats many of them up, and then gives them over to Liu so he can arrest them.

As a documentary-style crime film, *Big Jim McClain* focuses on the underworld in Hawaii.[6] Thus, the film frames the hunt for the Communists as being much like any other police investigation. But while the Communist spies have clear links to underworld corruption and crime, as in *Pickup on South Street,* they are far worse than the criminals they use to further their ends.[7] While the small-time crooks McClain encounters in his investigations are harmless and foolish figures— as is the landlady who offers to give him information about Nakamura, a Communist agent whom McLain and Baxter are hunting down, but will do so only in exchange for a date with McLain — the Communist spies are ruthless and inhuman. Dr. Gelster, the leader of the Communist cell, is revolted by the ideologically devoted amongst his group and callously urges Mortimer, a bacteriologist who works for the Party, to press on with the "creation of an epidemic in the harbor area." Nancy Vallon, McClain's fiancée and a former employee of Gelster's, describes Gelster in the following terms: "He doesn't draw affection from people ... He just is a neuter as a personality." Gelster's inhuman qualities show him to be far worse than the underworld thugs he employs to do his dirty work.

Big Jim McClain, like *Pickup on South Street,* highlights the corruption of the spy as worse than that of the underworld character who has become criminal due to class issues. Thus, as Joey is from a wealthy family, in contrast to the working-class backgrounds of the other characters in that film, so in *Big Jim McClain* the affluence of the Communist spies is highlighted as a contrast to the poverty of the underworld criminals. Gelster is obviously a wealthy physician. When Baxter and McClain are summoned by Ed White's parents so they can reveal his background to the agents, we learn that White is the son of political refugees from Poland who have worked their way up financially and have given White a good education. White has rejected his real name, Lexiter, and White's father has disowned him for having become one of the "men that have turned their backs on God." The class issue comes out most explicitly in the climax of the film when McClain invades the spies' meeting. One of the men working for Gelster insults McClain for being a poor cotton-picker from East Texas. McClain asks him if he has ever picked cotton, to which the man responds, "I'm from the country-club set. That chopping cotton is for white trash and niggers." McClain knocks the man out.

In Gabriel Almond's 1954 study of Communist conversion, he noted that amongst Americans party membership rarely correlated with class oppression, as it did in other countries (243). Thus, unlike the underworld criminal, who was frequently perceived as going into a life of crime out of economic necessity, the Communist spy was seen as having done so because of personal instability. This point is borne out in *Big Jim McClain* through the character of Namaka, whose mental instability finally causes the Communists to turn him into a vegetable so that he will not reveal any secrets to HUAC.

Thus, *Big Jim McClain*, like *Pickup on South Street*, uses the underworld element to highlight the incredible depravity of the Communist spy. By contrasting the spy with members of the barbaric underworld of crime, prime targets of hatred in Fifties society, the evil of the Communist becomes glaringly obvious.

The Big Rape, a pulp novel from the early Fifties, also highlights the corruptness of the Communists by contrasting them with another despised group — Nazis. Written by *Esquire*'s war correspondent, James Wakefield Burke, *The Big Rape* tells the story of Lilo Markgraf, a young German woman attempting to survive after the Soviet invasion of Germany at the end of World War II. Lilo's sister and mother are brutally raped by Soviet soldiers, and Lilo vows to one day get revenge upon the soldiers. Lilo tries to bring about a reunion between herself and her fiancé, Bruno, but finds him to have been driven insane from his work at Buchenwald as a member of the SS. Lilo begins an affair with an NKVD agent, Pavel Ivanov, in order to protect herself and her family from the Soviet brutes who are raping and killing all over Berlin. After Ivanov is called back to the Soviet Union, Lilo and her sister lure the rapists to their house in order to get revenge. Bruno helps them kill the soldiers. He is subsequently captured by the Soviet army and killed. Lilo welcomes the incoming American soldiers and gets a job working for the U.S. Press Center.

The Big Rape paints a portrait of the Soviet soldier as an inhumane beast. When the invading soldiers burst into the Markgraf home, they demand vodka. Because there is no vodka in the house, the family gives them lamp oil: "Finding this more palatable than the vinegar, the two soldiers sat down and ate and drank with much gusto" (84). Not only are the Soviet soldiers so barbaric that they drink lamp oil, but they immediately begin raping German women. Herr Markgraf gives razors to the women in the house, suggesting that they cut their throats if they are threatened with rape (87). Lilo, however, rejects this solution, concluding, "Life was always worth living" (88). When she sees the Soviet soldiers sizing up the German women like livestock, however, she is repelled: "The soldiers were stepping among the people with the air of county fair judges selecting prize beasts in the cattle pens" (89). Lilo's hatred for the brutality of the Soviets is solidified when she discovers her mother and sister, who have been raped and tied up with wire: "A wire had been passed in convolutions around each of their bodies binding their arms to their sides, and their legs were fastened to lengths of wire strung to the trees on either side of them" (96). Witnessing this sight, Lilo knows that "these two Russians had to die for what they had done this night" (97). Later in the novel, an elderly woman comments to Lilo that "The Russians are killing, looting, and raping. Like wild men they are" (163). In the novel, all the Soviets engage in sexual perversion, not just the brutal rapists found in the lower ranks of the military.

Pavel Ivanov initially emerges in the novel as a contrast to the Soviet soldier rapists. As a NKVD man, Ivanov has a more immediate connection with Communism than do the soldiers. Ivanov does not rape Lilo, but, rather, attempts to seduce her. He brings American rations to the house and provides protection to the women. He is so blinded by ideology, however, that Lilo initially wards off his advances by plying him with vodka and arguing ideology with him. Thus, Ivanov professes to Lilo his belief that the Soviet Union will win the Cold War: "The Superior Race doctrine is a good idea though, and is still usable. Either the Americans or we Russians will use for the next hundred years or so to come. I think it will be us, for the Americans ... are notoriously ignorant and docile in the art of aggression" (224). However, even though Ivanov appears more civilized than the rapist soldiers, the civilization he displays is merely a veneer — it has no substance, it is only an appearance. Once Lilo becomes his mistress, he begins to reveal his sexual perversions. Ivanov likes Lilo to wear black boots in bed, an action that enflames him with such passion that "Next day she was black and blue from head to foot" (265). Ivanov also likes to wear his gloves in bed, gloves that, as he has explained to Lilo, he uses to brutalize enemies of the state (265–66). On their last night of lovemaking together, Ivanov twists her arm behind her back, and then "bent down and sunk his teeth into the soft flesh of her side" (295). The narrator describes this as an act of rape: "Thus he took her by force" (295). Ivanov's sexual perversions reveal his brutality and corruption. The novel contrasts the brutality of the Communist soldiers with the morality of Lilo and her family.

The sympathy elicited for Lilo and other Germans indicates how, in some fictional manifestations in the early Fifties, the hatred of Germans prevalent during World War II had been transferred to a hatred of the Soviet Union. While Lilo has supported Hitler wholeheartedly in her past — "It was in the last year of school that Lilo found an interest against her loneliness. She discovered the greatness of Adolf Hitler" (38) — the novel portrays her as merely misguided in her discovery. While she may have admired Hitler the man, she has never been anti–Semitic. In fact, she helps two Jewish girls, former concentration-camp inmates, who have been raped by Soviet soldiers. Lilo's father praises her for helping the girls: "I am glad that you have no prejudice against the Jews. You will be much happier, and it will stand you well with the Americans" (304). Her father even goes so far as to praise the Jewish people as "truly the superior people" (305). Further, even though Bruno expresses some anti–Semitic ideas, the novel portrays them as a product of his madness. Lilo is forced to recognize Bruno's madness: "As she went upstairs she heard him chuckling darkly to himself in the recesses of his lair" (285).

The sympathy elicited for the German survivors of the war, in contrast to the lack of sympathy created for any of the Soviet soldiers is further highlighted by the positive attitude toward the Americans that Lilo's family has. Prior to the Soviet invasion, Lilo's father asks, "Why don't the Americans come?" He asks this question in "almost a wail" (35). When Lilo catches her first glimpse of American soldiers, she is struck by their majestic appearance: "Then came the 82nd Airborne. They were giants of men — tall, huge, powerful. There seemed to be no small or even medium-sized soldiers among them. They were giants— all! In contrast to the Russians there was something immediately sharp and commanding about these troops" (318). Lilo's ability to recognize that the American soldiers are superior to the Soviet ones indicates that even though she once supported the Nazi party, she now recognizes the true saviors when she sees them.

The Big Rape, by contrasting a German family with Soviet soldiers, works to highlight the corruption and animality of the Soviets. If Americans were not yet ready to hold a sympathetic view of Germans, when they are compared to the evil of the Soviets, the Germans come off as more human.

By comparing the Communist to the worst possible nightmares of American society — Nazis, underworld criminals — these examples of anti–Communist popular culture successfully highlight the evil of Communism. By choosing enemies that were seen to be corrupt and insane, Communism is presented as a sickness akin to Hoover's description of it as "an evil and malignant way of life" ("Testimony"120). Thus, the sickness of Communism is naturalized in these works as alienness, animality, and sexual perversion — all signs of the innate corruption of the Communist, whether he or she is American or Soviet.

If a work such as *The Big Rape* combines underworld motifs with anti–Communist feeling in order to comment upon post–World War II European society, illustrating ways in which a work can be both popular and politically aware, other uses of anti–Communism in popular culture display little or no political concern. One genre incorporated anti–Communist feeling as a plot device — the movie serial.

7. Anti–Communism and Movie Serials

One genre that easily incorporated anti–Communist plots was movie serials. Although movie serials were in their waning days in the Fifties, their melodramatic worldview easily accommodated a stereotype of evil Communists and good, brave American government agents. Gary Johnson characterizes the world of the serials in the following way: "These were the days when masked villains ... strove for world domination with a vast array of diabolical devices ... Meanwhile, courageous heroes valiantly struggled for justice, loyalty, and the American way" (1). The battle between a force of evil and a force of good fit the worldview of certain types of American anti–Communism very well. Joel Kovel defines extreme anti–Communist sentiment in the following terms: "The morality of anticommunism drives toward a state of all-goodness defining our side of things, surrounded, indeed defined, by a force of all-badness" (9). This extreme view of good and evil is not, however, the typical representation of the anti–Communist issue in Cold War America. In fact, the genre that comes closest to this polarization of good and evil, without asking serious questions about the American system, would appear to be the movie serial, where anti–Communism is a plot device overlaid onto a fictional world distinguished by its battles between good and evil.

Movie serials began in the silent era when *McClure's Ladies World Magazine* desired to expand circulation by linking stories with film adaptations. *What Happened to Mary* was the first serial and set off a popular trend (Johnson 1). Utilizing different genres, such as jungle tales, science fiction, espionage, westerns, and others, the serials continued to be a very popular form of entertainment until their demise in the late Fifties. Raymond William Stedman links the demise of the movie serial to increasingly formulaic action plots set around very thinly drawn characters of good and evil: "While the action scenes were reasonably well staged, the plots degenerated into tedious skirmishing between the goodies and the baddies" (140). Other influences, such as the increasing availability and popularity of television, certainly also contributed to the demise of serials.

The purpose of serials, however, was never art. The serials functioned as a hook device to draw audiences back to the theater week after week. Johnson comments that "that was the main purpose of the serial — to keep the theater seats filled with paying customers" (1). The fact that anti–Communist plot devices were incorporated into serials in the Fifties speaks to the studios' belief that anti–Communism was a means of luring people into movie theaters and away from their television sets. In this chapter, I will examine two Republic serials from the Fifties that utilized anti–Communist themes.[1]

Government Agents vs. Phantom Legion was a twelve-part serial released by Republic Pictures in 1951. It features government agents Hal Duncan and Sam Bradley in their attempts to stop a gang from highjacking trucks in order to obtain uranium and mechanical supplies needed to build nuclear weapons. A mysterious man known as the boss, whose identity is unknown to his two henchmen, Regan and Cady, heads the gang. Throughout the serial, Duncan and Bradley foil Regan and Cady's attempts to obtain material so that the boss can sell this critical material to the Soviet Union. At the end of the serial, Duncan finally stops the boss, at the same time revealing his identity as a member of the Interstate Truck Owners' Association.

Like many anti–Communist works discussed in this study, *Government Agents vs. Phantom Legion* attributes an aura of mystery to the Communist element. Not only is the gang working for the Communists known as the Phantom Legion, but the boss of the organization is given a godlike mystery. When the boss gives orders to Regan and Cady, he watches them through a two-way mirror, but they are never allowed to see his face. As Regan comments in Chapter One, "Don't forget, he can always see us." Much like Soberin in *Kiss Me Deadly*, the boss in this serial is given authority and mystery because he remains a voice. His face is never glimpsed until the final episode, when Duncan kills him. Furthermore, the buyers for the uranium retain a mysterious quality: they are never named directly as the Soviet Union or a Communist country, but referred to as "some enemy country." As in other anti–Communist works such as *Invasion USA*, a taboo exists against speaking the name of the Soviet Union: its mysterious quality is retained because it is spoken of indirectly. Thus, at times in the serial the enemy is given almost supernatural powers. For example, the enemy supplies the gang with M6 pills that place anyone who takes one" in a state of suspended animation." Thus, in Chapter Two, Regan is able to escape from the government agents by faking his own death through taking one of the pills.

At the same time that the Soviet enemy and its American allies are given powerful qualities of evil, they are also often portrayed as inept when faced with the bravery of the government agents. For example, in Chapter Four the boss has Regan and Cady give back some stolen electronic equipment in order to receive a $50,000 reward that the government is offering for the material. Duncan meets with Cady and Regan, but they rig an explosive device to the equipment so they can destroy it after they get the reward money. The boss has told them that "The government is urgently in need of this equipment," so their sabotage will harm the government and further the Communist world. When a fight breaks out between Duncan and Regan and Cady, Regan inadvertently trips over the explosives trigger and blows up the material. Duncan escapes with the government's money. Regan laments after this incident, "We'll have to tell the boss." Yet, for all his mystery, the boss never fires them, even though they make many buffoonish mistakes. In fact, Regan finally meets his death in a repetition of his earlier act of clumsiness. In the Final Chapter of the serial Regan dies when he trips over an explosives-triggering device he has rigged in a secret underground vault. *Government Agents vs. Phantom Legion* hence both attributes almost supernatural powers to the Soviet Union and their espionage agents, while simultaneously presenting them as inept.

The gang led by the mysterious boss also illustrates another idea present in some anti–Communist propaganda works, namely, that American espionage agents are amoral, motivated by money rather than by any ideological commitment to the Soviet Union. As Ellen Schrecker points out, espionage became the most popular device in anti–Communist propaganda because of its dramatic potential: "But espionage was easier to dramatize, and, as a result, became central to the popular perception that Communists endangered the United States" (*Many* 166). The boss's motivations appear to be solely monetary. In Chapter Five, he tells Regan and Cady that "I must have a supply of uranium for my foreign customer." The boss views his espionage activities as business propositions. Similarly, Regan and Cady display no commitment to Communist ideology. For example, in Chapter Nine, as Regan and Cady fall for fake information supplied to them by Duncan, Regan comments, "The boss'll pay us plenty for that uranium."

However, it is not only in the characters of the villains that ideology is absent. The trucking association seems to hold little or no concern for the fact that hostile enemies may be gaining access to uranium, their sole concern seems to be protecting their own business interests. Thus, in Chapter Three, when the association agrees to pay for extra security to guard their trucks, one member of the association comments, "Anything would be cheaper than losing our government contracts." In Chapter Five, as Duncan reports to the association of his near death at the hands of Cady and Regan, the association is concerned only with profits. One member remarks that Duncan's failure to capture the agents "won't help our reputation with the government." Another one demands to know from Duncan, "Just how much business will we get?" The closest that the association comes to being truly concerned about the fate of the world occurs in Chapter Eight when Duncan tells the association that the "government needs it [uranium] badly for the atomic bomb project." One association member then suggests that a "foreign government" wants it for the same reason. The larger threat of nuclear war that lurks behind the espionage occurring in the serial seems buried within a world in which everyday business concerns take predominance.[2]

Government Agents vs. Phantom Legion illustrates how a movie serial from the Fifties retains its cliffhanger devices— each chapter ends with the apparent death of Duncan — while overlaying an anti–Communist plot on the formulaic devices. The lack of concern that the serial displays for the Communist threat suggests that the serial was merely using the anti–Communist plot in order to be *au courant*. The serial clearly is not in the main aspiring to be a propaganda device to alert people to the dangers of Communist espionage.

Canadian Mounties vs. Atomic Invaders (1953) was a twelve-part serial that also used anti–Communism as a backdrop for its cliffhanging action. The serial focuses on Canadian Mountie Don Roberts who, along with government agent Kay Conway, searches for an espionage ring believed to be active in the Yukon. After battling Beck and Reed, two men who travel with them in the settling party they have infiltrated, Roberts and Conway finally discover that the leader of the espionage ring is Marlof, a Russian who has been masquerading as the village idiot, Smokey Joe. They are able to foil his plan to build a missile-launching base so that the Soviet Union can destroy all major American cities with nuclear missiles and then invade the United States.

Unlike the situation in *Government Agents vs. Phantom Legion* where Communism is aided by American financial greed, the motivation for the bad guy in *Canadian Mounties vs. Atomic Invaders* is mainly ideological. Marlof desperately wants to implement his leader's plan to destroy the United States with nuclear weapons. In Chapter One, Marlof speaks passionately to Reed and Beck about the plans: "Then our plans will bring in the rockets and start a bombardment of American cities in preparation for my country's invading force!" The serial portrays Marlof as an ideological slave, always radioing his leader and referring to him as "excellency." Marlof is the stereotypical drone portrayed by anti–Communist rhetoric. In *The Naked Communist*, W. Cleon Skousen describes rank and file Communists as "a regimented breed of Pavlovian men whose minds could be triggered into immediate action by signals from their masters ... a race of men who would no longer depend upon free will, ethics, morals, or conscience for guidance" (1). Marlof cannot tolerate any deviation from the orders that his leader has given him. In Chapter Three, Marlof tells Beck, "My country's plans are made and they must go through!"

In addition to representing the drone generated by the anti–Communist imagination, Marlof also represents an amoral, cruel force. He relishes the thought of American cities being destroyed by nuclear weapons, telling Beck and Reed in Chapter Five that when the missiles are launched, "Every important American city will be in ruins in a matter of hours!" In addition, Marlof coldly orders the murder of Roberts, a man he has pretended to befriend in his guise as Smokey Joe, telling Beck and Reed in Chapter Seven that "You must get rid of the Sergeant." Marlof conforms to the idea of the "Marxian Man" that Skousen puts forth in his anti–Communist propaganda: "The Marxian man has convinced himself that nothing is evil which answers the call of expediency. He has released himself from all the confining restraints of honor and ethics which mankind has previously tried to use as a basis for harmonious human relations" (3).

While Marlof conforms to the stereotypical evil fanatic of anti–Communist rhetoric, his henchmen, Reed and Beck, are more mysterious characters. While Cady and Regan have clear financial motives in *Government Agents vs. Phantom Legion*, Reed and Beck appear to be motiveless in their endeavors. They risk their lives again and again for Marlof, finally dying at the end trying to protect the launching site, yet they do not appear to be Communists and do not appear to be getting paid for their work. While they seem to have been involved in an espionage gang "from the East" that Kay had investigated earlier, their commitment to the destruction of the United States seems totally without cause. As the bad guys of a movie serial, maybe they have just been born cinematically bad — Marlof's slaves for no particular reason.

Like other anti–Communist works discussed in this book, *Canadian Mounties vs. Atomic Invaders* surrounds the Soviet Union with a cloud of mystery. While Marlof's home country is most certainly the Soviet Union — what other country would have had the capability of launching nuclear missiles on the United States in 1953? — the serial never mentions the Soviet Union by name. Marlof calls the force behind the attacks "my country." Robert and Conway refer to the agents as members of "the foreign spy group we're looking for" in Chapter Three. In the Final Chapter, Commissioner Morrison, discussing the agents' foiled plans with Conway and Roberts, comments that "This foreign country, and we can make a pretty good guess which one it is ..." hinting strongly at the country being the Soviet Union. Unlike works like *Invasion USA* that keep the enemy nameless in order to forge a connection between Nazism and Communism, the mystery around the foreign power in *Canadian Mounties vs. Atomic Invaders* does not work to align the Soviet threat with any other; not even the underworld connections forged in *Government Agent vs. Phantom Menace* is present.

Although Roberts and Conway defeat the agents in their plan for nuclear war, they do not seem to be very efficient or intelligent protagonists, especially Conway. As Gary Johnson notes, serials of the silent days were dominated by heroines (2).[3] While the presence of Kay Conway as a government agent would appear to be reviving this tradition, such is not the case. Conway is not a very successful agent. In Chapter One, after Conway and Roberts are shot at by Beck, Kay asks, "Do you think whoever it was knew who he was shooting at?" Roberts replies that if he did not know, "he certainly has a bad disposition." In Chapter Two, after Roberts and Conway have barely survived an avalanche caused by Beck, Conway asks, pointing at Beck, "I wonder if he started the avalanche?" Finally, after facing death several times by Chapter Three, Conway comments that Beck and Reed "could be agents for the foreign spy group we're looking for." Conway and Roberts both remain clueless about what the spy group is plotting. In Chapter Seven Conway comments, "That looks like a good location for whatever they're up to." Although Conway has lived with the spy group when it was in the East, she fails to recognize any of them until finally in Chapter Eleven when she begins to see something odd about Smokey Joe. At the conclusion of the serial, Conway is still amazed by what has happened, commenting, "It's fantastic how so few could expect to destroy two countries as powerful as the United States and Canada." Conway helps Roberts in the investigation, but as a clever espionage agent, she fails.

Overall, the serial points out that physical strength, not brains, will foil the Communist threat. While Conway is clearly the less intelligent of the two agents, Roberts relies on his fighting abilities to stop the plot. Thus, even though Morrison warns him to be on the lookout for strangers in town, he is completely fooled by Marlof's act as Smokey Joe, telling Conway that he is a man who is "a little hazy in the head." It is not until Marlof leads him to his cabin by hiding Beck and Reed there that Roberts catches on to his connection with the espionage ring. Even then, he searches the cabin and fails to discover Marlof's radio transmitter, which is hidden in a cabinet. He still believes Marlof to be a low-level part of the plot until Morrison reveals at the end of the serial that Marlof is a "famous foreign agent."

The movie serial genre used anti–Communism as a plot device for its action sequences. While the serials under discussion here partake of anti–Communist rhetoric, such as a connection between Communism and the underworld, as in *Government Agents vs. Phantom Menace*, and the maniacal drone of Communism, as in *Canadian Mounties vs. Atomic Invaders*, the anti–Communist threat remains oddly benign, even though Marlof is threatening the atomic destruction of the United States. Yet, the presence of Communism at all in such a formulaic genre as the serial again attests to how it invaded the popular genre, sometimes as real threat, sometimes as a phantom one.

The movie serial brought anti–Communist sentiment to almost comic levels. The ineptness of both the Communist and the American agents is often humorous. In the final chapters of both serials the good guys win because the Communist agents trip over their own booby traps. In the next chapter, we shall see how another genre took these comic elements of Cold War espionage to extremely humorous conclusions.

8. Cold War Parody

One of the more interesting genres that incorporated anti–Communist elements during the Cold War was parody. Linda Hutcheon argues that a key difference between satire and parody lies in the fact that parody does not always criticize its target negatively, whereas satire usually does. Hutcheon comments that "In modern parody, however, we have found that no such negative judgment is necessarily suggested in the ironic contrasting of texts. Parodic art both deviates from an aesthetic norm and includes that norm within itself as background material" (44). My interest here is in looking at Cold War texts that parody the U.S.–Soviet conflict, but do not necessarily satirize it. Thus, the work frequently highlighted as the first comic view of Cold War conflict, *Dr. Strangelove*, is, in my opinion, neither the first nor a parodic view. Stanley Kubrick's dark view of Cold War politics and their possible hideous outcome falls into the category of satire, as Hutcheon defines it: "Satire, like irony, possesses a marked ethos, one that is even more pejoratively or negatively coded. This can be called a scornful or distasteful ethos. It is that kind of encoded anger communicated to the decoder through invective" (56). *Strangelove* demonstrates moral objection to the Cold War and its illogical outcome: nuclear war. As Margot A. Henriksen indicates, "Even apocalypse and the extinction of human life were subjects of the satire that ruled the film as a whole, and it was this complete commitment to both satire and nihilism that made *Dr. Strangelove* a cultural tour de force and a cultural center of controversy" (327). As Henriksen indicates, critical opinions on the film center on the issue of its seriousness. Those like Lewis Mumford who saw it as a serious comment on nuclear war praised the film, while those like

Bosley Crowther who saw it as a sick joke condemned it (327–330). The heated reaction in the culture and the press over the film suggests that it was indeed satire, and not parody, that the film was premised upon. As I will argue in this chapter, parody is less likely than satire to cause such vehement reaction, because parody tends to reinforce, for example, dominant Western beliefs about the Cold War, while simultaneously exposing flaws in both the Soviet and American systems.

A television series that illustrates Cold War parody is *The Adventures of Rocky and Bullwinkle*, a continuing segment in both *Rocky and His Friends*, which ran on ABC from 1959 to 1961, and on *The Bullwinkle Show* from 1961 to 1964. This animated series, pitting a squirrel and a moose against foreign agents Boris Badenov and Natasha Fatale, parodies Cold War espionage openly.

Elements of the series exemplify the parodic mode in several ways. First, the series works within a clearly self-referential mode. In defining modern forms of parody, Hutcheon comments that "Imitating art more than life, parody self-consciously and self-critically recognizes its own nature" (27). *The Adventures of Rocky and Bullwinkle* constantly draws attention to itself as a television show. Thus, for example, in "Goof Gas Attack," an episode in which Boris and Natasha plot to destroy the U.S. by making its great minds idiots, Rocky expresses his worry to Bullwinkle that they will be caught by enemy agents. Rocky says, "I'm worried." Bullwinkle replies by asking "The ratings on the show down again?" In the same episode, Natasha expresses frustration with Boris by telling him, "Well, darling, you failed three times in one episode." In "The Treasure of Monte Zoom," in which Boris and Natasha try to recover a sunken treasure, Boris tries to shoot Bullwinkle and Rocky, but finds that the gun he is using is fake. Natasha comments, "Boris, we forgot. There's no violence allowed on television anymore." In this case the show parodies the strict guidelines regarding TV violence ushered in by the Kennedy administration. As Mary Ann Watson notes, "The Kennedy administration prepared to take office with the belief that government could play a part in the development of a democracy's cultural life. Robert Kennedy particularly found gratuitous television violence offensive and dangerous to the republic" (38). The characters also frequently exchange comments with the narrator of the show. On one level, then, *The Adventures of Rocky and Bullwinkle* works as parody of television and its standards. Thus, the target of parody on this level is simply the conventions of television, the importance of ratings, and the controversy surrounding violence in cartoons. Yet, even the concerns of the medium of television are related to the larger discourse that the show parodies, the discourse of the Cold War.

Cartoons from the 1950s and 1960s were not immune from scrutiny with regard to their stance on Communism. As Chris O'Brien notes, comic books became a center of controversy in the early 1950s: "Comic books, along with juvenile delinquency and crime, were initially branded a symptom of Communist infiltration and the loss of American morality" (90). As O'Brien notes, publishers of comics and creators of animation worked to "cleanse their product of anything that could be viewed as anti-American" (90). Thus, the very presence of Boris and Natasha on an animated television series indicates a concern with Communist espionage. As Hutcheon comments, "Even in mocking, parody reinforces; in formal terms, it inscribes the mocked conventions onto itself, thereby guaranteeing their continued existence" (75). As Hutcheon makes clear throughout her study of parody, parody reinforces the discourse that it parodies and only rarely projects a negative attitude toward the master discourse that it makes comic. Thus, *The Adventures of Rocky and Bullwinkle* reinscribe Cold War fears at the same time the show parodies them.

Boris and Natasha represent a complex coding of the Soviet enemy that was present in many propaganda films of the late 1940s and early 1950s. There are clear indications in the series that Boris and Natasha are meant to be Soviet agents. They have Russian names. Every time he is amazed, Boris exclaims "Raskolnikov," in reference to the protagonist of Dostoevsky's *Crime and Punishment*, and other images and ideas associated with the characters conjure up stereotypes of the Soviet Union. For example, in "Box Top Robbery," Boris and Natasha are ruining the world's economy by counterfeiting boxtops. When Natasha expresses fear about continuing with the boxtop counterfeiting once the police are on to them, Boris asks her, "Natasha, which are you more scared of, United States government or Central Control?" The answer is obvious: Central Control, the name for their government's organizational base, obviously alluding to the Soviet Communist Party Central Committee, is the more terrifying organization. Thus, the view that the Soviet system is more brutal than the American system is sustained by the parody. Cold War America believed that the Soviets deliberately manipulated language, an idea expressed in the Trojan Horse–theory strategy described by Harry and Bonaro Overstreet in their anti–Communist book as a ploy whereby the American Communist Party "abruptly abandoned its former revolutionary line — so far as public appearances were concerned — and began to call itself a 'progressive' American Party" (7–8). Thus, in "The Treasure of Monte Zoom," when Boris and Natasha want to blow up a treasure chest, the bag of TNT they use for the purpose is called a "Pottsylvanian Persuader." Yet, while there are many clear ways that Boris and Natasha are linked obviously with stereotypes of Soviet agents, part of the humor arises from the elements that do not fit into the stereotype.

Boris and Natasha display characteristics that contradict the stereotyped image of the Soviet agent. Murray S. Davis argues that this is how parody operates: "Since humor breaks down an expectation system by replacing congruous elements with incongruous ones, it informs us — indirectly — which elements belong in a system and which do not. Whatever threatens the system's continued existence is obviously out of place in it" (29). One of the most obviously incongruous elements in Boris and Natasha's behavior is their affection for each other. The Soviet Communist was typically stereotyped as an unemotional robot. Yet, Boris and Natasha continually refer to each other using endearments such as "darling" and "poopsie." Natasha expresses concern for Boris as he falls beneath the treasure chest they are trying to open, by stating, "Don't worry, darling. This is just cartoons," showing emotional concern for him and referencing the show's status as fictional animated series.

Other contradictions highlight not only incongruous elements in Boris and Natasha's behavior, but also illustrate how in *The Adventures of Rocky and Bullwinkle* parody reinforces the Cold War discourse out of which it simultaneously creates humor. Boris and Natasha's materialism point to the perceived hypocrisy of Soviet anti-materialism. When Boris and Natasha claim all the children's toys with the counterfeit boxtops they have made, Boris revels: "We are rolling in valuable consumer goods!" When Boris and Natasha discover that the buried treasure they have been seeking is a fourteen-karat gold car, Natasha says, "Let's face it, Boris, these Americans really know how to live." The view pronounced here was the recurrent one that underneath the Communist lurks the capitalist waiting to get out. As Davis comments, "The best parodies suggest a secret similarity between realms presumed to be very different" (22). Thus, the parody here suggests that Boris and Natasha are working to destroy a capitalistic system that they actually enjoy.

One interesting aspect of the threat of Boris and Natasha is that they represent a conflation of Nazi and Soviet threats that was common in anti–Communist propaganda. Thus, from anti–Communist propaganda films like *Red Planet Mars* and *Invasion USA* to pulp novels like *The Big Rape*, the threat of the Soviet and the threat of the Nazi have been viewed as a continuum. As I have discussed earlier, anti–Communist propaganda frequently made analogies between Communists and Nazis. So, while Boris and Natasha are visibly Soviet, Fearless Leader, the head of Central Control, and the dictator of Pottsylvania, the country Boris and Natasha hail from, conflates Soviet and Nazi stereotypes into one character. Fearless

Leader wears a German star on his military uniform and signs off when speaking to Boris and Natasha by saying, "aufweidersein." Yet, he wields a Stalin-like power over his subordinates. For example, he has a man imprisoned after Boris has used goof gas on the man and he tells Fearless Leader that "You are a mean, ugly schnook." Fearless Leader admits that these words are true, but says, "Nobody but an idiot would tell me so." Further, as Fearless Leader addresses his central council, he tells them that Pottsylvania has no raw materials, no consumer goods, no art, but only "mean," concluding, "We got to export mean to every other country." The common stereotype of the Soviet Union as a region with no raw materials, consumer products, or art was a common one. David Granick comments that "The Russian manager often feels loaded with money and is quite free in his spending precisely because he has no practical way of purchasing the things he would really like to have" (102).

Yet, the Soviet Union is not the only system parodied in *The Adventures of Rocky and Bullwinkle*. The American system is also an object of parody in the cartoons. In "Box Top Robbery," for example, the Coast Guard does not provide a safe haven for Bullwinkle and Rocky. After Boris rigs a bomb in the elevator they are traveling in, Boris and Rocky find themselves floating on the river in an elevator car. The Commodore in charge of the station believes that Bullwinkle's antlers are radar antennae and fires on them. After Bullwinkle and Rocky enter the station, the assistant to the commodore comments, "You sank a moose." The ineptness of American military figures is further emphasized in the character of Captain Peachfuzz, a reoccurring character in the TV series. In "Goof Gas Attack," Peachfuzz maintains the security of his mission by writing a memo to himself and then tearing it up. In the same episode, Boris and Natasha decide to use their goof gas on Washington. When they get to the Congress, senators on the floor make ridiculous comments. For example, one senator says, "I oppose foreign aid especially to places like Alaska and Hawaii." Boris and Natasha throw up their hands in despair, realizing that the effects of goof gas would be useless in Washington, where everyone is already an idiot. Thus, while the cartoons reinforce Cold War ideology by portraying the hypocrisy and ineptness of the Soviet system, they also parody American efficiency. When Fearless Leader plots to use goof gas to transform a country into one characterized by idiocy, he comments, "Let's pick an easy one. U.S. of A." By parodying both the Soviet system and the American system, the series points out what Gerald Mast sees as a major message embedded in comedy: "It [comedy] merely denies that men can be any better — or, rather, it denies that they can be anything but men, anything but foolish mortals" (340).

Another TV series from the 1960s illustrates Cold War parody. *Get Smart*, which ran on NBC from 1965 to 1970, focuses on the ongoing battle between Control, a secret U.S. agency, and its archenemy, Kaos, which is clearly intended to embody the Communist threat. Placed in Washington, D.C., the main characters are Maxwell Smart, Agent 86; The Chief, Smart's immediate superior; and Agent 99, Smart's partner and later wife. Like *The Adventures of Rocky and Bullwinkle*, the series is easily recognizable as a parody of Cold War politics. Hutcheon's theory of parody maintains that modern parody can be defined by the characteristic that its "'target' text is always another work of art, or, more generally, another form of coded discourse" (16). Like *The Adventures of Rocky and Bullwinkle*, *Get Smart* parodies specific movies and television shows and Cold War discourse itself. In the episode "The Apes of Rath," for example, *The Manchurian Candidate* is parodied by a plot involving a scientist who uses trigger sounds to transform a Control agent into a murderous ape. The episode also involves parody of *King Kong*, as Jocko the ape does not kill 99 because she has been kind to him. Jocko kidnaps her and takes her to the top of skyscraper where Max eventually saves her. In "Die, Spy," an episode whose title clearly references the TV series *I Spy*, the parody is made even more explicit by the fact that *I Spy* star Robert Culp appears in a cameo role.[1] Furthermore, since *I Spy* is a parody of the spy genre itself, this episode involves parody of a parody, a common occurrence in *Get Smart*, where the gadgetry typical of the James Bond films is exaggerated through the use of various ridiculous devices, especially unusual kinds of phones. Thus, while the shoe phone is the most common image associated with the television series, in "The Hot Line," by contrast, Max and the Chief must speak to LBJ through the horn of a longhorn cow. "Shock It to Me" involves a parody of *Frankenstein* and *The Island of Doctor Moreau* as Dr. Zarko reanimates dead bodies on a remote island off the coast of Newfoundland. The parodies involving specific TV shows and movies are numerous throughout the entire run of the series.[2] In addition to operating as a parody of different TV and movie genres, most notably the spy genre, the series also works to parody the larger discourse of the Cold War.

Like *The Adventures of Rocky and Bullwinkle*, *Get Smart* reinforces stereotypes of the Communist threat to an exaggerated degree. The split between Kaos and Control reinscribes broadly the split between the U.S. and its allies and the Soviet Union and the other Iron Curtain countries. In "Run, Robot, Run," a track meet becomes the site for a Cold War showdown as pennants bearing the insignias "Free World" and "Iron Curtain" are sold at the concession. In this episode, Kaos uses trickery to win the

Agent 99 (Barbara Feldon) and Agent Maxwell Smart (Don Adams) in the Cold War parody Get Smart.

games by performing acts of sabotage against the Control athletes. Control finally wins the competition by using its robot, Hymie. This episode reinforces the stereotypical image of the Communist as untrustworthy and only capable of succeeding through trickery.

A typical Cold War fear was that the U.S.'s own popular culture might be used against its better interests, were Communists to influence its content. Richard Maltby comments on the fear of Hollywood as a propaganda machine for the Soviets: "The Communists had done and were doing things to the movies, and they were so smart that Joe Public didn't even know he was being brainwashed. Naturally the Committee [HUAC] attacked the movies; they could not miss the opportunity to turn the dream factory into a paranoid fantasy. The concentration of their attack on writers and directors fitted equally well into the working of the Committee's paranoid style. They were the faceless ones, the backroom boys, the demonic brains behind the master-plan to destroy America's soul" (82). In "The Groovy Guru," Kaos has bought an influential rock and roll DJ called The Groovy Guru. He brainwashes American kids with his radio and television programs and changes them into Kaos zombies. The Guru broadcasts psychedelic messages like "Kaos swings" and "Rebellion is hip" in order to win American teenagers over to the Kaos side. *Get Smart* also emphasizes the notion that the Soviet Union was incapable of developing new technology and had to steal it through espionage, a viewpoint that high-profile cases such as the Rosenberg case emphasized to the American public. In "Pheasant Under Glass," Kaos has kidnapped the world's top nuclear scientist and is holding him in an impenetrable glass case and is brainwashing him in order to get information about secret weapons.

And just as the TV series emphasizes the sinister aspects of the Communist threat, it also emphasizes the incompetence of Kaos. Thus, in "The Day They Raided Knights," Kaos creates an elaborate plan to distribute stereophonic pistols to Kaos agents using a trading stamp redemption center. The goal of Kaos is armed revolution. Yet, "Kaos' new secret weapon" turns out to be faulty. When a Kaos agent attempts to kill Max with the pistol, it plays music instead of firing bullets. The Kaos agent laments, "It was Japanese. When we specified stereophonic they took us seriously." Thus, the threat of Kaos is sometimes diminished by the agency's own incompetence, especially with regard to technology. In his study of Soviet industry, David Granick emphasizes the danger of the Soviet factory: "One could not help being impressed by the relative absence of safety devices on presses and cutting-machine tools. This was despite the fact that, in each town, I was clearly taken to see one of the more efficient plants" (18). "The Day They Raided Knights" also emphasizes another element of the Kaos organization deemed worthy of parody: their slavery to bureaucratic rules, a common stereotype said to characterize the Soviet Union and its satellites. John Gunther, in *Inside Russia Today*, comments on the pervasive quality of the Soviet bureaucracy: "Everything must be continually referred to the next higher authority, which may be inordinately stubborn and slow-moving. Trotsky once made a little joke to the effect that the dictatorship of the proletariat had become the dictatorship of the secretariat" (203).[3] Examining their stockpile of stereophonic pistols, a female Kaos agent says, "Kaos is ready to launch its armed revolution." A male Kaos agent agrees, "We'll storm Congress ... but make sure when they pick up their weapons they pay the sales tax. We don't want any trouble with the government." Similarly, in "The Not-So-Great Escape," Siegfried, a Kaos agent running a prison camp for Control agents, fears arrest, saying: "When they find out we are running a prisoner-of-war camp without a license, we will be arrested." Siegfried, a reoccurring character on the series, represents another link between *Get Smart*'s Cold War parody and the parody of *The Adventures of Rocky and Bullwinkle*: the conflation of the Nazi threat and the Communist threat.

Siegfried, a vice president in charge of "public relations and terror" for Kaos, is clearly a stereotypical Nazi. In "The Mysterious Dr. T," Siegfried's heavy German accent and Nazi-style clothing mark him as an example of the old threat of Nazism reinscribed in the service of the new threat of Kaos. Siegfried reacts to each situation with violence, always having his pistols ready to fire. More blatantly, in "The Not-So-Great Escape," Siegfried and his associate Starker are running a World War II–style concentration camp for kidnapped Control agents. When Max enters the camp posing as the Beast of Buenos Aires, he is driving a Nazi-style car with red Kaos flags waving. While the plot behind the camp is a Soviet one — Kaos plans to take the Control agents behind the Iron Curtain, brainwash them, then return them to Washington to work for Kaos — the appearance of the camp is directly out of *Stalag 17*. Of the two threats, Nazi and Communist, the Nazi one is often the more visible, since there are more villains with German accents than there are ones with Russian accents. In "The Apes of Rath," Dr. Rath draws attention to this feature of the show, telling his Kaos contact, "I'll tell you what else is amazing ... that you and I can be here like this and converse in a German accent for hour after hour and neither one of us is German." Like *The Adventures of Rocky and Bullwinkle* cartoon, *Get Smart*'s parody of the enemy involves the incorporation in the show of elements reminiscent of both the Soviet and Nazi systems.

However, the Cold War parody in the TV show is not applied only to the enemy. While Control routinely beats Kaos in every episode, a large part of the parody of the program involves pointing out the humorous aspects of the American spy network. Maxwell Smart's physical bumbling is an obvious example of this, but so is his lack of commitment to any ideological or nationalistic cause. Thus, for example, In "The Mysterious Dr. T," when a prominent scientist working for Control is murdered by coffee

Max has brought him from a restaurant that is a Kaos front, 99 comments on how terrible the situation is. Max responds, "Certainly is. They had the best prune Danish in town." In "The No-So-Great Escape," when Max learns of Kaos' plan to brainwash Control agents into becoming Kaos agents, his response is: "I understand that Kaos pays a lot more than Control." In "Spy, Spy, Birdie," when a mad scientist threatens the existence of both Control and Kaos, Max responds in the following manner: "If he blew up the entire world, there'd be nothing for Control and Kaos to fight over. We'd be out of a job." Max's selfishness parodies the image of the ideologically committed spy. Yet, Max's lack of loyalty stems from problems within Control itself. Budget cuts are always an issue at Control. In "The Day They Raided the Knights," 99 is cut from Control because the computer has selected the agents who must be fired in order for the agency to be able to function within Control's budget. In "Tequila Mockingbird," Control cannot afford to buy Max a plane ticket to Mexico, so he must travel on transportation provided by "Rent a Burro." In "Classification: Dead," Max himself must pay for the antidote to the poison he has received from a Kaos agent while on a mission. In "The Not-So-Great Escape," Max must pay the electric and power company for damage incurred when he tries to dig out of the prison camp while a prisoner of Kaos. In "Run, Robot, Run," Max comments on the cheapness of the entire U.S. government: "Kaos knows that winning a track meet is more important to the U.S. than winning a war. Besides, it's a lot cheaper. We don't have to finance the losers." By portraying Control and the U.S. government as penny-pinching, the idea of Cold War espionage being financed ad infinitum from a bottomless government purse is called into question. As Murray S. Davis comments regarding parody, "A system's elements have degrees of essentiality; consequently, the various incongruities that annihilate them produce degrees of funniness. Conversely, the larger the laugh, the more essential the system's aspect that must have been annihilated" (14-15). Thus, the American public's belief that the U.S. government would spend an unlimited amount of money to combat the Communist threat was key to the master discourse of the Cold War. By portraying spies on a budget, *Get Smart* annihilates that notion, hence producing humor through that annihilation.

Another classic example of early Sixties Cold War parody shifts the focus from the world of spies to the corporate world: Billy Wilder's *One, Two, Three* (1961). The movie focuses on C.R. MacNamara, a Coca-Cola executive in West Berlin who longs to get posted to London. In order to impress his boss, Mr. Hazeltine, he agrees to look after Scarlett, the boss's daughter, during her trip to Berlin. Scarlett sneaks behind the Iron Curtain and marries Otto Ludwig Piffle, an East German Communist. MacNamara has Piffle arrested and tries to get the marriage annulled until he discovers that Scarlett is pregnant. Upon learning that, and with much ensuing difficulty, he retrieves Otto and has him adopted by Count von Droste Schattenburg. He then attempts to groom Otto to become a good capitalist. MacNamara succeeds so well that the London job he has been seeking is given to Otto.

By shifting the focus of the Cold War from the world of espionage to the corporate world, Wilder parodies the increasing power of American consumerism.[4] The battleground of the Cold War becomes consumer products as MacNamara attempts to establish bottling plants in the Soviet Union and other Iron Curtain countries. MacNamara brags to Hazeltine: "Napoleon blew it. Hitler blew it, but Coca-Cola is going to pull it off," setting up business as a successful Cold War battleground. The Russian trade commissioner, Peripetchikoff, is willing to negotiate with MacNamara, because espionage attempts to steal the secret formula of Coca-Cola have failed. MacNamara mocks the Soviet attempt to create a copy of Coca-Cola: "Kremlin Cola ... even the Albanians wouldn't drink it." In the end, the trade commissioner and his associates agree to MacNamara's arrangement for bottling plants but only because MacNamara has implied that they will have sexual access to his beautiful secretary, Ingeborg. Thus, in *One, Two, Three*, the Communists are shown to harbor the same desire as Westerners for consumer products and beautiful women, though they conceal these desires under an ideological hatred for all that is capitalist. Thus, for example, MacNamara easily bribes the border guards at the Brandenburg Gate by giving them free Coca-Cola. Otto's quick conversion to capitalism, which takes place in a few hours, also highlights the powerful allure of capitalism and consumerism. Thus, like the parodies discussed previously, *One, Two, Three* reinforces Cold War ideas by demonstrating the seductive nature of the American system, which allows Americans to win the Cold War through an alluring way of life based on easy access to consumer products. As David Granick points out, by the late 1950s, active interest in obtaining consumer products had made an inroad into everyday Soviet life: "Save, the Russian is urged, in order to buy a car, build a house, purchase a refrigerator or a TV set" (99).

What Wilder's vision suggests is that it will be the corporate world and not the espionage world that will win the Cold War. In their negotiations, MacNamara and Peripetchikoff both make references to peaceful coexistence. In an address to the UN General Assembly on September 23, 1960, Nikita Khrushchev commented: "The policy of peaceful coexistence assumes a readiness to solve all outstanding issues without resort to force, by means of negotiations and reasonable compromises" ("Address"). This is what MacNamara does in the film, negotiating with both Peripetchikoff and Otto in order to achieve reconciliation between the two systems. Naturally, since this is an American Cold War film, reconciliation means a conversion of the Communist into a capitalist, which is what occurs with both Peripetchikoff and Otto.

Like *Get Smart* and *The Adventures of Rocky and Bullwinkle*, *One, Two, Three* relies upon references to other discourses in order to create its parodic humor, references to other fictional works, and references to the master discourse of anti–Communism and the Cold War. The most obvious film parodies that are part of *One, Two, Three* rely upon James Cagney (who plays MacNamara) and his background as a star of gangster films. When MacNamara discovers that Scarlett is pregnant, he says, "Mother of mercy, is this the end of Little Rico?" quoting the last line of the gangster classic *Little Caesar*. When he is trying to teach Otto proper table manners, he threatens to hit him in the face with a grapefruit, a reference to Cagney's classic gangster film *The Public Enemy*. Red Buttons, in a cameo role as an American MP, breaks into a Cagney imitation in sarcastic response to MacNamara. By creating these parodic allusions to Cagney, the film suggests a similarity between gangsterism and the Cold War corporate world. Certainly the tactics that MacNamara uses in order to achieve his goals in the film are gangster-like tactics of blackmail and less-than-ethical bargaining. Yet, while the film parodies the American corporate world, it also makes the Communist an object of parody.

In a review of *One, Two, Three* that appeared in *Variety* on January 1, 1961, the reviewer comments that the film "pulls no punches and lands a few political and ideological haymakers on both sides of the Brandenburg Gate" ("One, Two, Three"). Wilder parodies Communist attitudes in both Otto and the Soviet trade commissioner and his associates. Otto is the stereotypical Communist ideologue. He brags to MacNamara about his and Scarlett's wedding rings having been "forged from the steel of a great cannon that fought at Stalingrad." He threatens MacNamara, echoing Nikita Khrushchev's famous 1959 speech to the UN: "You and your kind are doomed.... We will bury you!" to which MacNamara replies, "Bury us. Don't marry us." Otto castigates American consumerism and popular culture. When MacNamara says, "To hell with the revolution," Otto replies, "To hell with Frank Sinatra." Otto accepts the inefficiency of the Communist system, telling Scarlett that "the 7:00 train for Moscow leaves promptly at 8:15." As MacNamara is trying to transform Otto, Otto lectures the manicurist working on his nails: "A strong, healthy girl like you, you should not be cutting nails. You should be cutting wheat in the Ukraine." When Otto realizes that he will hold a corporate position in Coca-Cola as Hazeltine's son-in-law, he envisions his role as a leader of a worker's revolution: "Soft drink slaves of the world arise!" While Otto represents the young, passionate Communist idealist, Peripetchikoff and his associates reference Soviet bureaucratic corruption.

When Peripetchikoff gives MacNamara a Cuban cigar that, so he tells him, has been exchanged for rockets, MacNamara comments that the Soviets have been cheated, because the cigar is lousy. Peripetchikoff replies, "Not worried. We send them pretty crummy rockets." When MacNamara meets Peripetchikoff and his associates at the Hotel Potemkin in East Berlin, the decadence of the Soviet officials is revealed as the men drink vodka, eat caviar, and watch Ingeborg perform a strip tease. Later in the film, we learn that Peripetchikoff has defected, turning in his two associates as spies in the process. The character of Peripetchikoff, like that of MacNamara, indicates the amorality of their respective systems, as both characters are motivated by selfishness rather than by any kind of ideological commitment.

Similarly, the naïveté of Otto is doubled by Scarlett's innocence. If Otto represents the young Communist blinded by ideological fervor, Scarlett represents the naïve, apolitical American teenager. At seventeen, Scarlett has been engaged four times. The film portrays her attraction to Otto as teen rebellion. Scarlett has come to Berlin because she has misinterpreted political commentary about the city: "Everybody says Berlin's the hottest spot in the world." Scarlett is easily and superficially converted to Communism by Otto: "I wash his shirts, and he broadens my mind." She has been helping him blow up balloons emblazoned with the slogan "Yankee Go Home." When MacNamara accuses her of anti–Americanism, Scarlett, a Southern belle from Georgia, retorts: "It's not anti–American. It's anti-Yankee. Where I come from everybody's against the Yankees." Scarlett views the ideological clashes of the Cold War through a sexual prism. She tells Phyllis, MacNamara's wife, "Those subversives, they're the wildest!" Phyllis replies, "I thought we were just lagging behind in missiles." Scarlett characterizes her father's anti–Communism in the following terms: "Daddy has a fit any time I order anything with Russian dressing." The film matches Otto's naïve political commitment, one shattered when he learns of Peripetchikoff's defection, with Scarlett's political ignorance and innocence.

American capitalism and Soviet bloc Communism are not the only political systems parodied in *One, Two, Three*. Like *The Adventures of Rocky and Bullwinkle* and *Get Smart*, this film also parodies the Nazi system.

However, instead of linking Nazis and Communists as one continuous enemy, Wilder's film deals with the danger of Nazis working as part of the American alliance.[5] MacNamara's assistant, Schlemmer, clicks his heel habitually when taking orders from MacNamara, yet denies having had any participation in the Nazi regime. When MacNamara labels his heel-clicking "that old Gestapo training," Schlemmer professes ignorance: "Adolf who?" Yet, Schlemmer's Nazi past saves the day for MacNamara as he recognizes a reporter who threatens to expose Otto as a Communist in the newspapers. Schlemmer identifies the reporter as an SS man he served under during the war, and this results in the reporter printing the views about Scarlett and Otto that MacNamara desires. A subtle link between the Nazi system and the U.S. corporate world is forged in other ways as well. When a cuckoo clock in MacNamara's office strikes, a small flag-waving Uncle Sam emerges. Schlemmer clicks his heels at Uncle Sam. Phyllis sarcastically accepts orders from her husband by replying, 'Yes, Mein Fuhrer." In a study of the uses of Nazism in Cold War discourse, Barton Byg argues that Nazism stood as a femme fatale in the Cold War: "In connecting Nazism with seductiveness and with capitalism, films imply that the danger indeed does not come from outside, but arises from one's own desires" (182). Desire is what wins in *One, Two, Three*: desire defeats any political ideology. The allure of American consumerism captivates all the characters, capitalists, Communists, and Nazis alike. Refuting Otto's nihilism, MacNamara comments, "Any world that can produce the Taj Mahal, William Shakespeare, and striped toothpaste can't be all bad."

Thus, the pervasiveness of anti–Communist rhetoric is indicated in one way in Cold War society by the ability of it to work within a diverse array of genres.

The last section of the book examines anti–Communist rhetoric's engagement with historical concerns of Cold War American society, beginning with the fear of nuclear holocaust and its connection to anti–Communism.

9. Nuclear Apocalypse and Anti–Communism

In post–1945 America, the fear of nuclear war pervaded many aspects of American life. At first, the United States turned a mirror on itself, fearing the power it had unleashed with the Manhattan Project and the two atomic bombs dropped on Hiroshima and Nagasaki. After 1949, however, the perception of the bomb changed radically as by that point it was in possession of the Soviet Union, not just the United States. As Paul Boyer comments, "On September 24, 1949, a terse announcement from Washington struck a largely unprepared nation: the Soviet Union had tested an atomic bomb!" (336). Since the government and military had been predicting that the advent of the Soviet bomb lay as far as twenty years in the future, the sudden realization that a nuclear war was potentially imminent came as a terrible shock to many. Questions concerning nuclear warfare shifted from being an internal matter plaguing Americans and their consciences to ones concerning the truly frightening potential outcome of a Cold War gone hot. The fears that nuclear scientists had been living with since the inception of the Manhattan Project — and especially since its successful culmination — came to color the everyday images and concerns of the American public, to a great extent via Civil Defense drills and films. Richard Feynman, a junior member of the Manhattan Project, describes his post–Hiroshima reaction in the following terms: "I sat in a restaurant in NY, for example, and I looked out at the buildings and I began to think, you know, about how much the radius of the Hiroshima bomb damage was... And I would go along and I would see people building a bridge, or they'd be making a new road, and I thought, they're *crazy*, they just don't understand, they don't *understand*. Why are they making new things? It's so useless" (132). Feynman's intense personal fear that nuclear bombs could destroy New York at any moment was echoed in the Fifties by intense nationwide fear, fear that helped fuel and then powerfully intensify anti–Communist sentiment. In this chapter, I explore three works from the Fifties that intertwine fear of Communism with fear of nuclear war.

"Atomic Attack," an episode of *Motorola TV Hour,* was broadcast in 1950.[1] The drama focuses on a Westchester family before and after an H-bomb attack on New York City. Mr. Mitchell, the father of the house, goes to work, and his two daughters, Barbara and Ginny, go to school. Gladys Mitchell, the mother of the house, stays home and does ordinary household chores. At 10:50 that morning, an H-bomb is dropped on New York. Barbara and Ginny come home, but there is no word about Mr. Mitchell. The Civil Defense system soon billets some lodgers with the Mitchell home: first, there is a young girl and her grief-stricken mother who is sure her husband is dead; then there is another woman who is certain she is dying from radiation sickness; finally, there is a man who is a former naval commander. In addition, Mrs. Mitchell allows her former science teacher, Dr. Garson, to stay with the family, since he fears being hunted down because of his pacifist beliefs. After facing general uncertainty, conflicts with their new lodgers, and attacks from people trying to break into their house, the Mitchells suffer two final blows: first, they discover that Mr. Mitchell is dead, then they find out that Ginny is suffering from radiation sickness and must undergo a long course of treatment, treatment whose chances of success are minimal at best.

While the Soviets never appear in the drama, their destruction of everyday American life through an unprovoked H-bomb attack indicates their inhumanity.[2] For the Fifties, the nuclear family often symbolized what was best about American life: the home as the ideal middle-class space. As Elaine Tyler May summarizes, "In the postwar years, Americans found that viable alternatives to the prevailing family norm were virtually unavailable. Because of the political, ideological, and institutional developments that converged at the time, young adults were indeed homeward bound, but they were also bound to the home" (15). Television provided the perfect medium for this idealization of the domestic, as Fifties shows such as *I Love Lucy, Leave It to Beaver, Father Knows Best,* and *The Donna Reed Show* attest. Lori Landay comments, "Television brought the world into the home and the home into the world. Because American culture was engrossed in the ideas and commodification of domesticity, postwar society was a fertile field in which television expanded" (32). Part of the eeriness of "Atomic Attack" lies in the fact that i the beginning of the episode it operates within a sit-com mode. We see the Mitchells at the beginning of an ordinary day laughing over breakfast. Mr. Mitchell laments that the family isn't normal, but Gladys reassures him that it is. Ginny's biggest problem is that she must leave behind her stuffed horse, Michael. Then, into the safety of the domestic, horror suddenly intervenes, and familiar objects of comfort become radioactive objects of horror. Thus, for example, Ginny's horse, Michael, a favorite toy, becomes drenched with black rain and contaminates her with radiation.

Suddenly nothing is normal or funny in the Mitchells' world. When Ginny and Barbara return from school, Ginny is excited by the "big bang" she has seen, but Barbara is hysterical. Gladys tries to calm her down by making her see that nuclear war always has been inevitable: "We've been living with this thing in the back of our mind for years." By disrupting the contentment of the nuclear family, the Soviets have shaken what many in the Fifties saw as the cornerstone of their society: the family. Even though Gladys steps in as a source of strength for her daughters and the lodgers who are staying with her, Mr. Mitchell is dead, and the ideal breakfast with which the film begins can never be enjoyed again. However, because the attack in "Atomic Attack" is deliberate and not an accident (as, by contrast, it is in *Fail-Safe*, for example), the episode raises issues about the necessity of nuclear weapons as well as the horror of them.

The subplot that most emphasizes the necessity of nuclear stockpiling involves Barbara's science teacher, Dr. Garson, who has once worked on the Manhattan Project, but has given up that life in order to become a teacher. He is a pacifist and believes that violence of any type is wrong. He regrets the role that he has played in the creation of nuclear weapons. Garson's views reflect the short-lived scientists' movement of the late 1940s. Many Manhattan Project scientists favored international control of nuclear weapons and set about through a propaganda campaign including such publications as *One World or None* (1946) to convince the American public of the necessity of implementing this idea. As Boyer comments, "Though the scientists consciously manipulated the public's fears, they did not do so cynically. They were genuinely convinced that the atomic devastation they described was a strong likelihood, if not a near certainty; that time was desperately short, and that the remedies they proposed offered at least a slim hope" (71).[3]

By 1950, however, support for the views of the scientists' movement had been eclipsed by anti–Communist sentiment that advocated an arms race rather than international control of nuclear weapons. Boyer comments of Edward Teller, the father of the H-bomb: Teller succumbed "increasingly to an all- encompassing suspicion of the Soviet Union, Teller championed development of the hydrogen bomb, challenged nearly all arms-control efforts as naïve and dangerous and advocated a nuclear arms build-up almost without control or limit" (101). In "Atomic Attack," in order to protect the Mitchell family, Garson must learn to abandon his pacifist attitude. Thus, he fires Mr. Mitchell's rifle at some men who are trying to break into the house, and then is overcome with guilt over what he has done: "Why did I have to use this gun?" Mrs. Mitchell replies savagely, "Isn't that a luxury, that kind of sentimentality?" Garson's limitations are further highlighted in the film by his hiding out in the Mitchell house. Because he is a pacifist who has opposed the arms race, Garson fears that he will be killed as a collaborator with the enemy. However, when Dr. Spinell discovers that Garson is hiding in the house, he informs Garson that the authorities have been looking for him merely because they want him to help with the treatment of patients who are suffering from radiation sickness.

Although "Atomic Attack" is a very sobering drama, it still promotes the notion that nuclear war is winnable, thus advocating a continued arms race between the United States and the Soviet Union. Bomb shelters and civil-defense drills of the Fifties promoted just such a vision of nuclear war. Articles in popular magazines of the late Forties and early Fifties bore such titles as "How to Survive an Atomic Bomb" and "Survival Secrets for Atomic Attacks" (Boyer 310). In "Atomic Attack," the Soviet Union launches H-bombs in the form of missiles targeted on twelve American cities simultaneously. Yet, recovery happens very quickly. Mrs. Mitchell is almost immediately visited by her block warden, Jim, who tells her that "We trained for it long enough"—he seems almost relieved that something has finally happened. At eight the same evening, when the Soviet missiles have reached their targets and wreaked their havoc, the radio reports that "we have taken the offensive to pay the enemy back on his own terms." The twelve Soviet hydrogen bombs have not crippled the United States, since it has been able to strike back at the Soviet Union. On the third day of the war, the radio announcer reports that "Every single major city in the enemy's homeland has been hit." By the tenth day, the announcer reports that "The enemy's will and ability to fight have virtually been broken." At the breakfast table, Gladys promises a sick Ginny that the United States will triumph: "We are going to win."

"Atomic Attack" frightens its audience about the unpredictable Soviet Union, which has a government that might decide to drop H-bombs on the U.S. for no particular reason, yet the episode also reassures the audience by propagating the belief that nuclear war is both winnable and survivable.

The Atomic City (1952), a feature film from the same time period, deals with the issue of the development of the hydrogen bomb and with the threat posed to U.S. safety by Soviet espionage. The film focuses on the top nuclear scientist at Los Alamos, Dr. Frank Addison, who finds his world turned upside down when his son Tommy is kidnapped by a fellow scientist who is working for the Soviet Union. In collaboration with the FBI, Addison passes phony information relating to the H-bomb to the contact. Later, working against the FBI's wishes, Addison physically beats a contact in order to discover Tommy's whereabouts. Tommy is being held in the ancient Indian cliff dwellings outside of Los Alamos. The traitor is caught, and Tommy is saved after dangling in extreme danger outside one of the caves.

At the very beginning of the film, we see the supposedly normal domestic life at Los Alamos as one that has been frighteningly altered by the scientific work occurring there. Thus, we are shown the Addisons' irregular domestic life at Los Alamos and how that irregular life has come to be perceived as normal by the family. Over lunch, Tommy says to his mother, Martha Addison, "If I grow up, do you know what I'm going to do?" Martha is horrified by his use of the word "if." As Eleanor Jette's account of life at Los Alamos maintains, this was a common expression used by the children who grew up there. She relates that a friend of hers was horrified by her son's expression when he says to her, "If I grow up —" (82). The children who lived at Los Alamos openly expressed their uncertainty regarding the world's future as a result of the radical scientific changes being created where they lived. Tommy, however, is unruffled by this uncertainty and repeats the phrase to his friend Peggy. A man who is installing the Addisons' new television overhears this conversation and witnesses Martha, Tommy, and Peggy being unmoved by a routine test that shakes the entire house. The television man, an outsider, registers shock at what is perceived as normal by Los Alamos residents.

When Addison returns home after an ordinary day of work at the lab—a day that has included one of his colleagues being burned by overexposure to radiation, Martha expresses anxieties about life at Los Alamos and shows discontent with the barbed wire, the FBI, and the secrecy that is characteristic of routine life at Los Alamos.

Yet, her discontent is dispelled somewhat by the casting of the atomic scientist as a savior figure, a move that serves to further conflate the mythical and the modern. One figure that stood as a savior figure in postwar American society was the atomic scientist. Postwar perceptions of the atomic scientist saw him as one in whom the sites of moral considerations for the Atomic Age were located. On the one hand, the atomic scientist was perceived as the culprit behind the anxieties introduced into American society via nuclear weapons. On the other hand, the scientist stood as a new moralist who could help Americans come to terms with the radically unfamiliar postwar world. As accounts of the Manhattan Project make clear, after the use of atomic bombs on Hiroshima and Nagasaki, many scientists, especially nuclear physicists, began to perceive themselves as potential savior figures. This image was largely fashioned by J. Robert Oppenheimer and the scientists' movement that he led. *One World or None* best expressed the movement's view that there was an urgent need for Americans to look to atomic scientists for moral guidance. The scientists contributing to the volume projected an image of themselves as the promoters of a peaceful atom, and portrayed the nation state as a demonic force that could very well bring about world destruction.

This perception of the atomic scientist as the upholder of a new morality and justice outside the traditional channels of authority links the atomic scientist with the figure of the detective. As Sherlock Holmes attests to Victorian England's need for an alternative justice apart from that provided by Scotland Yard, and as Philip Marlowe indicates weaknesses in the LAPD that must be answered by a knight-detective who polices the mean streets, in much postwar popular culture, the atomic scientist serves as a savior-detective figure.

In *The Atomic City*, Dr. Addison, the top scientist at Los Alamos, must work outside the traditional channels of authority in order to save his kidnapped son, Tommy. *The Atomic City* deals with ethical complexities of the atomic age by portraying Addison as both the cause of the crime and the solution to it. Further, the film works to reduce postwar anxieties about nuclear weapons to a kidnapping scenario that has a positive outcome.

In the film, the strange newness of life at Los Alamos is played out against a backdrop of the older traditions of New Mexico life. At one point the film cuts directly from Addison's radically new work at the lab as he works on the H-bomb project to a scene of the Santa Fe Fiesta. Tommy is kidnapped at the fiesta, and the Addisons attend a square dance that evening to await word from the kidnappers. The kidnappers ask Martha to meet them near the Nuestra Senora de Guadalupe church in order to receive a phone message. The climactic scene is played out in Frijoles Canyon, home to 12th century Indian cliff dwellings and surface villages. Here, as the representatives of the modern world — Soviet agents — attempt to kill Tommy after discovering the passed information is false, the ruins themselves seem to come to the aid of the child and allow him to escape. Because he can fit in a small crevice in one of the caves, he eludes the attempt on his life. Even as he dangles from one of the caves, the landscape seems to take mercy on him and allows him to hang on until the FBI can rescue him. If the modern, dangerous world of Los Alamos, a world in which Tommy can become a pawn in a Cold War game of espionage, endangers the child, the natural landscape protects and saves him.

In the film, the Soviets pose the threat of disrupting the normality of American family life. Although life in Los Alamos is not average, the Addisons, much like the Mitchells in "Atomic Attack," represent an average nuclear family. Early in the film, Frank attempts to comfort Martha about her worries about Tommy growing up in Los Alamos by scolding her, "You make it sound like Siberia." And, middle-class normality does exist in the film. Tommy goes to the Fiesta and wins a bicycle; Frank and Martha go to a square dance. What makes these events nightmarish in the film is the intervention of the Soviet Union. Soviet agents use the opportunity of a school outing to the Fiesta to kidnap Tommy; they use the square dance as a contact point with the Addisons. As the narrator of the film reminds us in the semi-documentary style of its opening, Los Alamos must develop new weapons, "because the spirit of aggression is not yet dead in the world."

The Atomic City portrays the Soviet Union as the aggressive force that invades the normality of American life. As FBI agents trail a courier working for the Soviets, they follow him to a baseball game. He appears to enjoy the game, but passes information to another agent who is posing as a vendor. Thus, something as American and innocent as a baseball game is invaded by the corrosive power of the Soviet spy network. *The Atomic City* suggests that the Soviet threat is dangerous because it plays on the good qualities of Americans. Thus, the Addisons' love for their son is a positive quality, yet it makes them vulnerable to espionage. Inspector Mann of the FBI tells Addison that the Soviets have used the kidnapping as an occasion to "turn you into a traitor," so they can "have a pipeline into Los Alamos." As scientist-hero, Addison is able to solve the problem by keeping the secret of the H-bomb and rescuing his son. Addison's success in the film reaffirms the positive image of Los Alamos, a place that the narrator tells us is striving in its weapons development to "at last to free man from his long bondage to power." *The Atomic City* illustrates that in order to succeed in the Atomic Age the detective figure must understand the confusing new world everyone lives in. By contrast, conventional detectives increasingly find themselves useless and ineffectual in a world dominated by nuclear weapons and foreign espionage. Mike Hammer, in *Kiss Me*

Deadly (1955), is the epitome of the outdated hard-boiled private detective baffled by the confusing complexities of the Atomic Age.

Kiss Me Deadly begins with Christina Bailey flagging down Mike Hammer on a dark road. Christina has escaped from an insane asylum and asks Mike to take her to the bus station. On the way, they are forced off the road and kidnapped. Christina is tortured to death. The torturers then place Christina and Mike in his car and push it off the road. Mike survives the accident and begins his own investigation, despite the warnings of his acquaintance Pat Murphy. Mike follows up leads that suggest that a conspiracy has been organized against a scientist named Raymondo by a local gangster, Carl Evello. Hammer traces Christina's roommate, Lily Carver, and hides her in his apartment. Nick, Mike's mechanic friend, is murdered while helping Mike follow leads. Mike is then kidnapped by Evello's men. After escaping, he discovers that Velda, his secretary and girlfriend, has been kidnapped. With Lily's help, Mike breaks the coded message Christina mailed to him prior to her death, "Remember Me." At the morgue, he retrieves a key Christina swallowed prior to her murder. He finds a locker at the Hollywood Athletic Club and discovers a strange box. He tries to open the box, but burns his wrist. Pat reveals to Mike that the box contains radioactive material that foreign agents are attempting to steal. The box is stolen from the locker, and Mike follows a lead to Dr. Soberin's beachouse. Arriving at the house, Mike learns that Lily, who is really Gabrielle, is Soberin's lover, and that she has killed him to gain possession of the box. Lily shoots Mike, then opens the box, catching herself on fire and starting a chain reaction. Hammer and Velda struggle to escape the house. In the last shot, the house explodes.

"Atomic Attack" and *The Atomic City* juxtapose the insidious threat of the Soviet Union with the normality of American middle-class life. The Soviets are thus shown to be villainous because they disrupt a happy and peaceful society. *Kiss Me Deadly*, however, while also emphasizing the ruthlessness of those working for the Soviets, highlights the horror of atomic espionage by contrasting it with an already corrupt American society.[4] While the Americans are hardened and corrupt in the film, they are no match for the ruthless, unseen Soviet force controlling events in the film.

Two characters serve to highlight the manner in which American corruption is no match for Soviet-backed ruthlessness. Mike Hammer is the epitome of the corrupt, selfish private detective.[5] Christina labels him accurately as "one of those self-indulgent males." At a questioning by the Interstate Crime Commission, the officials express contempt for Mike, labeling him a "bedroom dick." When Mike leaves the hearing, one of the agents comments, "open a window." Indeed, Mike pursues the investigation purely for selfish reasons. He believes as he discovers the vastness of the conspiracy that there may be a profit in pursuing the question. Mike tells Velda they are going to stay away from divorce cases for a while, because "I've got a line on something better." Mike tells Velda that he is after "something very valuable." And yet, for all his corruption, Mike is an innocent.

Despite clues that suggest atomic espionage, Mike never catches onto what the object he is seeking truly is. When he visits Ray Diker at his apartment, Diker has obvious radiation burns on his face, yet Mike never questions him as to what has happened. Carmen Trivago, Raymondo's friend, tells Mike that Raymondo spoke of possessing a secret, "a riddler without any answer." Velda tells Mike that through seducing an art dealer, Mist, who is part of the conspiracy, has learned the name Soberin. Velda even indirectly reveals the answer to Mike when she speaks of "the nameless ones who kill people for the great whatsit." While Mike is being held at Soberin's beachhouse, Soberin tells Mike that "as the world becomes more primitive, its treasures become more fabulous." Even when he burns his wrist from attempting to open the box, Mike still does not perceive a solution to the mystery. This happens only when Pat tells him, "Now, listen, Mike. Listen carefully. I'm going to pronounce a few words. They're harmless words, just a bunch of letters scrambled together, but their meaning is very important. Try to understand what they mean: Manhattan Project, Los Alamos, Trinity." Mike responds to Pat by saying, "I didn't know." Within the complex world of Soviet-backed espionage, the street smarts of Mike Hammer are useless. Even when he does track down Soberin, he is too late, and can only watch helplessly as the chain reaction starts.[6]

Mike's corrupt double in the film, Gabrielle, also indicates the limitations of the corrupt American mind in grasping the significance of atomic espionage. Gabrielle is the typical femme fatale of the noir world.[7] Gabrielle has used her sexual appeal to forge a bond with Soberin. She uses her sexuality on Mike to gain his trust and protection. Like the typical femme fatale, she turns on her men, shooting both Soberin and Mike in an attempt to have the mysterious box entirely to herself. But, as is the case with Mike, her ignorance works against her. She, too, has not caught on to what the contents of the box are, even though she is Soberin's mistress. Soberin's warnings to her against opening the box fall on deaf ears, because Gabrielle does not understand the allusions to mythology that Soberin makes—he mentions Lot's wife and Pandora, and tells Gabrielle that "the head of the Medusa, that's what is in the box." Prior to his death, he tries to warn Gabrielle not to open the box, but, rather, to turn it over to his contact. He tells her that he is "Cerberus barking with all his heads," warning her stay away from the gates of hell. But Gabrielle does not understand what he is implying. Like Mike, she is continuing to live in a world in which valuable objects cannot be imagined to be dangerous. She believes that by opening the box she will become rich, not set off an atomic chain reaction.

In the complicated world of *Kiss Me Deadly*, it is Soberin, with his scientific knowledge and brutality, who functions best. Soberin's motives for espionage are unclear. That they are possibly ideological is suggested when, prior to being murdered by Gabrielle, he tells her that "Where I am going it is not possible for you to go," implying that he is defecting to the Soviet Union with the radioactive material he has procured for the Soviet government. Soberin's power comes from his vast knowledge and mysterious qualities. The film affords him a godlike power by creating him as a faceless voice, visible only through his pinstriped suit and blue suede shoes. When one of the torturers offers to revive an already-dead Christina, Soberin comments, "Who do you think you are that you can raise the dead?" Soberin, however, seems to be godlike in his ability to organize such a vast conspiracy and successfully arrange for so many murders. Yet, he is not the selfish loner that Mike is. When he phones Mike to threaten him, he speaks of "our intentions." At the beginning of the film, Soberin and the torturers are a faceless mass, suggesting the ruthlessness and lack of individuality often associated with the Soviet Union. Yet, Soberin fails as well. If Mike and Gabrielle fail because they do not understand the discourse of the Atomic Age, Soberin fails because he does not understand the language of the underworld. His trust in Gabrielle and belief that she will let him leave with the box indicate his naïveté.

In the world of *Kiss Me Deadly*, the arms race has created a corruption deeper than the existing corruption of the urban world. Nuclear weapons and the espionage associated with them have made old rules and old emotions meaningless. The signature tune of the film, "I'd Rather Have the Blues," indicates this changed world. Over the credits, Nat King Cole's lyrics exemplify the feeling that being sad is better than the way everyone feels at the time. They would rather just be sad rather than deal with their current situation. Later, Mike listens to a torch singer sing the same song. Cold War society suffers from a malaise worse than the blues, but one for which there is no name. The apocalyptic ending of the film suggests what the final result of the arms race and atomic espionage may be ... complete annihilation.[8]

While "Atomic Attack" and *The Atomic City* emphasize the horror of the Soviet threat via nuclear weapons, they both suggest that American bravery and ingenuity will be able to obviate total destruction. Informed, moral scientists like Frank Addison can stop espionage; Americans can survive nuclear war and strike back at their enemy. *Kiss Me Deadly* offers no such hope, since, in the film, the government and law enforcement are powerless to stop atomic espionage, and American ignorance and greed lead to inevitable nuclear destruction.

The espionage that informed anti–Communist representations of nuclear weapons was also part of a popular strain of anti–Communism that combined history and fantasy. The next chapter explores the careers of two famous FBI informants.

10. Cold War Confessions and the FBI Plant

Matt Cvetic and Herbert Philbrick were household names in early 1950s America, both famous for their roles as FBI plants within the inner-circles of the American Communist Party. Their own nonfiction accounts of their experiences and media representations created from those experiences revealed to a frightened American public the dangers implicit in internal subversion. The realities and myths that have become associated with these two anti–Communist icons reveal a strain of anti–Communist discourse that was popular in early 1950s American society. In this chapter, in order to explore how both men contributed to anti–Communist mythos in mid-century American culture, I will discuss both the real experiences of these two men and the fictional representation of their exploits.

In the minds of many, anti–Communism is frequently associated exclusively with McCarthyism, but anti–Communist sentiment in post–World War II America encompassed a variety of sentiments and discursive strategies. As Richard Gid Powers notes in his history of American anti–Communism, there were two clear camps of anti–Communists in late Forties and Fifties America: the liberal anti–Communists, who viewed the Party as "despicable and annoying," but did not perceive a real threat of subversion from American Communism (214); and the countersubversives, who perceived the Communists as an immediate danger because "they were infecting the country with collectivist values incompatible with American traditions, with the goal of eventually imposing a Soviet-style system on the United States" (214).

In the United States, a plethora of anti–Communist discourse was produced in the 1950s, discourse representing both major strains of anti–Communism. Sidney Hook, a representative of liberal anti–Communism, in an article published in the *New York Times Magazine* in 1950, argued that the Party represented heresy, but not conspiracy. Thus, for Hook, the Party as heresy was "a set of unpopular ideas or opinions on matters of grave concern to the community" (237), but in this view there was no way that the Party could be labeled a conspiracy. As defined by Hook, a conspiracy is "a secret or underground movement which seeks to attain its ends not by normal political or educational process but by playing outside the rules of the game" (237).

In stark contrast, countersubversive anti–Communist discourse clearly labeled the Party as a conspiracy seeking to overthrow the U.S. government. J. Edgar Hoover, in his *Masters of Deceit*, paints a portrait of a Communist Party that is dangerous, threatening subversion of the government on a mass scale: "These fronts are a vehicle for communist pressure. They are highly fissionable. From many comes one; from one come many. They can be cut, sliced, slivered, or compounded to fit any need" (218). Countersubversive anti–Communism proved in the 1950s to be the type of anti–Communism most readily embraced by the media. Hence, the best-selling accounts of anti–Communism tended to come from this camp. Powers traces the dominance of countersubversive anti–Communism to the liberal's elitism, an attitude that implied that "anticommunism was something that could be properly understood only by the elite" (262).[1]

The stories told by the FBI plants within the Party formed a subgenre of countersubversive anti–Communist discourse. Both Cvetic and Philbrick fall clearly into this camp of anti–Communism. Further, the accounts written by Cvetic and Philbrick and by other "reformed" Communists such as Whittaker Chambers indicate how the first-hand account of experience in the Party relates very clearly to confessional discourse.[2] In his study of confessional literature, Dennis A. Foster argues that the literary confession "involves a narrator disclosing a secret knowledge to another, as a speaker to a listener, writer to reader, confessor to confessor. A full confession would presumably require that a private knowledge be revealed in a way that would allow another to understand, judge, forgive, and perhaps even sympathize" (2). The unique positions of both Cvetic and Philbrick required that while working undercover for the FBI they showed themselves to be convincing members of the Party. Once the cover was broken through important testimony, the need to confess the truth, to distance themselves from the sin of Communism, was a factor in both of their first-hand accounts. As Foster argues, confession involves a need to reconstruct the self after a "disruptive, transgressive experience" that has caused one to see the self "as strange, beyond familiar boundaries of comprehension" (15). Both Cvetic and Philbrick, by posing as Communists, experienced a fragmentation of self and also came to possess forbidden knowledge, the knowledge of the inner-workings of the Communist Party. Because countersubversive discourse labeled communism as a disease and a sin, the need to confess having had close contact with the force was paramount.[3] Within such a rhetorical framework, Cvetic and Philbrick stand out as epic American Cold War heroes, heroes who have been to the underworld and survived to tell of it, but bear with them the taint of that unclean experience. Yet, the celebrity status of these two figures stems partly from a public ready and willing to embrace the FBI informant as a cultural icon.

The FBI was skilled in public relations and by the late Forties had successfully promoted itself as a paragon of virtue. As Ellen Schrecker argues in *Many Are the Crimes*, under Hoover's leadership, the FBI successfully created an image of itself as a nonpartisan and completely ethical organization. This image allowed the FBI to enjoy unconditional political and public support. Schrecker argues, "By insisting that it was above political considerations, the Bureau ensured that it would receive support from all constituencies and that few restrictions would be placed on its activities" (218). Trust and belief in the FBI extended beyond political groups to the public in general. As Schrecker argues, the FBI made Americans aware of the threat of internal Communists and then constructed itself as the only institution capable of effectively battling that threat: "Together Hoover and his men had alerted the rest of the nation to the alleged dangers of domestic Communism and then had created and operated much of the machinery that was used to combat that menace" (239). Within the FBI system, the informant was all-important, providing inside information about the workings of the Communist Party.

The FBI informant obviously stood in an ambiguous position: potentially hero, but nevertheless a person courting the stigma of informer. As Schrecker argues, the FBI deliberately used the word "informant" to distance these people from the "negative connotations of the word 'informer'" (*Many* 228). However, informants were a constant source of trouble for the FBI. While they were needed for information, they constantly posed the threat of humiliating the FBI and harming its public image. With around a thousand informants working for the agency during the late 1940s and 1950s, there were ample opportunities for these informants to harm FBI image, either deliberately out of bitterness or because of carelessness (Schrecker, *Many* 228–229). Because the informant was such an unstable variable in the eyes of the FBI, the need to construct heroic media images for these figures was crucial. Yet, while the FBI willingly continued to help a discreet agent like Philbrick, they were eventually forced to wash their hands of the self-aggrandizing and unstable Cvetic. In addition to the need for the hero-informant to booster the FBI's image, a public living within a world in which informing on one's friends, co-workers, and even family was frequently presented as a matter of national security would most likely be comforted by a vision of the informant as national hero.

One problem with constructing the FBI informant as heroic stemmed from anti–Communist propaganda itself. The Communist was sometimes demonized as a cog in a heartless machine who would stoop to informing on his own family for the good of the state. The inhuman informer, therefore, was an image often associated with Communism itself. Because the FBI informant had to sacrifice his personal relationships and feelings to the cause of anti–Communism, his image became perilously similar to that of the emotionless Communist ideologue. In *What We Must Know About Communism*, Harry and Bonaro Overstreet describe the Communist system as one within which "the individual is 'downgraded'" (261). They argue that Communism forces the individual to sacrifice "the emotions we have counted basic to sound human relationships: love, friendliness, compassion, neighborliness, tenderness" (261). One way in which both Cvetic's and Philbrick's accounts of their experiences skirt around this uneasy comparison is through creating worlds in which the people who are informed upon are all clearly bad people: no innocent people get hurt in the situation because only bad people associate themselves with the Communist Party.[4] Furthermore, Cvetic and Philbrick's years as emotional vacuums are presented as temporary states, ones which can be easily overcome as soon as the FBI has gained the necessary testimony from the informants. Yet, as discussion of the true and fictional experiences of these two men illustrates, the difficulty and ambiguities involved in the process of changing an informer into an informant were always at hand.

Matt Cvetic's career as a FBI plant reveals that there are many sharp contrasts between anti–Communist icons created by the media and the reality experienced by the flesh-and-blood behind those constructed images, the men who actually worked as undercover FBI informants. As Dan Leab's biography of Cvetic relates, Cvetic worked undercover for the FBI for seven years. In 1943, he was asked by the FBI to join a Pittsburgh Communist Party unit. In the event, Cvetic did actually provide valuable information to the FBI, but as the result of his erratic behavior, including alcoholism, violent outbursts, and constant demands for more money, he was secretly fired by the Bureau in 1950 (2).[5] Subsequent to his firing, and after his story had been told in several media, Cvetic emerged as an icon. In July 1950, he appeared on a popular radio program called *We, the People*. In the same month, a series of articles appeared in *The Saturday Evening Post* relating his adventures as a FBI informant. As Leab notes, "The *Post* at that time had 'a unique place in the heart of Middle America'.... Probably for that reason, during the Cold War years, the *Post* was the favorite vehicle for the stories of recanters, defectors, and government types peddling mainstream anti–Communism" (73). Subsequent to the publication of the *Post* articles, Jack Warner purchased the rights to Cvetic's story, and in 1951, the film *I Was a Communist for the FBI* was released and became a financial success. It was even taken seriously enough to be nominated for an academy award for best documentary of 1951. Cvetic's articles in the *Post* and the film version of his experiences illustrate how reality and fiction merged to create the myth of Matt Cvetic, anti–Communist crusader.

In the *Post* articles—which were actually written by Pete Martin, to whom Cvetic told his story—Cvetic casts himself as a self-sacrificing patriot who in the service of the FBI has lost everything. Cvetic argues that because of is work within the Party, his family ceased to love him. He relates that his mother "died thinking I was a traitor to my country, and I couldn't run the risk of telling her I wasn't" ("Part One" 17). According to Cvetic, right before her death his mother "begged me to change my name, so I wouldn't humiliate the other Cvetics" ("Part One" 95). Cvetic also lays blame for his divorce on the FBI and blames the agency too for loss of contact with his twin sons, concluding that there certainly "wasn't anything funny about my family thinking me a jerk and a traitor. That was the biggest price I paid for the work I did" ("Part One" 93). As Leab's biography makes clear, these images of self-sacrifice are pure fiction: it was Cvetic's alcoholism and womanizing that broke up his marriage and alienated him from his sons. In addition, his parents and siblings were not at all horrified by his Communist ties, but, rather, playfully teased him about the association. One sister stated that the family "kidded him about being a Communist and laughed at him" (qtd. in Leab 16).

Curiously, the myth that is created in Cvetic's articles is one exclusively about his private life. As Leab relates, post–Cold War revelations have proven that some of Cvetic's testimony about the workings of the Party was true (74–75). The lies in Cvetic's articles relate primarily to his personal life and character. Cvetic evidently felt impelled to create an image of himself as a spotless self-sacrificing man, but the lure of Communism never touched him—a situation in stark contrast to that of Philbrick, who does seem to have been profoundly touched by it.

In his study of forbidden knowledge, Roger Shattuck argues that one type of forbidden knowledge is the type that straddles the boundaries between objective and subjective knowledge: "This fifth form of forbidden knowledge arises from a familiar fissure at the heart of our thinking. Hard as we may try, we cannot be both inside and outside an experience or a life — even our own" (334). The role of the plant is dangerous precisely for this reason: the individual must at the same time be both inside and outside the camp of both the friend and the enemy. Cvetic, however, unlike Philbrick, remained ideologically untouched by his work for the Party. His objective approach to the Party he traces back to ignorance: "Communism is based on dialectical materialism. I never got it straight in my mind exactly what that is, but I know it's atheistic" ("Part One" 95).

In fact, the real villain that emerges from Cvetic's articles is not the Communist Party, but the FBI, which Cvetic blames for ruining his life: "Before I'd gone to work for the FBI, I'd been a happy go lucky type. I'd enjoyed taking my twin sons camping, fishing, and to the Pirates' ball games. But when they grew up, they began to be ashamed of me" ("Part Three" 99).[6] Cvetic's account of his experiences as an informant tell the reader very little about the inner-workings of the Party. What the reader hears is Cvetic's confession, an attempt to justify his life, and scapegoat the FBI for his personal problems. The threat of Communism fades into the background and the sad, self-sacrificing life of Cvetic moves to the forefront. Thus, Cvetic's articles serve as a confession aimed at reestablishing his credibility as a citizen. As Peter Brooks argues in his study of confession, "The confessional subject thus is obliged to perform a scrupulous self-examination and to submit the results ... to an examiner who holds the power to absolve, and, in absolution, to acknowledge and legitimate the individual as a valid part of the community" (100). Because Communism never touched him, Cvetic did not need absolution for his actions within the Party; he needed absolution for the personal failings that led him to be fired by the FBI. What better confessor than a huge portion of the American reading public? The film version of Cvetic's story retains the self-sacrificing element, but works to create an evil Communist Party, an exaggerated version of the Communist conspirators of countersubversive discourse.

Between 1948 and 1954, Hollywood produced more than forty anti Communist films (Zinn 427). *I Was a Communist for the FBI* is one of the best known. The film recasts Cvetic, who in reality worked in a very low-level Party position, as the chief Party organizer of the CP in Pittsburgh. Through his job as a foreman at North American Steel, Cvetic aids in infiltrating Communist workers into the labor union there. Cvetic gets in trouble with the Party when he tries to protect Eve Merrick, a high-school teacher who openly expresses her doubts about Party procedure. Cvetic saves her from being killed by two Party assassins, but is himself almost killed by Party members. However, the FBI steps in and saves him by accusing him of the murder of an FBI agent who was protecting Merrick. Cvetic escapes from his role as informant when he is called before HUAC and testifies about his knowledge of the inner-workings of the Party. This results in his being reunited with his brother and son.

While the myth of Cvetic's personal sacrifice persists as a key element of the film, much more emphasis is placed on the nature of the Party's conspiratorial activities than is to be found in Cvetic's articles. In one *Post* article, Cvetic provides a very simple explanation for the appeal of Communism to Americans: "Given youngsters who've never had much in the way of opportunity and who know what it means to suffer from malnutrition, the offer of an auto to use on party business, together with a few dollars to carry in their pockets, plus an introduction to attractive girl party members, are lures hard to resist" ("Part Three" 102). While Cvetic's article suggests that the real presence of poverty in the U.S. abets the Communist Party, the film denies this, substituting a well-organized and insidious conspiracy as the basis of the Party's success.[7]

The voice-over narration at the beginning of the film establishes the tone, stating that "Pittsburgh, the strong heart of America's industrial might" is being threatened by the arrival of Gerhardt Eisler, a Communist mastermind. At a Party meeting during which Eisler and Cvetic toast Comrade Stalin with champagne and caviar, Eisler reveals his plan of conspiracy: "We must incite riots, discontent, open warfare." Jim Blandon, a Moscow-trained Communist and Cvetic's immediate superior, uses "the old rule of divide and conquer" to implement Eisler's plan. Blandon speaks of equality before a meeting of African-Americas and then after his speech comments that "those niggers ate it up." The film illustrates a primary tenet of countersubversive anti–Communism, that the CP mouths ideas of equality while cynically using minorities to further internal unrest. Hoover comments that "This is the terrifying danger of communist discipline — that in the name of freedom, by appealing to the most noble qualities in man, the human being is pushed into deepest tyranny" (*Masters* 165).[8] Later in the film, Blandon asks a German-American Party member to pose as a Fascist in order to create dissension in his neighborhood.

Because *I Was a Communist for the FBI* portrays the CP as such an insidious threat, the myth of Cvetic's sacrifice proves to have a huge payoff in the film. Whereas Cvetic's articles underplay the value of his "sacrifice" and play up his own personal suffering, the film argues that the sacrifice is necessary in order to destroy the vast CP conspiracy that threatens all Americans. Cvetic must face abuse from his family members, such as his brother, Joe, who calls him a "slimy Red" and beats him up after their mother's funeral. He must also endure the hatred of his neighbors, such as one man who upbraids him for teaching his son how to bunt, proclaiming, "Baseball's an American game. I can show him that without your help." In the end, all of Cvetic's suffering proves to have been worth it when he testifies before HUAC, exposing the American Communist Party as "a vast spy system" that is designed "to deliver the United States into the hands of Russia as a slave colony." After his testimony, the celluloid version of Cvetic is reunited with his brother, Joe, and his son, Dick. Both admire his heroism and regret their earlier bad treatment of him.

I Was a Communist for the FBI is a very melodramatic example of countersubversive anti–Communism. Its Oscar nomination for best full-length documentary of 1951 illustrates the blurring between fiction and reality that often occurred in anti–Communist propaganda of the early Fifties. With Cvetic's confession to HUAC in the film a moral cleansing takes place: the dirty secret of Communist conspiracy is aired and by implication due to Cvetic's testimony society will be at least partially purged of the disease of Communism. Brooks argues that "confession plays a crucial role in moral cleansing and also in moral discipline: it works both to console and to police" (2). *I Was a Communist for the FBI*, with its confessional title, solidified Cvetic's image, thus cleansing him of his real-life sins, but also stood as a warning to those who would get involved with the CP: someone is watching you.

While Cvetic's career and fictional representation of self deals with the problem of an informer who had an embarrassing private life — a man who provided valuable information to the FBI, but was ultimately fired, only to recast himself as a paradigm of virtue, much to the FBI's chagrin — the career of Herbert Philbrick illustrates the model FBI plant. However, as was the case with film representation of Cvetic's experience, for fictional representation, Philbrick's story was changed. Philbrick was a man who approached the FBI in 1940 upon realizing that the Massachusetts Youth Council he was involved with was a Communist-front organization. The FBI asked him to remain within the organization and provide the Bureau with information. Philbrick became a member of the Communist Party in 1944 and continued to work as a counterspy until 1949, when he appeared as a surprise witness at the trial of eleven Party members in New York. Based to a large extent on Philbrick's testimony, the eleven were convicted under the stipulations of the Smith Act. In 1951,

Philbrick began writing his memoirs for the New York *Herald Tribune*: his book-length memoir grew out of those articles (Klingaman 303–304).

Philbrick's memoir, *I Led Three Lives: Citizen, "Communist," Counterspy* (1952), was written with the unacknowledged aid of the FBI's public-relations team and became both a best-seller and the basis for a very successful TV series produced by ZIV (Leab 115).[9] Unlike Cvetic's *Post* articles, Philbrick's book paints a very positive view of the FBI. Philbrick's account of his first visit to a FBI office underscores the efficiency of the Bureau. Philbrick goes to the FBI to tell of his suspicion that he is working for a Communist-front organization: "Yet within moments the F.B.I. had me talking to exactly the right man. Obviously, the F.B.I. knew a lot more about the Cambridge Youth Council than I did — and I was the chairman of it" (29). Philbrick also emphasizes that the FBI never forced him to continue with his undercover work. Discussing a Party meeting, Philbrick comments that one agent told him, "Try to get there if you possibly can": Philbrick comments that "It was about as close as the Bureau ever came to giving me a direct order" (195). In addition to the positive image of the FBI conveyed in *I Led Three Lives*, Philbrick provides concrete verification of many of the ideas found in the countersubversive discourse of Hoover.

One idea key to Hoover's lectures and writings on anti–Communism was the idea of the misguided American who has been tricked through naïveté into becoming involved with a Communist organization. Hoover pointed out that the greatest weakness Americans possessed with regard to Communism was ignorance ("Testimony" 119). Philbrick portrays his own involvement with the Party as beginning because of ignorance: "I had always been a non-Communist.... The fact is that I knew so little about communism and its hidden aims and methods that, like the average person of those times, and many even today, I regarded the movement more as a nuisance than as an acute menace" (64). Thus, the liberal anti–Communism view is seen by Philbrick, as it is by Hoover, as a dangerous stance, one that might easily allow people to become dupes of the Communists. Further, Philbrick discusses his own experiences with recruitment in the CP as playing on the good intentions of the people approached: "Each front group in the network is baited with idealism. It is usually based on a legitimate and sincere motive" (104). Additionally, when discussing Communism, Philbrick takes up Hoover's disease metaphor, stating that the Party leaders "rendered me susceptible to their infectious poison. Wouldn't it be a fine thing, I often thought, if the evil I was trying to fight consumed me instead?" (86). As this quote illustrates, while Philbrick's account lauds the FBI for their hard work and fairness, it also, like Cvetic's articles, emphasizes the intense personal strain that Philbrick endured during his role as counterspy. However, unlike Cvetic, who seems to blame the FBI for his woes, Philbrick blames the Communist Party for his loss of identity.

Philbrick's memoir charts a loss of identity that occurred increasingly during his nine years as an informant, a loss of identity that was only righted with his act of confession at the Smith Act trials. Foster argues that a confessional memoir functions to "objectify the self — to represent it as a knowable object — through a narrative that 're-structures' ... the self as history and conclusions" (10). *I Led Three Lives* fulfills just this purpose for Philbrick. Unlike Cvetic, who apparently was able to keep his distance and obtain only objective knowledge of the Party, Philbrick's account indicates that he risked his identity by becoming too involved with the Party. Shattuck's definition of subjective forbidden knowledge is stated in terms of a process in which we "enter into, sympathize with, and unite with the thing known in order to attain subjective knowledge" (332).

Philbrick describes his loss of identity: "Nine years with my face smothered in a mask that could never be taken off; no face of my own to look at man in the eye and say, 'I am Herbert Philbrick'" (3). Philbrick relates that he had to obtain subjective knowledge of the Party in order to fight it: "One thing I did know. There is only one way to find and expose the underground Communist. You have to get in there with him, down in the muck and mud. There is no other way" (219). Yet, Philbrick paid a price for his subjective knowledge of Communism. He diagnoses his condition as one of "manufactured schizophrenia" (86). He admits his "dual personality" (237), and even indicates that when the FBI offered him a way out, he volunteered to continue working: "But I'm in there now. And I think I ought to stay" (247). Yet, when Philbrick does confess to his role as counterspy, he is relieved of the mental strain he has been suffering under.

Philbrick describes his testimony as a moment within which he gained back a sense of self. The testimony justifies his existence: "For this moment my presence, my very existence had been meticulously guarded.... For this moment I had somehow managed to live through nine years" (2). Brooks discusses the modern confession as "the justification of existence" (110). Philbrick describes the intense relief that he felt after the testimony in the following confessional terms: "Now for the first time I was permitted to speak them [the words "The Federal Bureau of Investigation"] in public. With five words I was able to shrug off the burden of those nine years, and to square myself with my family, my friends, and the world" (268). Philbrick's memoir, like Cvetic's articles, illustrates the importance

of the confessional mode to countersubversive anti–Communism. However, just as Cvetic's image was changed in its filmic representation, so was
Philbrick's image altered as he was transformed into a television character.

I Led Three Lives ran for 117 episodes, from 1953 to 1956. Reruns of
the series continued to be popular until the mid–Sixties (Leab 131). While
in comparison with Cvetic, Philbrick was obviously the ideal counterspy,
the character created by the series contrasts in several important ways
with that of its real-life original. First, the TV program makes Philbrick
a family man. In the book account of his experiences, Philbrick is not
married and mentions no romantic involvements; however, the Herbert
Philbrick of the television series has a wife and daughters. The addition
of a family allows the viewer to see the insidious disruption that the Communist Party could bring to the average nuclear family of the 1950s. In one
episode entitled "The Big Fear," the Philbrick household has a typical
middle-class morning. Eva, Philbrick's wife, prepares to go shopping, and
their daughter, Constance, studies for a history exam. As Philbrick takes
Eva out to the car to give her a ride, Comrade Jack tells them that Party
headquarters has sent for Eva. When Philbrick expresses concern over the
welfare of his wife, Jack replies: "You sound like the typical bourgeois
husband." In this episode, Philbrick threatens to blow his cover in order
to keep Eva out of danger. He tells FBI agent Jerry Dressler, "Those guys
have got their sticky little fingers on my wife." Eva comes away safely from
the assignment due to an error on the part of one of the Party members,
but the episode underscores how the Communist Party disrupts the normality of the American family: Eva misses the sale at the department store;
Constance is frightened by Philbrick's concern over Eva. Michael Rogin
has argued that Cold War rhetoric set up domesticity as a buffer against
the Communist threat: "Domestic ideology promised that the American
family would triumph over Communism" (17).

Accordingly, the TV Philbrick is provided with a family in order further to establish him as a normal hero. In her study of 1950s masculinity,
Barbara Ehrenreich notes that, in the 1950s, twenty-three was the average
marrying age for a man, "and according to popular wisdom, if a man held
out much longer, say even to twenty-seven, 'you had to wonder'" (14–15).
Sexual and marriage handbooks published in the Fifties attest to this same
suspicion surrounding men unwilling to marry. In a handbook entitled
Attaining Manhood: A Doctor Talks to Boys About Sex (1952), George M.
Corner associates unmarried men with homosexuality and with imma-
turity. The one blemish that might have been adduced to the real-life
Philbrick's character is hence corrected by the TV series that makes his

normality beyond reproach by adding a wife and children to his life. Further, Fifties perceptions of totalitarianism often focused on a definition of the totalitarian system as one devoted to "replacement of the family by the government" (Bethelard and Young-Bruehl 533). Thus, Philbrick's family has a clear ideological meaning — democracy and its freedoms.

Also from the ideological point of view, another way in which Philbrick's image is enhanced in the TV series results from portraying Philbrick as a man who has always been an anti–Communist. As has been mentioned previously, in his memoirs Philbrick relates that he had been neutral about Communism before he became involved with the Party. The TV Philbrick, however, has an anti–Communist past. In an episode entitled "The Candidate," an old friend of Philbrick's, Dr. Kettner, approaches him to ask him to help do PR work on a campaign for an anti–Communist running for Congress, George Reynolds. Philbrick refuses to help, and Kettner points out that three or four years previously Philbrick would have gladly helped; he asks Philbrick if his politics have changed. As a result of the meeting with Kettner, Philbrick is summoned to Party headquarters, and he has to recant his anti–Communist past: "We all committed sins against the masses" before joining the party, he tells the comrades. Philbrick is then involved in a Communist plot to smear Reynolds. He is asked to help him run the campaign and then arrange for a CP member, Mrs. Dayton, to make a huge donation to the campaign. The Communists hope then to expose Reynolds as funded by the CP and thereby produce the result that the "people begin to lose faith in their elected representatives." Through Philbrick's work, the FBI is able to inform Reynolds of the donation, and the Communist plan is foiled. By making Philbrick a character with an anti–Communist past, the TV series absolves him of the role of Communist dupe that in the memoir he identifies as his sin. Thus, in the TV series that remakes him into an ideal, informed man, the confessional aspect of Philbrick's book is lost.

While the series boosts Philbrick's image, it retains the positive representation of the FBI that was core to Philbrick's memoir. Philbrick is continually amazed at the efficiency of the Bureau. In one episode, which is entitled "Caviar," the FBI emerges as both caring and efficient. When Philbrick volunteers to get a suspicious pamphlet from an NKVD man's house, his FBI contact, Agent Henderson, tells him, "I can't ask you to take a chance like this, Herb." Philbrick, however, gets the pamphlet, and, through the FBI's brilliant and efficient team, the manual is decoded. Shipment of other copies of the manual is then stopped. The work itself is described as "a highly technical manual on the art of sabotage," and, in transmission, copies of it were intended to be concealed in boxes by being placed under layers of caviar. The FBI seizes the manuals and places only caviar in the boxes.

Further, Philbrick's suffering is blamed on the Communist Party, not on the FBI. For example, in an episode entitled "The Secret Police," a call from the Party summoning Philbrick to meet with a NKVD man interrupts his dinner with Eva. In "The Big Fear," when Philbrick is forced to lie to his daughter, Constance, he comments, "When you're working for the Party, you've even got to lie to your kids." Unlike Cvetic's articles, but like the film version of his career, *I Was a Communist for the FBI*, *I Led Three Lives* absolves the FBI of blame, singling out the Communist Party as the cause of disruption in domestic life.

The memoirs of Cvetic and Philbrick and the fictional representations of their lives illustrate countersubversive anti–Communist myth-making. While both men use memoir as a means of confession, their purposes are very different. While Cvetic uses confessional discourse to absolve himself of personal sins, Philbrick confesses to his audience the fine line he walked between role-playing and reality. He illustrates how close he was to removing the quotation marks from "Communist" in his experiences with the Party. Both accounts illustrate how the confessional mode was an important aspect of anti–Communist discourse. The fictional transformations of Cvetic and Philbrick demonstrate how anti–Communist television and film worked to create icon images of spotless crusaders against the Communist threat. Cvetic gets extensively made over as an ideal man in *I Was a Communist for the FBI*, while Philbrick gets a minor makeover in *I Led Three Lives*. Both in reality and in fiction, the lives of Cvetic and Philbrick illustrate how during the years of the Cold War, a new type of hero, the FBI informer, made a powerful impact on American popular culture.

While FBI informants worked undercover in the Communist Party to reveal a secret world of espionage, other fictional and nonfictional works engaged the issue of the overt world of capitalism — the business world — and its relationship to Communist espionage.

11. Anti–Communism and the Business World

One staple of anti–Communist propaganda from the Cold War was the notion that the Soviet system desired the dismantling of capitalism and consumerism. In *Masters of Deceit*, J. Edgar Hoover paints a portrait of the Communist as one who threatens the American Dream: "The communist leader rammed home his point. 'I'm working all the time, so much that I can hardly sleep at nights. You can't allow personal problems to take your mind off the Party. You've got to fight that kind of pressure. Your allegiance to the Party comes first. I never let my wife interfere. She knows her place.'"(79). The Cold War seemed to promise more leisure time for the breadwinner to spend with his family and more money for consumer goods. Yet, Communism often appeared as the specter threatening this dream. While blatant propaganda films from the Fifties through the Sixties seek to construct a rhetoric within which Communism and Capitalism are irreconcilable social and economic systems, nonfiction writings from the same time period portray a Soviet business world that is very similar to the American business world.

A striking example of a propaganda film that argues for capitalism and Communism as being polar opposites is a film made by Warner Bros. for the Department of Defense in 1962, *Red Nightmare*, narrated by Jack Webb, which begins by showing the audience a fake American city behind the Iron Curtain where Communists are being educated. In this "College town, Communist style," Communists create a replica of an American city that they then proceed to destroy through their studies in propaganda, espionage, and sabotage. The focus of the film then shifts to an ordinary American, Jerry Dawson. He is a man who takes his freedoms for granted, so Jack Webb causes him to have a nightmare, a nightmare about his hometown, Mid Town, being transformed into a Soviet satellite. Jerry learns from his nightmare and, as a result, becomes a better American citizen.

Red Nightmare focuses on the transformation of both home life and business life in the U.S. under Soviet domination. In the nightmare, Jerry's personal life evaporates. Hoover comments that "The Party's instructions must always take precedence. This constant stealing of time, never allowing the member to relax, develop a hobby, or enjoy a family, provokes the most searching doubts" (*Masters* 114). In the red nightmare he experiences, this is the type of world that Jerry finds himself in. Jerry's wife has become a cold woman, urging him to give to the PTA meeting a Party-scripted lecture entitled "How the New Communist Life Benefits Children." She eventually turns him in for deviationist behavior and testifies against him at his trial by the Party. Jerry's older daughter, Linda, volunteers for farm work and leaves home, declaring: "It's true, Daddy, I did volunteer for farm work…. The Party convinced me that I should free myself of the lingering bourgeois influence of family life." Jerry's younger children also become family-hating drones. His younger daughter tells him that she has decided to go away to boarding school, because "We learned in school that home life does not encourage the growth of the collective character." His son threatens to report him to the Party for not raising him properly.

In addition to all semblance of a private life being destroyed under the Communist system, business and industry are also affected by the Communists. Jerry works at an industrial factory. In his nightmare, he is given a quota that he must meet, causing him to have to work through his lunch hour. The freedoms of consumer society disappear as well. At a local diner, Jerry attempts to make a phone call home to his family, but the operator tells him that he cannot make a personal call unless he has "a permit from the Commissar." Thus, Communist domination has erased typical American business practices and the consumer culture.

As a result of experiencing the nightmare, Jerry learns to value what is important in American society. When he wakes from his dream and comes downstairs for breakfast, his son asks him if he can have a new space helmet. Jerry gladly agrees, happy that consumerism is alive and well. He allows his daughter to get married to her fiancé, a marriage he has opposed prior to his nightmare. He learns to view his freedom as a responsibility. Webb comments that "Freedom has a price. And its price is vigilance."

Red Nightmare is a strong example of government anti–Communist propaganda. By focusing on the nuclear family and the threat that Communism supposedly posed to the family and to the consumer culture of Fifties America, the film indicates the binary oppositions that were dear to anti–Communist propaganda. To threaten consumerism and the family is to threaten what it means to be American. Communists can never have similar desires to Americans, films like *Red Nightmare* tell us. Other propaganda films from earlier in the Cold War, while not as blatant as *Red Nightmare*, also extol American consumerism and the American business world in contradistinction to Communism.

The Woman on Pier 13 (1949) is about Brad Collins, a man who in his youth was a member of the Communist Party, but who left the Party, assumed a new identity, and became executive vice president for the Cornwall Shipping Company in San Francisco.[1] Brad steals Nan Lowry from his friend Jim Travis and after a whirlwind courtship marries her in less than a week. During their honeymoon, Brad is confronted by Christine Norman, an old girlfriend from his Communist past who works for a fashion magazine. When Brad returns home, Vanning, a Communist Party leader, visits him, threatening that he will reveal Brad's Communist past to his employer and to Nan unless he works for the Party. Brad refuses until Vanning threatens to frame him for murder. Thereafter, Brad works for the Party, creating tension between management and labor until the company's waterfront operations are shut down. Meanwhile, Christine seduces Nan's brother Don, a union dockworker, and tries to convert him to Communism. She fails, however, and the Party has Don killed in a hit-and-run accident. Vanning then kills Christine, making the death look like suicide. He then kidnaps Nan. Brad rescues her and kills Vanning, but is shot in the process, and dies at the end of the film.

The film portrays the capitalistic business world as the polar opposite to the Communist Party. For Brad, the corporate world provides a means to rehabilitate himself after his youthful mistake of joining the Party. Vanning describes Brad as "typical of the lost generation of the Thirties." Prior to his death, Brad confesses to Nan the reason that he joined the Party: "I was a kid out of a job. I wanted to get even with somebody." While Depression Era factors played into his conversion to Communism, success in the business world reformed Brad into an ideal American, wealthy, romantic, willing to bring about compromise between management and labor. Nan praises Brad for reforming Don by giving him a job on the waterfront; she tells him, "You're quite a man yourself."

Because of his success in the business world, the Communist Party preys on Brad: during a dinner party he and Nan are giving for his boss,

Cornwall, Communist agents intrude and take Brad to their secret head-quarters on the waterfront. While there, Brad witnesses the interrogation and murder of a Communist suspected of being an FBI informant. Vanning tells Brad that he has "used the Party" to get ahead in the world, but that now the Party is going to use him by forcing him to bring manage-ment and labor negotiations to a stalemate. Vanning tells Brad that the "Party decides who's out and when." Vanning then informs Brad that he must deposit two-thirds of his salary into a Communist Front organiza-tion called "Mankind Incorporated." The result is that Brad's success and marriage become endangered, because he must follow the Party's orders.

The Woman on Pier 13 portrays Christine and Don, like Brad, as vic-tims of the Party's ruthless practices: they are all dupes of the Commu-nists. Christine and Brad's naïveté and poverty have drawn them into the Party during their youth. When Christine shows Nan a photograph of Brad and herself, she describes their relationship in the following terms: "Young love among the lower classes. Two young Communists out to save the world." Even though Christine has stayed in the Party, she is motivated by emotion. Her love for Brad and Don cause her death. Vanning contin-ually expresses contempt for Christine's motivating factor: "Call it what it is: emotion." Likewise, Don is a naïve young man who is easily trans-formed into a Communist dupe. At a party given by Christine, a Party member describes Don as "Ideologically uninformed but emotionally, very receptive." Jim confronts Don and tells him that "love-sick kids like you" are ideal Communist stooges. Thus, most of the Party members in the film work against the business world because of youthful mistakes.

Even though Brad, Christine, and Don work against capitalism only because they have been fooled into doing so, and even though all three at-tempt to reform themselves by leaving the Party, they must all pay the price for their youthful mistakes. The deaths of all three characters at the hands of the Communist Party not only emphasize the ruthlessness of Party tac-tics, but simultaneously suggest that, though reformed, they somehow cannot be trusted to be good members of the business world. The elimi-nation of these tainted characters and the impending marriage of Nan to good businessman Jim was probably intended to reassure American au-diences that the business world is safe. *The Woman on Pier 13* suggests that American business is threatened only to the extent that some of its mem-bers have a Communist Party past. Thus, by implication, if the business world can rid itself of Communists and former Communists the threat will disappear. By the Fifties, however, the threat of Communism within the business world was not so easily dispelled.

That such is the case is well exemplified by *The Fearmakers* (1958), which tells the story of Alan Eaton, who, prior to the Korean War, ran a polling agency along with his partner Claude Baker. While in Korea, Alan is captured by the Chinese and tortured and brainwashed in a prison camp. Upon returning to his business, he discovers that his partner has died in a mysterious hit-and-run accident, and that, before the accident, a man by the name of Jim McGinnis had taken over the business, apparently with Baker's blessing. The polling agency has now branched out into the business of political lobbying. At the request of Senator Walder, Alan works at the polling agency, eventually uncovering the fact that the company has become part of a Communist conspiracy to get a political candidate elected by using forgeries and false polling data. With the help of his secretary, Lorraine Dennis, Alan foils the plot and brings the Communist agents to justice.

In the film, disruption of ethical business practices is traced back to Communist influence. First, Alan's absence caused by his having to fight the Communists in the Korean War undermines the integrity of his polling agency, a fact graphically emphasized when the first images we see in the film are of Alan being physically tortured by his Chinese captors. Later in the film, the American Communists who have taken over his business, Eaton Baker Associates, are portrayed as analogous to the Chinese Communists who have tortured and brainwashed Alan. When McGinnis and his associate Hal Loder work Alan over after discovering that he has broken into the office to secure evidence against them, McGinnis remarks that they are going to complete "what those Chinese Commies didn't finish." Alan responds to his beating by saying, "I've been worked over by professionals. They call it coexistence." Thus, the American Communists are seen as an extension of Chinese Communism, though the extension is weaker than the original. The film thus emphasizes the notion of a Communist conspiracy with American Communist-front businessmen being in a continuum with Communist Chinese prison-camp officers.

The Fearmakers also emphasizes the changing face of the American business world by pointing out how easy it is for a Communist-front group to pose as a legitimate business. The film highlights the surveillance aspect of the American business world. William Whyte's 1956 book, *The Organization Man,* also found popularity because it lamented a society of increasing conformism, in this case conformism created by the ability of organizations to encroach on every aspect of the individual's life. Whyte comments, "Group-relations advocates have been saying, it is the whole man the Organization wants and not just a part of him. Is the man well adjusted? Will he remain well adjusted? A test of potential merit could not tell this; needed was a test of potential *loyalty*" (172). Two characters in

The Fearmakers emphasize the Organization Man mentality of American business. Lorraine wants to confide in Alan that she believes that unethical practices are occurring at Eaton Baker Associates, but hesitates because she fears that when Alan asks her questions he is "testing my loyalty to the team." Loraine finally does confide in Alan and is able to help him foil the Communist plot, but only after overcoming her suspicion, suspicion bred by the corporate environment.

In the film, Barney Bond likewise also indicates the presence of the Organization Man mentality: McGinnis refers to Barney as one of the "drones," and, indeed, Barney seems to be working for the organization, not because of any ideological commitment to Communism, but because he is unthinkingly an organization man. Barney tries to justify the manipulation of polling statistics to Alan after Alan asks him, "Are we running an honest survey, or aren't we?" Barney dodges the issue by arguing that truth is relative and that every poll has an agenda behind it. Barney fits into Whyte's category of "A Generation of Bureaucrats," men who "do not question the system.... They want to get in there and lubricate and make them run better. They will be technicians of the society, not innovators" (74). Thus, Barney is serving a Communist-front organization simply because he has gone with the flow. Had Alan been in charge, Barney would have supported *his* views, as is made clear when Barney expresses his admiration for Alan and his work at their first meeting.

Even Alan initially rejects any suggestion that there is something sinister about the changes at Eaton Baker Associates. After his first meeting with McGinnis, Alan opens the wrong door and overhears a man lecturing some employees, saying, "All right, then, so much for the Jews. The way we handle the labor unions...." Alan seems only mildly interested in the speech and closes the door. It is not until Senator Walder convinces him that McGinnis has a "connection with certain groups in this country that are out to sell us peace at any price," that Alan takes up the cause of exposing the agency as a Communist-front group. Even then, he sees the greatest threat of the agency stemming from the American public's blind conformism. He tells Lorraine that "most people from Main Street to Madison Avenue prefer to go along with the majority." Therefore, Alan concludes, if the Communist-front group can manipulate statistics to make its ideas seem to be the ideas of the majority, Americans will follow like sheep.

While *Red Nightmare*, *The Woman on Pier 13*, and *The Fearmakers* all deal with the dangers of external threats to the business world brought about by Communist infiltration, the 1950s were also fraught with concerns about possible internal collapse that might be brought about due to a creeping national conformity for the most part created by the business world and its influence on individuals' lives. David Riesman's book *The Lonely Crowd* helped chart this fear by looking at how the American personality had shifted from inner-direction to other-direction and done so independent of any direct influence from the Soviet Union.[2] In contemporary American culture, according to Riesman, individuals were becoming other-directed, less autonomous as citizens, and much more influenced by the media and peers. As Adam Wolfson notes, "What most disturbed the fifties social critics was the bogy of conformism. They believed that the American people were becoming ever more alike.... There was also a note of pathos in their descriptions. Plasticity and malleability of the other-directed man" ("Individualism"). Wilfred McClay has argued that Riesman and his collaborators sought to write a neutral description of personality shifts in American culture, one not necessarily viewing the other-directed man as negative. The American public, however, responded to the book because they read the other-directed personality as a sign of cultural doom for the United States. McClay comments that "the public embraced *The Lonely Crowd* because they found it a great secular jeremiad against other-direction" (41). Comments such as these suggest that the organization of American life was eerily like the invasive power of the Communist Party. Thus, though Communist drones like Barney may be under the thumb of the Communists, ironically they may have been produced by the American system.

Within this climate of worry over how close business techniques in the U.S. really were to Soviet-style domination of individuals' lives, David Granick published *The Red Executive: A Study of the Organization Man in Russian Industry* (1960).[3] Granick's study is a comparison and contrast of the business world in the United States and the political and economic organization of the Soviet Union that seeks to dispel many American myths about Soviet life, while also reassuring Americans of their superior position vis-à-vis Soviet business life.

Granick helps to comfort a society fraught with concern over conformity, by pointing out that while the Soviets are not the drones that extreme anti–Communist propaganda imaged, they are still more conformist than Americans. His views in this regard contrast with those of Hoover, who, for example, describes Party members in the following terms: "Communist members learn what to think, how to vote, what to say by a process of automatic osmosis— the seeping of predigested thoughts along the Party line into all subordinate minds, disciplined to accept. The members become ideological sleepwalkers, drugged into complete obedience by an unconscious discipline" (*Masters* 136). Granick's Soviets are not mindless drones, but are, rather, educated in a system that does not reward open-mindedness. For example, Granick reports that he was allowed to watch Soviet students taking comprehensive exams. Granick asked one student whether he wanted on his reading list works that presented views in opposition to those of the Party. "The student seemed puzzled and somewhat shocked at my questions. He was reading true views of the situation from the original documents, and achieving a true insight into the Opposition ideas. Why should be possibly be interested in reading the Opposition documents themselves?" (59). As Granick concludes, Americans, by contrast, are taught the opposition's viewpoints and are trained to think for themselves. Granick's work reassures its audience that Americans are not becoming mindless conformists. Comparison with Soviet education indicates how open-minded and problem-solving oriented American education really is.

Granick's study also reassures American audiences by pointing out the flaws that exist within the Soviet business-and-industry sector. Granick cites figures that accidents at Soviet iron and steel plants are twenty-three times as high as those that occur in the American steel industry (16).[4] Women are required to work in heavy construction jobs, which causes Granick to comment that "a policy of keeping women off heavy jobs is unlikely to be carried out in Russia until the never-never end of Communism, with its two free mink coats per customer" (222). Granick points out use of secret police informants in business and industry and the outlawing of strikes as further ills that make life difficult for management and workers alike (183).

Yet, *The Red Executive*'s novelty lies in the ways that it draws very close comparisons between the American and Soviet business worlds. Like other works from the same time period, such as *Fail-Safe* and *Main Street U.S.S.R.*, the book puts a human face on the Soviet people. Thus, whereas John Gunther, in *Inside Russia Today,* emphasizes the dehumanized life of Russia workers, noting that cattle and milkmaids are equated: "Each cow is numbered and named.... Then at the end of the corridor is a large sign listing all the milkmaids. They too have their names on display, just like the cattle, together with a tally sheet showing exactly how many hours they have worked" (358), by contrast, Granick shows how similar Soviet life is to its American counterpart. He does this especially through his focus on rising consumerism in the Soviet Union. Granick begins his studies by emphasizing the similarities between the United States and the Soviet Union, titling a section "Brothers Under the Skin?" He points out that both societies have a rapidly growing industry, frontier aspirations, and "a worship of size, speed, and material success" (6). Granick emphasizes how living conditions in the Soviet Union are rapidly approaching living standards in the United States: "The Soviet public has been demanding and getting better food, clothing, and furniture.... In short, the Soviet public has been getting — and seem scheduled to keep getting — higher living standards both in the form of more goods and more leisure" (255).[5]

Granick reassures his audience that the Soviets are consumers in the making and discounts the notion that Soviet business is dominated by ideological concerns: "Moreover, there seems no reason to categorize the Party official as the fire eating ideological fanatic, thus contrasting him with the businesslike manager who has strong vested interests in existing society. The Party official, after all, is also primarily an administrator" (265). For Granick, the fear the United States should feel with regard to the Soviet business world is not that it is run by ideological robots and represents a direct contrast to the American system, but, rather, that its efficient use of American business techniques makes it a threat in terms of world power. Granick argues that "Comparison of the American and Soviet rates of growth has, for several years, been giving concern to American policymakers as well as to the American public" (251). Granick's vision of the Cold War is one in which an increasing consumer culture in the Soviet Union combined with high productivity and efficiency rates will lead to the Soviet Union dominating the economic scene in world politics. This is a very tempered fear when compared with earlier propaganda films that painted lurid pictures of the Communist's difference and his desire to destroy American business practices altogether.

In the late Forties and Fifties, the Soviet Union served as the primary source for anti–Communist sentiment in the United States. From government propaganda films to movie serials to cartoons to television shows, the often unnamed enemy threatening American security was the Soviet Union. While fear of and hatred for the Soviets continued in the Sixties, historical events began to cause a shift in anti–Communist rhetoric, one that began to see the Yellow Peril of China as increasingly more threatening than the Red Menace of Russia.

12. The Bear and the Dragon: Representations of Communism in Early Sixties American Culture

By the early Sixties, American attitudes toward the Soviet Union began to alter. Instead of the Soviets being represented consistently in the entertainment media as an inhuman threat, as was the case in early Fifties propaganda films such as _Invasion USA_, a process of looking at the Soviets, both government and people, in a more favorable light emerged. With this shift in perception in the United States, images of China as demonic Red force began to supplant postwar images of a brutal and monstrous Russia. As a result of examining government propaganda films, television shows, Hollywood films, and sociological studies, in this chapter I explore the crucial shift in anti–Communist sentiment from a stance that demonized the Soviets to one that made China the often more frightening of Cold War threats.

In the early Sixties, the foreign policies of both the Khrushchev and Kennedy administrations began to promote friendlier relations between the two superpowers. Indeed, in _American Military History_, a textbook published by the Center of Military History, the period of the early Sixties is portrayed as a time of reconciliation between the two superpowers. Kennedy's policy of flexible response brought about a lessening of the threat of nuclear war by stressing "the need for ready nonnuclear forces as a deterrent to limited war" ("Global Pressures"). And at the same time, United States' military policy was seeking to lessen the threat of nuclear confrontation between the two superpowers, many Americans were beginning to view the Russian people not as monstrous drones of a totalitarian system, but as human beings very much like themselves.

During this time period, Irving R. Levine's *Main Street, U.S.S.R.* became a best-selling book that painted a picture of the Soviet Union not as some fantastic mythical land, but as a place of real people with recognizably human lives and struggles. Levine, who worked for NBC in Moscow for four years, was the first accredited U.S. correspondent to operate in the Soviet Union. He captured a huge audience for *Main Street, U.S.S.R.,* because of the inside information the book provided about life in the Soviet Union.

Levine's study presents a humanizing vision of both the Russian people and the Soviet government and does so in several important ways. Thus, for example, the book points out the hatred of war that was then dominant element in collective social psyche of the Soviet Union. Levine comments that "the fear of war, and especially the propaganda that tries to convince Russians that capitalistic nations have aggressive intentions, motivates Russians to ask Western visitors, 'Why do you want war?' or 'Are you for peace?' (14). Levine's text emphasizes the intense fear of war that was then felt by a country that had suffered truly catastrophic loss of life in both World War I and World War II, a fear that had led to an absence of nuclear culture in the country, an absence underscored by the fact that civil defense drills and visible air-raid shelter signs, commonplaces of postwar U.S. life, were absent in Russia because the Soviet government feared "that near-hysteria might be created among a populace which has known war as intimately and tragically as Russia's if alarms were given simply to conform with external propaganda" (168). Levine further humanized Russians by emphasizing that the average Russian did not hate the American people. His book discusses a radio commentator who explained to him that "of course we feel friendly toward the American *people*. Neither our radio nor our newspapers have any complaint against the American people. It is only the American ruling circles whom we attack for seeking war" (72).

Yet in the midst of a train of developments through which political policy and sociological studies were gradually furthering a more humane Western Cold War attitude toward the Russians, a crisis suddenly erupted that severely tested this new attitude. The Cuban Missile Crisis of October 1962 brought the world to the brink of nuclear war. Recently declassified documents reveal that even though the crisis was dangerous, it resulted more from misunderstandings that arose between the U.S. and the U.S.S.R. than any desire to escalate Cold War tensions. In a memorandum from presidential advisor Chester Bowles to President Kennedy on Oct.

13, 1962, Bowles discusses a meeting he had had with Anatoly Dobrynin, the Soviet ambassador to the United States. Dobrynin had expressed shock that the United States could be so disturbed about "a small island" like Cuba. Bowles emphasized to Dobrynin the history of U.S.-Cuba relations and stressed that the Kennedy Administration "had hoped and expected that we could in fact negotiate a more rational set of relationships" (*Foreign Relations*).

Even before declassified information about the Cuban Missile Crisis became generally available to the American public, the events that transpired during that crisis had had the effect of making Americans see the Soviet government as reasonable. As Mike Moore notes in an article in *The Bulletin of the Atomic Scientists*, the Doomsday Clock remained at seven minutes to midnight during the Cuban Missile Crisis because it was "a frightening exception to the still developing rule that the U.S. and the Soviet Union should not directly confront one another."[1] As Moore notes, a year after the crisis, the clock was moved back further from midnight due to the partial test-ban treaty that had been signed by the Soviets and the United States. Commenting on Ernest R. May and Philip D. Zeilkow's book *The Kennedy Tapes: Inside the White House During the Cuban Missile Crisis,* one reviewer remarked that "In retrospect, the clearest lesson of the crisis is that neither Kennedy nor Khrushchev was seriously ready to risk a nuclear war ... the real danger was the cold war itself, with its underlying assumption that the whole world was a zero-sum game: blind man's ideological bluff with megaton weapons" ("Kennedy Tapes").

And it was not only in long historical retrospect that the crisis was perceived in such terms: one 1964 film, Sidney Lumet's *Fail-Safe,* indirectly evaluated the potential for rationality of the superpower leaders while condemning the horror of nuclear weapons. The film focuses on the issue of accidental nuclear war. A squadron of SAC planes receives a mistaken order to drop their H-bombs on Moscow due to a combination of a mechanical error on the part of the United States military and Soviet jamming of the U.S. planes' radios. The President orders that American fighters must shoot down the errant planes, but the fighters fail to do so. He then contacts the Soviet Premier and tells him about the situation. The President orders the U.S. military to cooperate with Soviet military personnel in their attempt to shoot down all the bombers. When this plan fails, the President proposes to the Premier a solution to the crisis that would involve a drastic U.S. sacrifice to compensate for the certain destruction of Moscow, a sacrifice that would have the effect of avoiding total nuclear war. The President tells the Premier that when he hears from the U.S. ambassador to the Soviet Union from his post in Moscow that the city is about to be destroyed, he will order American bombers to destroy New York City. The Premier consents to this plan. H-bombs destroy both cities.

Fail Safe labels machines, and especially the machinery of war, as the enemy to be feared — not the Soviet Union. Before setting off to command the ill-fated plane that will bring about the destruction of Moscow, its pilot, Colonel Grady, argues with a colleague about changes in society that have taken place since World War II. Grady laments the general mechanization that has evolved. War has become mechanized and so

The American President (Henry Fonda) represents a new, more sympathetic attitude toward the Soviets in Fail-Safe.

have humans, particularly the SAC pilots he flies with. Grady comments, "I like the personal factor." Yet, later in the film, at the height of the crisis when his military orders dictate that he must ignore all incoming messages, he has to reject the personal touch in favor of orders from a machine. The President appeals to him to stop the mission, but Grady has been trained to suspect that in such situations the President's voice could be being imitated by the Soviets. In a later even more disturbing scene, Grady feels forced to reject emotion-filled pleas from his wife to stop the mission.

In many of its scenes, the film makes it clear that it does not intend its viewers to believe that the evil Soviet Union is solely to blame for the Cold War, but, rather that rapid technological development is the demon.[2] When Congressman Raskob tours the base prior to the crisis, he is horrified how mechanized the instruments of nuclear war are. He comments, "The only thing that everyone can agree on is that no one is responsible." Humans, not wanting the moral weight of nuclear war on their shoulders, mechanize it. As *Fail-Safe* warns, mechanization is not flawless. When an electronics expert, Knapp, is consulted about the probability of mechanical error causing the planes to continue, he does not reassure the military leaders and the President, but tells them that "the more complex a system, the more accident prone it is ... humans just can't know whether a machine is lying or telling the truth." All the sympathetic characters in the film share a horror of the mechanization of war and the absence of the human factor in reaching crucial military decisions. General Black, General Bogan, Colonel Grady, Congressman Raskob, and the President all lament the fact that the human element has been removed from decisions involving nuclear war. In *Fail-Safe*, recognizing the human element means abandoning postwar hatred of the Soviet Union.

The film portrays the old-style Cold Warriors as insane and very dangerous. In particular, Professor Groeteschele, a political scientist who advises the Pentagon, advocates limited nuclear war, even going so far as to suggest that the U.S. strike the Soviet Union first in order to test out his theory. Groeteschele advocates the replacement of manned bombers with nuclear missiles, yet the film suggests that manned bombers and their ability to be shot down are the only elements that save this crisis from being transformed into one involving total nuclear war.[3] Groeteschele is the epitome of the mechanized human. He speaks coldly about limited nuclear war, and cannot see beyond his view of the Soviets as "Marxist fanatics." He labels the Soviet government as a group of "calculating machines," yet it is Groeteschele himself who is the machine. While all the other characters are too horrified to respond to the impending bombing of New York, Groeteschele calculates the number of people who will die immediately and later and worries about retrieving corporate records because "our economy depends on this." While Groeteschele is the most monstrous of the characters in the film, other hard-line Cold Warriors are also portrayed as dangerous. Colonel Cascio and unnamed Soviet military officers try to convince their respective leaders that the situation is a trap.[4] In the case of Cascio, his attempt to sabotage the negotiations is explained through insanity. Under the stress of personal problems as well the crisis, he attempts a mutiny. Yet, General Bogan forgives him for his actions, stating that "anyone could crack under this strain."

The film finds reassurance, however, in the fact that the two world leaders are balanced and rational people who can see beyond ideology and consider the horror of total nuclear war.[5] In *Fail-Safe*, the President approaches the crisis with rationality and humanity from the beginning. He tells the military leaders that the problem is big, "but it still depends on what each of us does." He takes a conciliatory approach to the Soviet

Premier, telling the translator, Buck, that he wants to understand what the Premier is feeling. The Premier initially takes a hostile stance toward the President, asking "Are these planes being flown by crazy men?" Yet, he displays the same calm rationality in the face of the unthinkable as the President does. The Premier tells the President, "This is time for common sense. I must have proof, Mr. President, that neither of us wants war." During the development of this tense situation, both the President and the Premier gain respect for each other. The President says that the Premier has acted exactly as he himself would have done under similar circumstances. Although the Premier and the President are equal in their rational response to the situation, the President proposes an end to the Cold War. When the Premier tells the President that "this was nobody's fault," the President reacts by saying "we let our machines get out of hand ... Men are responsible." The President, who has not only been forced to give the order to destroy New York, but also incidentally to kill his own wife, since she is on a visit New York at the time, suggests that the Cold War can be resolved. He tells the Premier that "what we put between us we must remove." Thus, while the film represents a horrible solution to a frightening mistake, it is optimistic that tensions between the United States and the Soviet Union can be reduced.

The crisis in *Fail-Safe* teaches everyone involved to respect the Russians as people and to despise the insanity of the Cold War. When General Bogan speaks to a Russian general they reminiscence about their mutual love of London. The Russian general tells Bogan "Goodbye, my friend," and Bogan responds by calling the Russian general "my friend" also. One facet of the Cold War of the early Sixties was the abating of intense American hatred of the Soviet Union. Most works, however, were not quite so willing as *Fail-Safe* is to embrace an end to the Cold War. A common strain in the texts of ongoing anti–Communist discourse was the move toward a hatred for Chinese Communists. In fact, the conciliatory attitude the Soviet Union began to adopt toward the United States "may have resulted partly from the growing independence of China," a country that never "embraced the concept of peaceful coexistence with the capitalist countries" ("Global Pressures").

The alliance of Chinese and Soviet Communists had been an uncomfortable one. In his 1951 book, *Chinese Communism and the Rise of Mao*, Benjamin Schwartz portrays the uneasy alliance between Chinese and Soviet Communists, thus questioning the American fear that Chinese and Soviet Communists together represented a monolithic threat. Schwartz states that "We must therefore conclude that Moscow's recognition of the Mao Tse-tung leadership was essentially in the nature of an acquiescence to a *fait accompli*" (187). Schwartz's argument is that the Chinese divergence from Marxism, by severing the Communist Party from a proletarian base, was an embarrassment to the Soviet Union. Schwartz implies that in some respects Chinese Communism is worse than Soviet Communism because it hides its totalitarian impulses behind a rhetoric of Communism that it does not really believe in. Schwartz emphasizes the danger of China by stating, "Totalitarianism, I think, will be inhibited in Communist China only by limits imposed by external circumstances" (203). Although, in representations in the Fifties, the Soviet Union would remain the primary Communist enemy, by the early Sixties, the image of a China more deceitful than Russia began to emerge.[6]

Red Chinese Battleplan, a propaganda film made by the Department of Defense in 1964, is a good example of an anti–Communist film that has moved away from hatred of the Soviet Union to intense hatred of Communist China. In the film, the narrator tells us that the goals of China are to "conquer and enslave" the world. The film relates the history of China, tracing its Communist tendencies back to the time of the building of the Great Wall, a time in which China became "the first police state, complete with slave labor and thought control." The film tries to instill a fear of Chinese Communism into the viewer by showing images of a giant dragon that first conquers the map of China and then conquers the map of the entire world. Quotations from Mao portray China as an aggressive and intolerant state. An actor playing Mao says, "Political power grows out of the barrel of a gun."

While the film portrays China in 1964 as the current world threat, like *Fail-Safe*, it portrays the Soviet threat as a weakened one. Although after Korea, as the narrator tells us, "all is harmony between the Chinese dragon and the Russian bear," by 1956 a rift had grown between the two countries as a result of Khrushchev's policy of peaceful coexistence. The film states that while in 1963 the Soviet Union was signing a test ban on atmospheric explosions of nuclear weapons, at the same time China was denouncing Moscow as a traitor to the Communist cause. As this film suggests, even in explicit propaganda films of the early Sixties, the attention of anti–Communists had turned to China and away from Russia. Two dramatic representations of this idea characterize anti–Communist film and television of the early Sixties.

John Frankenheimer's *The Manchurian Candidate* (1962) focuses on the brainwashing of Raymond Shaw and members of his troop during the Korean War. The Chinese and Soviet Communists together kidnap Shaw and his men in order to make Raymond into an unknowing assassin for them. Shaw is chosen because his mother, the wife of Senator Iselin, is a

Senator Joseph McCarthy, anti–Communist demagogue, served as the inspiration for Senator Iselin in The Manchurian Candidate. *(Courtesy of the Library of Congress, Prints and Photographs Division, USZ62 094487.)*

Communist agent who is helping the Chinese and Soviets in an elaborate plan to get Iselin elected as the U.S. president. The Communists' plans for Shaw begin to be thwarted when Major Bennett Marco starts an investigation based on traumatic dreams he has experienced, dreams that relive for him the brainwashing episodes he, Shaw, and the other men had been subjected to. Eventually, Marco is able to undo the Communists' brainwashing of Shaw, but only after Shaw has killed several people, including his own wife. After Shaw's brainwashing has been counteracted, his Communist contact, unaware that Shaw has been turned, gives him one final set of instructions: during the Party Convention that has chosen its presidential candidate, he is to assassinate that candidate, and, by so doing, elevate Iselin, the vice-presidential candidate, to take his place. Instead, Shaw assassinates his mother and Iselin. Shaw then kills himself.

The Manchurian Candidate, then, illustrates the shift in anti–Communist sentiment from demonizing the Soviets to demonizing the Chinese. Although the film still retains an image of the Soviets as a threat, it represents the Chinese Communists as worse than the Soviet Communists.

Curiously, while the film portrays the Chinese Communists as more ruthless in the use of knowledge, it affords the Soviet Communists the status of highly intelligent enemy. The basis for the brainwashing techniques comes from Russian psychology: two Russians, Ivan Pavlov and his disciple Andrew Salter, developed the theoretical basis for the experiments conducted by the Communists on Raymond. In the film, the ability of the Soviets to utilize knowledge in such a striking way illustrates American insecurity with regard to Soviet accomplishments. Levine also illustrates this insecurity in *Main Street, U.S.S.R.* In the book, he points to the superiority of the education system in the Soviet Union: "However, there is no arguing with the fact that the Soviet educational system produced scientists and engineers capable of launching a sputnik before the USA did, and then following it with sputniks of enormously greater size" (155). In the film, the fact that the Soviets are more advanced in their knowledge of brainwashing is underscored by the fact that the U.S. military officials will not listen to Marco's contention that brainwashing has been a key factor in the Manchurian situation involving himself and Shaw. They put Marco on sick leave, to which he protests, "What the hell does the medical core know about intelligence work?" Marco's perception is correct, but only when Al Melvin, another member of Marco's troop during the Korean War, reports similar dreams, do the officials take Marco's ideas seriously.

The idea of Pavlovian-based brainwashing experiments relates to the very different ways in which the United States and the Soviet Union viewed the purpose of psychiatry during the Cold War. As Levine relates, "In the words of a Russian psychiatrist, Soviet psychiatry depends on suggestion, hypnosis, and re-education, not on prolonged analysis" (123). This view is in direct opposition to the Freudian-dominated view of the mind prevalent in the 1950s and 1960s in the United States. While Freudian ideas are largely incompatible with political brainwashing, behaviorist notions of re-education that dominated the Soviet psychiatric world easily meshed with policies of political re-education. Anti–Communist works emphasize the horror of brainwashing as lying in its ability to kill the personality. Fred Schwartz, in his 1960 study of Communism, describes the brainwashing process, then concludes that "by such processes as these, a mental breakdown is induced. The old personality pattern is shattered and the victim is ready to be molded according to the desires of the Communist Party" (135). In his account of his own captivity in enemy prison camps during the Korean War, British journalist Philip Deane notes the characteristically horrible sense of loss of control that accompanied the brainwashing administered to him by the Communists: "I felt my thinking processes becoming tangled, my critical faculties blunted. I could not think, and I was afraid.... If you cannot think, it frightens you by its immense repetition, just as the immense repetition of the ocean swell frightens the shipwrecked non-swimmer" (173). While *The Manchurian Candidate* portrays the Soviets as possessing frightening knowledge, knowledge that is even superior to that possessed by the United States, the Soviets are portrayed as using that knowledge more responsibly than do the Chinese.

In the film, the notion of conflict between Soviet and Chinese Communism emerges through two representative characters — Yen Lo, a Chinese Communist, who is also the director of the Pavlov Institute, and Zilkov, a KGB officer in charge of Soviet security on the Eastern seaboard. Zilkov is a very conscientious man who takes the job of testing Raymond as mechanism extremely seriously. Additionally, Zilkov is ideologically committed to Communism. Yen Lo, by contrast, is amoral, a man who shows no real commitment to Communism and who finds the psychological manipulation of Raymond highly amusing. When Yen Lo goes to

Ben Marco (Frank Sinatra) helps Communist brainwashing victim Raymond Shaw (Laurence Harvey) out of Central Park Lake. (Courtesy of the Library of Congress, Prints and Photographs Division, USZ62 129065.)

the New York sanitarium where Raymond is being held, the conflict between the views of the two Communist characters emerges. Zilkov, describing the sanitarium, which is owned by the Soviet government, comments that it is "one of the few Soviet operations in America that actually showed a profit." Yen Lo mocks him and tells him he is being seduced by capitalism. Zilkov is horrified by this accusation, but Yen Lo tells him that he must "cultivate a sense of humor." Yen Lo smiles and jokes with Zilkov, then ruthlessly turns to question Raymond. Yen Lo's amorality emerges when he describes Raymond's brainwashing as having relieved him of "those uniquely American symptoms of fear and guilt." Yet, Zilkov's nervousness suggests that he suffers from these symptoms as well. Further, Yen Lo's lack of commitment to Communist ideology emerges when he leaves Zilkov with Raymond because he has to go to Macy's because "Madame Yen has given me a most appalling list." Zilkov again registers shock at Yen Lo's contempt for Communist ideology.

Yen Lo's flippant attitude toward the brainwashing process is underscored in the flashbacks to the initial brainwashing sessions in Korea. In these scenes, Yen Lo, as opposed to the Soviets present, Gomel and Berezovo, gets great pleasure out of the process of brainwashing the men. In Richard Condon's novel, on which the film is based, Yen Lo's whimsical attitude toward the process is particularly evident: "There were cigarettes and cigars for everyone, and Yen Lo had allowed his boys to have a little fun in the selection of outlandish tobacco substitutes because he knew that word of it would pass through the armies, based upon the sure knowledge of what made armies laugh, rubbing more sheen into the legend of the Yen Lo unit" (31). In the film, Yen Lo laughs heartily at the fact that he has given the men yak dung to smoke: "Yak dung. Tastes good like a cigarette should." By contrast with the attitude of Yen Lo, the Soviets seem horrified by the murders that Raymond commits in order to demonstrate his adeptness as a killing machine. In the novel, Berezovo's assistant vomits and leaves the room after Raymond kills Ed Malvole (48). Thus *The Manchurian Candidate* suggests that the Chinese are more amoral and cruel than are the Soviets.

The amorality of Chinese Communism finds shape in the character of Raymond's mother as well. The film works visually to associate her with Chinese Communism. In several scenes, Raymond's mother wears Asian-style clothing as a visual reminder of her amorality and her connection to threatening Chinese Communism. As she is telling Iselin that he should not think for himself, but, rather, "say what you're supposed to say," she wears a silk dress designed in an Asian manner. In a flashback that deals with how Raymond was parted from Jocie, his girlfriend, the daughter of Senator Jordan, a man opposed to Iselinism, when Raymond's mother brainwashes him against Jocie, she wears a silk robe with a dragon embossed on it. In Condon's novel, the garment is described as "a fantastically beautiful Chinese house coat" (94). In the film, the addition of the dragon symbol suggests the threatening power of amoral Chinese Communism seen in films like *Red Chinese Battleplan*. Raymond's mother's

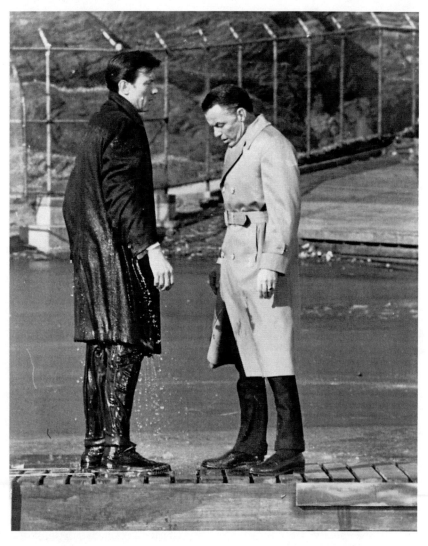

Marco stands amazed at the power that the Communists have over Raymond's mind. (Courtesy of the Library of Congress, Prints and Photographs Division, USZ62 129059.)

amorality comes out particularly clearly near the end of the film when she vows to Raymond that she will double-cross the Communists she has seemingly served and get revenge on them for "so contemptuously underestimating me."[7] Thus, *The Manchurian Candidate* supports the notion put forth by authors such as Schwartz that Chinese Communism was not ideologically motivated, but a mask for naked abuse of power.

The fear expressed in *The Manchurian Candidate* that Chinese Communists could infiltrate the inner sanctum of the United States government is also expressed in a television show of the early Sixties, "The One Hundred Days of the Dragon," an episode of *The Outer Limits* that aired on Sept. 23, 1963. This episode focuses on Chinese Communism's attempt to take over the American government. Because they have a serum that allows human flesh to be molded, the Chinese devise a plan to kill an American presidential candidate and replace him with a Chinese official. The plan succeeds, and after the candidate's election to the presidency, the Chinese proceed in a similar way to replace key cabinet members. The vice-president, however, catches on to the plot and is eventually able to stop the takeover from being completed.

This television episode clearly underlines the increasing fear of Chinese Communism that dominated early Sixties American culture. At the beginning of the episode, the narrator tells viewers that the Chinese Premier, Li Chin Sung, has caused China to awaken from years of inactivity, describing this awakening in these terms: "A slumbering giant has shaken itself to wakefulness." The narrator also tells the audience that only the Chinese approve of Sung's methods, and that he is perceived as an "irresponsible threat to peace in the eyes of the rest of the world." The implication, then, is that even the Soviet Union sees China as irresponsible and dangerous.

The Soviet threat is present in the episode only in the form of Soviet knowledge. As is the case with *The Manchurian Candidate*, the idea here is that the greatest danger the world faces is in Chinese Communism abusing Soviet ideas. Bob, President Selby's brother-in-law, tells Ted Pearson, the vice-president, that the "Russians have been conducting experiments on molecular rearrangement." He finds a study of Russian experiments on monkeys, and assumes, correctly, that the Chinese have applied these procedures to human beings. The Soviet threat is not present. Unlike the situation in *The Manchurian Candidate*, in the television episode there is no visible collaboration between the two powers.

In the episode, the Chinese Communists are detached, cold-blooded killers. The face of Major Ho Chi-Wong, the agent who is to assume Selby's identity, is molded before he kills Selby, thus sadistically forcing Selby to look at his own double before his death. When Wong meets with Premier Sung before Wong's transformation, the pair gloat over their plans for political takeover, and Wong comments that "not a single shot will have been fired." It is the very cold-bloodedness of the Chinese Communists that eventually undermines the plan.

After the substitution, those who have been close to Selby begin to recognize details that seem wrong about him. Ted is shocked by the transformed Wong's hunting skills and the rapid change in policy he adopts when he gets to office, a change featuring open negotiations between the Americans and the Chinese. Selby's daughter, Carol, voices her concerns about her father to Ted, telling him that "He's polite ... but it's as if he turned to stone. Suddenly, I don't love him anymore." Indeed, it is the dehumanized aspect of the Chinese Communists that finally gives their plan away.

While this television episode underlines the insidious threat of Chinese Communism, it also argues against nuclear war with the Communist enemy. After Ted exposes Wong as an impostor in front of an international gathering, the secret-service man who has been helping Ted suggests that they declare war on China. Ted refuses to do this, even though he has labeled the Chinese actions as the "most monstrous act of international espionage." The narrator tells us that Ted refuses to start a war with China "because there is no war as we knew it. Only annihilation." While this episode was aired before the Chinese explosion of an atomic bomb in 1964, it nevertheless encourages its audience to perceive the threat of starting war with a country that clearly is advancing technologically, even if those advances are simultaneously perceived to be the result of ideas taken from the Soviet Union.

Early Sixties American culture displays a shift in anti–Communist sentiment. After a decade in which the atmosphere of this culture was partially characterized by intense hatred of the Soviet Union, it began to refocus its hatred on China. China emerged as the Communist force to be hated as the political policies of the United States government gradually transformed so as to promote peaceful coexistence with the Soviet Union. Propaganda films and the products of popular culture alike illustrate the steps needed to make this transition. And it was through a process of gradually humanizing American images of Russia, while at the same time demonizing those of China, that such a transition in representation became possible.

Conclusion

Suspicion of and hatred for Communism, and especially Soviet Communism, formed the backdrop for Cold War politics from the late Forties through the Sixties. Popular culture both contributed to anti–Communist sentiment in the United States and helped interpret that sentiment. Anti–Communist feelings continued to pervade U.S. culture until the end of the Cold War in the 1990s. A resurgence of television and movie anti-Soviet propaganda predominated the Reagan years, in works such as *Red Dawn* and *The Day After*. These forms of anti–Communism are beyond the scope of this study, but are well worth exploring.[1]

Examination of popular works dealing with anti–Communism reveals that a simplistic Red Scare was not what dominated the popular mind. While a good versus evil mentality that pitted Capitalism against Communism was always part of anti–Communist rhetoric, popular culture, like many nonfiction works from the period, reveals complexities instead of a simple black and white morality regarding the Communist threat. This book tells only part of the story of Cold War demonizing. The Soviets' construction of the United States as an evil enemy is the other side of this complicated story.

In Adlai Stevenson's 1958 account of his travels within the Soviet Union, he concludes that anti–American and anti–Capitalist propaganda had a much stronger hold on the Soviet people than the anti–Communist rhetoric had on the United States. Stevenson states, "I felt that the Russian people are really more fearful of the United States than we are of them, which is not hard to understand in view of our ring of air bases and the incessant propaganda about the hostility of the 'ruling cliques of the imperialist-capitalist powers'" (xiii). Nevertheless, as an example of an American Cold War reflection on the U.S.–Soviet conflict, Stevenson ultimately points the finger at the United States itself, seeing our internal weaknesses as encouraging anti-American sentiment in the Soviet Union: "My conclusion is that our Russian competitors are much tougher than most of us have yet realized — and that this time we might get licked, unless we are willing to change our habits, our political behavior and our complacent outlook on the world" (xxii). With regard to Communism and anti–Communism, the American writer or filmmaker most often blames the United States for Cold War problems, both internal and external. This self-blame has largely been the intellectual heritage of assessments of anti–Communism in America.

There were abuses that occurred under the banner of anti–Communism. As Haynes points out, segregationists, haters of rock and roll, and anti–Semites, among others, jumped onto the bandwagon, claiming that their cause was anti–Communist. Other, stranger abuses existed as well, such as the case of Kenneth Goff, an ex–Communist who along with anti–Semite Gerald L.K. Smith "promoted the notion that fluoridating drinking water, approved to prevent cavities, was a Communist plot" (184). While popular culture of the Cold War dealt with varieties of anti–Communism, it rarely criticized anti–Communism itself, though often criticized American weaknesses. Even the criticism of McCarthy in *The Manchurian Candidate* argues that the demagogue Iselin conceals a more insidious Communist plot to take over the government. Nevertheless, a real threat of Iselinism comes from an uninformed American public that would support such a political demagogue. Thus, while much revisionist scholarship, especially post–Vietnam, has focused more on the abuses of anti–Communist politics than on the presence of a Communist threat in Fifties and Sixties America, popular culture charted no such territory. Popular culture largely argues that the anti–Communists were right, and that the problems within our system stemmed from our laziness, idealism, and confusion.

As Haynes points out, "The broad anti–Communist consensus in American politics was not seriously questioned until the Vietnam War" (195). Popular culture, even television comedies like *Get Smart*, did not question the existence of a Communist threat, but, rather, posed the question as to what particular form the threat would take. Haynes argues that "The only common thread of the different varieties of anticommunism was their disdain of communism" (197).[2] The popular culture artifacts discussed in this book reflect this commonality. While different works argue for a different shape that the Communist threat takes — to name a few:

organized crime in *Kiss Me Deadly*; Foreign Invader in *Invasion USA*; The American CP in *I Led Three Lives*; a dashing British officer with a revolutionary past in *Conspirator*—all the works argue that there is a threat, whether it is perceived as an internal one in the form of American Communists and profiteers, or an external one in the form of Soviet, Soviet Bloc, Korean, or Chinese Communists.

Anti–Communism in popular culture reveals a familiar cultural pattern of constructing the enemy. In *Constructing the Political Spectacle*, Murray Edelman discusses a common construction of the enemy that characterized twentieth-century politics. He argues that one form the political enemy takes is an essential one in which the enemy force is "characterized by an inherent trait or set of traits that marks them as evil, immoral, warped, or pathological" (67). The inherently evil enemy of *Invasion USA* illustrates just such an ahistorical and unexplained force of evil by deciding to use a nuclear attack and invade the United States for no apparent reason. Edelman also argues that twentieth-century political enemies were often characterized by the home country feeling ambivalence, making a distinction between a system and the people. Edelman comments that, regarding the construction of an enemy, a small portion feels unconflicted hatred, but "most of the population displays a substantial measure of ambivalence" (71). The conflict in popular culture between a fondness for the Russian people and a hatred of Communist ideology, in works such as *Guilty of Treason*, clearly illustrates this ambivalence.

Other views of Edelman about the general construction of the enemy clearly apply to representations of the Communist enemy in mid-century popular culture. Edelman argues that one rhetorical strategy used to make the enemy seem more powerful is to refuse to name it specifically: "Beliefs in political enemies seem to influence public opinion most powerfully when the enemy is not named explicitly, but evoked through an indirect reference" (73). The refusal to name the enemy of anti–Communist fantasies as Soviet is witnessed in such works as *Invasion USA*, *Get Smart*, the movie serials discussed in this book, and other works. Edelman also points out how several enemies are often condensed into a single form in political rhetoric: "As times change and fashions in naming threats change with them, enemies often succeed one another, though new enemies also coexist with older ones" (81). The conflation between Communist and Nazi, Communist and organized crime, Communist and psychotic, just to name a few, is a common feature of how popular culture presents the Communist threat. Edelman states that "Enemies become whatever claim works for the situation and moment" (74), and popular culture illustrates that point clearly as the Communist enemy appeared in many forms from the late Forties through the Sixties.

In examining the chronological development of anti–Communist sentiment in the popular, trends emerge. The move toward comedic representation of the threat appears to occur in the Sixties. Even so, *Jet Pilot*, with its romantic comedy frame for Capitalism vs. Communism, was a product of the Fifties.[3] Additionally, some of the most extreme countersubversive anti–Communist works, like *Red Nightmare*, were also products of the Sixties.

Similarly, while in many examples the Sixties represent a transitional period during which Chinese Communism increasingly became more of a concern in representations, anti-Soviet sentiment was still alive and well in the Sixties. In a television documentary entitled *The Red Myth* that aired on public television in 1962, the Soviet threat is framed within familiar terms. Thus, while the documentary admits that the Soviet Union appears to be more conciliatory under Khrushchev, rather than under Stalin, suspicion wins out because "The evidence indicates that communists still aim at world domination, but with more sophisticated techniques than in the past. They hold to the Khrushchev prophesy that the Red Flag will fly over the entire world" (115).

Popular culture of the Cold War represents, then, the complexities of anti–Communism as it was experienced by Americans. Additionally, it illustrates that the deepest political, social, psychological, and moral fears of the time could be transformed into entertainment. With the exception of government or military propaganda films, the works discussed in this book were produced for reasons of entertainment. Translating anti–Communist fear into something engaging and often fun was the feat accomplished by popular culture's incorporation of anti–Communist sentiment.

In a book entitled *I Was a Slave in Russia*, John Noble, an American citizen living in Germany at the end of World War II, recounts his nine-year imprisonment in Soviet work camps from 1945 to 1954. The book illustrates an anti–Communism born of terrible suffering under the Stalin regime. The book is a catalogue of anti–Communist views of the Soviets, but also a moving account of Noble's suffering at the hands of the abusive Stalinist government. Noble's father, for example, immediately sees a connection between the brutality of the Communists and the brutality of the Soviets going to the city officials in Dresden only to find "that the Communist officials, by and large, were simply Nazi officials with new armbands" (8). When Noble and his father take an injured man to a hospital run by the Soviets, they find the stereotypical drunk, looting, and raping Russians of the anti–Communist imagination (8–9).

Noble's suffering in the prison camps points to a horrible dehumanization that reduced humans to starving animals. Prisoners were convicted in mock trials: "If the person was innocent, the whip would pound and lash the desired 'guilt' into the person's back muscles, nerve fibers, mind, and consciousness" (33). When Noble and the other prisoners were transported from Germany to Russia, they were packed on shelves in the train "like sausages on a tray" (70). Once inside a Soviet camp, Noble finds himself in "a human jungle, smelly, overcrowded" (87). Noble's isolation was extreme as he did not speak Russian and was forced to engage in heavy manual labor on a daily diet of 1,400 calories. Noble comments that "I felt more and more like a primitive slave, my starving body pushing a two-ton car in an age of mechanization" (104).

As is typical in anti–Communists accounts, Noble discovers that most of the Soviets he encounters are hypocritical, not really Communists in any true sense. In describing the Communists he encountered in the Soviet camps, he mentions that "The Party was strictly a means to a career for them. Few had any idealistic concern with communism" (133). The director of the mine group at Vorkuta, a mining camp where Noble was imprisoned, walked the streets with his wife in expensive furs, but "called himself a 'true Communist'" (131).

I Was a Slave in Russia is representative anti–Communist propaganda from the Fifties, yet, it also reminds the reader that there were horrible, inhuman abuses that existed within the Soviet Union. Anti–Communism did not stem solely from Americans' imaginations.

Americans might well feel and express sympathy for the Soviet Union in regard to population losses of up to thirty million caused directly by the German invasion of 1941 and its extended aftermath. Neither United States nor British losses in the same cause even reached the million-person figure. However, a very large number of these Soviet deaths certainly resulted from Stalin's fanatical callousness, killings carried out probably out of a rigid but quite sincere commitment to his brand of Leninist Marxism. Unfortunately for his harassed forces, Stalin, as military commander in chief, learned his business on the job and, instead of being able to take into account sensible military considerations, often gave his orders at the beginning of the war as if he were dealing in his accustomed brutal way with domestic political enemies. It is true that in the end, being a relatively quick learner, Stalin did come to respect the ideas of his military experts and so the rate of losses to military personnel gradually dwindled; however, by that time the damage had been done.

All revolutions entail brutality, and, in spite of a tendency to turn Lenin in retrospect into a saint, he and his initial regime were brutal enough. Later, however, whether or not such was bound to have been the case with any Communist government, the Stalin regime gradually evolved into what must have been one of the most brutal regimes known to the history of the human race.

It seems as if Stalin felt he had to destroy anyone who had the slightest chance of ever opposing him, not simply those who really had been expressing open opposition to a point of policy, let alone actually organizing opposition. Up to the time of the Gorbachev regime, it was never fully revealed through official Soviet sources what kind of horrendous depredations the Stalin regime had perpetrated. Anti–Communist rhetoricians, of course, painted a consistently ugly picture of the state of affairs thought to exist in the Soviet Union and its satellites, but this, no matter how factually based, was propaganda — necessary propaganda, doubtless, but inevitably to a degree fanciful and all too full of categorical conclusions.

In 1988, in the waning years of the Gorbachev regime, Colonel General Dmitri Antonovich Volkogonov, then head of the Soviet Institute of Military History and a people's deputy in the Soviet Parliament, brought out his book *Stalin: Triumph and Tragedy*. He had worked in Stalin's immediate military entourage in World War II and seen many of the dictator's methods at first hand. His very detailed and carefully reasoned book does not blaze with the starry hyperbole of the convert. His assessment of all aspects of Stalin's life and political career is even-handed, accounting for the dictator's undoubted achievements even as he documents his works of grisly horror. Volkogonov's book and its successors deserve close reading from persons desiring to understand the period and its personalities better. No doubt the actual figures for Soviet internal casualties of Stalin's actions will gradually solidify; Volkogonov himself, a man who had access to the great majority of the necessary documents, was uncertain of the exact figures, but recognized that large-scale forced emigrations, prolonged and agonizing torturings, and callous deaths reached into many millions, these quite apart from the known military casualties.

At the time he wrote *Stalin: Triumph and Tragedy*, Volkogonov was still an official of what seemed to be a viable if radically changing Soviet Union, a country he supported, a county run by the reformer Gorbachev, whom he also supported. The general's revelations may have been in part written in order to give wide notice of what had happened in the past and what must not be repeated in the future. The book doesn't just generalize, does not just make a statement that unspeakable horrors emanated from the pen of the dictator and his cronies; it actually accounts in detail for lives and groups of lives first transformed through sufferings akin to those suffered by the inhabitants of Dante's Hell, then brutally squashed out through a combination of unspeakable tortures, physical and psychological.

Particularly horrifying and apparently illustrative of a typical undeserved fate is Volkogonov's description of the tragic end of Marshal Vasili Konstantinovich Blyukher, brutally tortured and killed on 9 November 1938 at the time of the great and nationally devastating military purge of that year. The marshal, one of the truly competent military commanders of the entire Soviet period, had been using his own initiative regarding the timing of air attacks in the current Soviet war against Japanese invaders. He had delayed ordering the attack planes to take-off because of bad weather, instead of carrying out command orders to the letter issued far away from the actual situation. Stalin, ever paranoid, recalled the marshal and shortly ordered him into the Lubianka meatgrinder, where he was savagely beaten and otherwise tortured day after day, hour after hour —finally succumbing, but without writing any kind of fake confession.

Members of the Communist party apparently accounted for the vast majority of the people who suffered and perished, but in Stalin's Soviet Union nobody was safe. The secret police arrived in the middle of the night and carried off people from all walks of life, with or without reason, either to be tortured then shot behind the ear or tortured and sent to join the millions in the great empire of forced-labor camps known as the Gulag, where many eventually perished through the very rigors of the monstrously harsh conditions.

Stalin had created five Soviet Marshals (five-star generals in American terms): two of them, Voroshilov and Budyonny, courageous enough, no doubt, but toadies to Stalin, and altogether too lacking in flexibility and initiative to be good generals in modern warfare; the other three, Blyukher, Tukhachevsky, and Yegorov, were well-trained and experienced military men with appropriate initiative. They were, however, loyal to Stalin and the Party, even though independent-minded enough when it came to strategy. Nevertheless, Hitler planted in Stalin's mind, through a rumor spread innocently enough by Eduard Benes of Czechoslovakia, the notion that these three men might seek to topple Stalin in a coup d'état. So, in 1938, without a shred of real evidence, these three men and thousands of other military officers thought to be possibly in sympathy with them were simply tortured and destroyed, thus, of course, as Hitler had wanted, leaving the Soviet armed forces at their hour of crisis in the hands of the untrained and untried as well as the completely incompetent. The story of the rise and fall of Marshal Tukhachevsky as outlined in Victor Alexandrov's book *The Tukhachevsky Affair*, despite its occasional inaccuracies, deserves reading as a salutary example of Stalin's thoroughly deceptive and despicable methods.

Stalin had his relatives, friends, and close colleagues killed on a whim and knew no mercy. His closest colleagues have been criticized for not having stopped him, but his was a bureaucratic tyranny and he had carefully woven his minions into structures in such a way that the slightest dissent on the part of one of them would have inevitably resulted in the others carrying out orders to destroy the dissenter. Consequently, when Stalin died, because, however willingly or unwillingly, his successors had been incriminated in his extra-legal actions, it was hard for them to blow the whistle on his actions without indicting themselves and endangering the continuation of the regime. Eventually, Khrushchev's Secret Speech started a gradually unfolding revelation of the full extent of the Stalin horrors. Gradually thereafter, the Gulag was dismantled and the Lubianka cellars quietened down, and, in the end, in spite of sporadic attempts on the part of the Brezhnev regime to rehabilitate the reputation of Stalin, the true dimensions of the previous horrors were made public by the Soviets themselves, and it came to be seen that in some respects the hyperbole of the Cold War anticommunists, even if on occasion inaccurate, probably for the most part erred in mildness.

Stalin's Soviet Union and the international Communist movement he headed seem to have been a many-limbed monster quite on a par with that of Hitler and very likely exceeded it in sheer awfulness.

Not all the motives of Cold War anticommunists were pristine pure, and some of their assertions were clearly inaccurate; nevertheless, Soviet Communism really was a diabolical monstrosity and a danger to the peace and prosperity of the rest of the world. The history of the Stalinist Communists should continue to give us all pause for thought.

Notes

Introduction

1. See Chapter Five in John Haynes' *Red Scare or Red Menace?* for a discussion of the different varieties of anti–Communism present in Cold War American life.

2. J. Laplanche and J.B. Pontalis define paranoia as "chronic psychosis characterized by more or less systematised delusion, with a predominance of ideas of reference but with no weakening of the intellect, and, generally speaking, no tendency towards deterioration" (296). In speaking of paranoia as a dominant feature of anti–Communist fictional worlds, I am, of course, discussing cultural paranoia, following Richard Hoftstadter's distinction in *Cold War America* between paranoia as a psychosis and as a cultural symptom.

3. Curtin links the common Cold War association between Fascism and Communism to Arthur Schlesinger Jr.'s concept of the vital center (47).

1. The Seduction of Communism

1. Robert L. Sandels argues that what Hammer seeks to do in Mickey Spillane's series of novels about the character is avoid women because he perceives them as a threat to his autonomy: "Hammer may easily fool the reader by his compulsive sexual banter into assuming that his adventures are chiefly in bed. In fact, he uses every excuse to avoid or to postpone sex" (353).

2. The majority of critics accuse Spillane of misogyny. For a sampling, see Tim Dayton, James Shokoff, Kay Weibel, Robert L. Sandels, and Tony Hilfer.

3. Almond makes a distinction between Communist affiliation in various countries. He argues that American and British Communists are largely motivated by rebellion against the norms of society, while French and Italian Communists display ideological commitment to the cause (243).

4. After a ten-year hiatus from Mike Hammer novels, Spillane published *The Girl Hunters* in 1962. In it, Spillane reveals that Velda had been an OSS agent during World War II and had during the past seven years been an agent "behind the Iron Curtain causing trouble for the Commies" (Collins and Traylor 88).

5. See also Jennifer Terry for a discussion of Momism and Communist infiltration.

6. Spillane exposes Lee Deamer, who is a McCarthy-type character, as a Communist who hides behind anti–Communist rhetoric to further the cause of the Soviet Union. As Collins and Traylor note, "The 'kicker' is that the figure in the novel representing a thinly disguised Joe McCarthy proves not only to be a murderer but a Communist agent" (19). The notion that McCarthyism conceals the real Communist threat is also played out in Richard Condon's novel *The Manchurian Candidate* (1959) and John Frankenheimer's film based on the novel (1962). See Chapter 12 of this book for a discussion of *The Manchurian Candidate*.

7. As Charles L.P. Silet notes, Spillane was attacked by critics who argued that the novels "promoted anti-social behavior through their excessive violence and sadistic treatment of women, homosexuals, and Communists. He was blamed for juvenile delinquency, increased sexual immorality, and the breakdown of other traditional values" (199).

8. Eric Smoodin argues that *Jet Pilot* uses the narrative of the typical Hollywood film to tell the audience that communism is "an impediment to typical narrative closure" (40). Thus, the pleasure we feel at the end of the film in seeing the couple reunited reminds us that "only American values can produce a happy ending" (40).

2. Paranoiac Discourse and Anti–Communism

1. J. Laplanche and J.B. Pontalis define paranoia as "chronic psychosis characterised by more or less systematised delusion, with a predominance of ideas of reference but with no weakening of the intellect, and generally speaking, no tendency towards deterioration" (296).

2. Ellen Schrecker paints the anti–Communist sentiment as one of paranoiac delusion: "It used all the power of the state to turn dissent into disloyalty and, in the process, drastically narrowed the spectrum of acceptable political debate" (*Many* x). Whereas, John E. Haynes comments that while anti–Communism was an important issue of the Cold War, "the notion that most Americans were so obsessed with domestic Communists that hysteria ruled the land for more than a decade, a notion found in some historical accounts, is myth" (189).

3. The figure of the messianic savior of mankind is a common motif in 1950s genre films, especially science-fiction films, as works such as *The Day the Earth Stood Still* (1951), *This Island Earth* (1954), and *Killers from Space* (1954) attest. See Hendershot's *Paranoia, the Bomb, and 1950s Science-Fiction Films*.

4. For discussions of the either/or fallacy as characteristic of paranoia, see Prado de Oliveira and Norman Cameron.

5. Wylie was a successful writer for women's magazines. His concept of Momism, expressed in an essay from his book *Generation of Vipers*, has made him notorious. See Chapter 1 of this book for further discussion of Wylie.

6. See, for example, Chapter 6 of this book.

7. Additionally, Peter R. Chadwick comments on a paranoiac patient who believed "women were coming into his room while he was asleep and having intercourse with him while his penis was erect during REM (rapid eye movement) sleep" (22).

8. *I Spy* ran from 1965 to 1968 on NBC. The series chronicled the adventures of two Pentagon agents who traveled the world on exotic adventures in the guise of being a world-class tennis player and his trainer. Kelly Robinson (Robert Culp) was the consummate tennis bum — a drinker, a smoker, a womanizer. He was born in Ohio, raised by a single mother, and joined the intelligence service early in life. In a job that could have hardened him, he was never at a loss for a quick witticism, and seemed always on the lookout for a good time.

Alexander Scott (Bill Cosby), or Scotty, was a Temple University graduate and a Rhodes Scholar. He didn't drink or smoke, and was endlessly dedicated to his mother and sister in Philadelphia. He was multi-lingual, and generally the more serious of the two— although he had quite a quick wit himself. This series had the distinction of being the first drama series on American television to cast a black man in a starring role, and was the series that launched Bill Cosby's acting career.

3. Internal and External Communism in Popular Film

1. In 1948, the FBI learned that Army intelligence had decoded 2,900 Soviet intelligence messages known as the Venona Documents. These documents listed 349 spies in the U.S., some of whom were high-ranking government officials. These documents were not made public until 1995, but at the time they justified the FBI view that "the Communist Party was a fifth column and spurred them on to destroy the party once and for all" (Schmidt 364–365). In 1997, Joseph Albright and Marcia Kunstel published *Bombshell*, an account of the life and career of Manhattan Project scientist Ted Hall, an American working as a Soviet agent. He passed information about the atomic bomb to the Soviets, crucial information that greatly cut down the time needed to complete the Soviet bomb project, reducing it perhaps by as much as ten years.

2. Herbert A. Philbrick unwittingly became involved with a Communist front organization in 1940 in Massachusetts. He took his information about the group to the FBI, which asked him to operate as a counterspy within the Communist Party. He fulfilled this role for nine years. In 1949, he broke cover to testify about eleven Communist leaders. All eleven were convicted. Philbrick subsequently became a public figure with the 1952 publication of *I Led Three Lives*. See Chapter 10 for a detailed discussion of his career.

3. For example, both *Red Planet Mars* (1952) and *Invasion USA* (1952) focus on the German threat as either part of or worse than the Soviet threat. See Chapter 5 for more detailed discussion of these films.

4. *One World or None* seeks to frighten its audience with the inevitable horrific outcome of atomic bombs if a world government is not formed and if nuclear weapons are not put under international control. Arthur Compton's introduction

to the collection sets up the "either-or" logic that lies behind the rhetorical strategies of the scientists' movement. Compton argues that either wars will be outlawed by international agreement or "catastrophic conflict" will result (v). The atomic scientists contributing to this collection characterize themselves as saviors, as the promoters of the peaceful atom, and portray the nation state as the demonic force that may bring about world destruction. The division of the world into heroes and villains characterizes the paranoiac worldview and this is also the view *One World* promotes. In his contribution to the volume, Niels Bohr predicts a nuclear holocaust that in its extremity will outstrip the imagination: "The grim realities being revealed to the world these days will no doubt, in the minds of many, revive the terrifying prospects forecast in fiction" (ix–x).

5. In recently declassified Soviet documents, Col. Gen. D.A. Volkogonov translates a memo from Stalin to Mao in which Stalin seems to accept the inevitability of world war: "Together we are stronger than the United States and England while the other capitalist states of Europe, excluding Germany, which is not able to render any sort of assistance to the U.S. at this time, do not add up to a serious military power. If war is inevitable, then let it be at the present time and not several years from now when Japanese militarism reestablishes itself and becomes an ally of the United States" (qtd. in Petrov 55).

4. The Individual Russian and the Communist System

1. Mindszenty opposed both Fascism and Communism. He was arrested in 1919 and 1944 for opposing totalitarian regimes. In 1945 he was made primate of Hungary; he became a cardinal in 1946. Because he opposed the closing of Hungary's Catholic Schools by the Communists, he was arrested in 1948 and convicted of treason. His sentence was life imprisonment, but he was released in 1956 during the Hungarian Revolution. When the revolution failed and the Communists regained control of Hungary, he sought asylum at the U.S. embassy in Budapest. He lived in the embassy for fifteen years. At the request of the Vatican, he settled in Vienna in 1971.

2. The film is based on a book entitled *As We See Russia*, a compilation of articles on the Soviet Union and the Communist bloc countries written by members of the Overseas Press Club of America. The book was published in 1948.

5. Anti–Communism and Ambivalence in Science Fiction

1. Peter Biskind argues that "[s]ci-fi films that presented Communists directly, like *Invasion U.S.A.* and *Red Planet Mars*, were rare. The analogy was usually oblique, but so close to the surface ... as to be just below the level of consciousness" (132).

2. Anti-Communist propaganda took various forms during the Cold War. While retrospective accounts of the era tend to emphasize the hysteria of Mc-

Carthyism, anti–Communist rhetoric was much more complicated and multi-layered that many of these retrospective accounts suggest. In his book *Not Without Honor: The History of American AntiCommunism*, Richard Gid Powers provides an in-depth analysis of the various forms of anti–Communist propaganda.

3. Many Cold War horror/sf films used the metaphor of dehumanization to convey evidence of the Soviet threat. Films such as *Invasion of the Body Snatchers* (1956), *Invaders from Mars* (1953), and *I Married a Monster from Outer Space* (1958) utilize this metaphor. Criticism on *Body Snatchers* indicates the pliability of the metaphor in the film: Anti-Communism, Anti-McCarthyism, and Anti-conformity are all labels that have been attached. For example, see Ernesto G. Laura for a mid-century article establishing a metaphorical link between body snatcher and Communist. See Le Gacy, Samuels, and Hoberman for analysis of the film's relation to the McCarthy Era and issues of conformity. Leonard Quart and Albert Auster label the film "an exaggerated version of Riesman's Lonely Crowd" (54).

4. See Chapter 10 for detailed discussion of Philbrick.

5. This view of women as scientifically informed, which dominates many 1950s science-fiction films, presents a stark contrast to the culture of secrecy that pervaded wartime scientific discovery. Women at wartime Los Alamos, even those scientifically informed like author Eleanor Jette, were kept ignorant of the scientific discoveries taking place there. See Eleanor Jette's account of her experiences at Los Alamos in *Inside Box 1660*. See also the accounts of other Los Alamos wives in *Reminiscences of Los Alamos*. Mark Jancovich notes one common aspect of many Fifties sf films was the "new breed of woman," the women concerned having qualities combining scientific knowledge with emotional nurturing (61).

6. Other Fifties sf films featuring women scientists include *The Thing* (1951), *It Came from Beneath the Sea* (1955), *This Island Earth* (1955), and *Earth vs. the Flying Saucers* (1956).

7. A typical association made in anti–Communist propaganda was between the homosexual and the Communist. The connection between criminal tendencies and transgressive sexuality was a commonplace of Cold War society. Harry Benshoff notes that the most visible link between homosexuality and criminality in the 1950s was the direct connection between Communism and homosexuality: "Homosexuality became directly connected to communism both in the popular press and in the public gestalt from February of 1950, when hearings before the Senate Appropriations Committee revealed that homosexuality had been the reason for recent dismissals of government workers" (130).

8. This collection consists of essays published between 1947 and 1954.

9. This is true not only of B films like *The Beast of Yucca Flats*, but also A films like John Frankenheimer's *The Manchurian Candidate* (1962). See Chapter 12 for a discussion of this film.

10. See Chapter 3 for further discussion of Korean POWs.

6. Criminals and Communists in Fifties Popular Culture

1. Philip L. Gianos notes in his study of Cold War films that "The bipolar stalemate that was at the heart of the cold war and the policy of containment that

underlay it drove an essentially defensive cultural mindset: the point was as much to defend the United States from internal adversaries as from external ones" (133–134). These adversaries converged in the underground criminal and the Communist spy, both of which spoke to weaknesses in the American system.

2. Silver and Ward note that the criminals "fight for their country even though they will remain in its gutter" (227). Thus, neither Candy, nor Skip, nor Moe will benefit financially from their fight against the Communists; their motives are purer than are the motives of the Communist spies, who expect financial reward for their treason.

3. Foster Hirsch notes that in *Pickup on South Street* "Fuller endows these people, who live on the margins of the city, with greater human dimension than is usual in *noir*" (133).

4. Hirsch comments that "Fuller has fashioned a punchy valentine to the big city underworld, with petty hoods and bag-lady informers stirred to their finest hour as they vanquish the communist threat" (133–34). Whitfield comments that in the film "the 'Commies' are *more* dangerous and *more* brutal than ordinary criminals, who at least adhere to their own code of honor" (135).

5. See also Jennifer Terry for a discussion of Momism and Communist infiltration.

6. Quart and Auster note that the documentary style of the film serves to "exalt the FBI and HUAC while condemning communists more for their character traits (they were criminals, idealistic dupes, nymphomaniacs, or disturbed fanatics) than for their ideology" (46).

7. As Larry May notes, in *Big Jim McClain* and other anti–Communist propaganda films of the Fifties, the threat of the spy was the closeness between him or her and normal society: "These films suggest that 'Reds' could number among one's old friends and their ideas could be part of one's former identity" (221).

7. Anti–Communism and Movie Serials

1. In 1935 Republic Pictures was created. It soon became the most popular and largest producer of serials until it stopped serial production in 1955 (Johnson 3).

2. Johnson argues that by the mid–1940s serials began to be plagued by "the scenarios becoming increasingly silly and lazy with each week" (5). Maybe this trend helps explains the cavalier attitude toward espionage and nuclear war that *Government Agents vs. Phantom Legion* takes.

3. Some of the most popular female-dominated serials were *The Perils of Pauline* and The *Exploits of Elaine*, both starring Pearl White. Buck Rainey comments of movie serial heroines that "In their own diminutive kingdom, their royalty was as real as that of the big-name and better-paid actresses at the prestige studios, and the faithfulness of their fans was often greater" (1).

8. Cold War Parody

1. *I Spy* ran from 1965 to 1968 on NBC. See Chapters 2 and 4 for discussion of the series.

2. A survey of the titles of the episodes makes this clear. A few addi[tional] examples include "Tequila Mockingbird," which puns the title of *To Ki[ll a Mock]ingbird* and parodies *The Maltese Falcon*; "Leadside," which through its title and main character parodies *Ironside*; "The Not-So-Great Escape," which parodies *The Great Escape, Stalag 17,* and *Hogan's Heroes*; "The Impossible Mission," which parodies *Mission Impossible*; "Run, Robot, Run," which in its title parodies John Updike's *Rabbit, Run,* while parodying *The Avengers* in its content.

3. Gunther was a *Daily News* correspondent who wrote a series of "Inside" books, such as *Inside Europe, Inside Asia,* and *Inside Africa*.

4. Mast notes that the Berlin of *One, Two, Three* is "slick, skyscrapered, and bureaucratized, retaining very little of its original German soul, capitulating completely to the dollar, the bomb, and Coca-Cola" (272).

5. Barton Byg comments that "Although Wilder treats Nazism and Communism as sources of humor, the latter always appears the more harmless of the two. Both the Cuban missile crisis and hidden Nazi pasts supply laughs in *One, Two, Three* (1961), for instance, but the Communists are seen as both guileless and easily seduced by consumer capitalism, while the Nazis remain part of the latter system yet continue to conceal their secrets" (185).

9. Nuclear Apocalypse and Anti–Communism

1. The episode was based on Judith Merrill's novel *Shadow on the Hearth*.

2. Although 1950 marked the year in which Truman gave scientists approval to go ahead with the hydrogen-bomb project, it was two years before such a bomb was created. Edward Teller and other U.S. scientists developed the first H-bomb and tested it at Eniwetok atoll (Nov. 1, 1952). The Soviet Union first tested an H-bomb in 1953.

3. Even as late as 1980, Joseph O. Hirshfelder, a scientist at the Manhattan Project, was still advocating the line of the scientists' movement: "We have reached the point where we can annihilate the world and make it uninhabitable by civilized people. This is not a sensible way of solving any disputes. We just cannot afford to have a nuclear war. There is no protection from nuclear warfare" (88).

4. The film represents a radical change by comparison with the Mickey Spillane's novel from which it was adapted, a novel that focuses on underworld drug trafficking. As Telotte comments, "While the Mickey Spillane novel on which it is based clearly focuses on a menace of a tangible criminal underworld ... the film substitutes an unnamed, apparently international, evil at work" (*Voices* 200).

5. R. Barton Palmer notes that "the film's Hammer is no longer much of a detective, but, apparently like everyone else in L.A., has become a hustler looking for a big score" (96).

6. Critics have commented on how the film highlights the failure of the traditional detective in the complex age of nuclear weapons. Peter Biskind comments on the significance of the film: "The age of the private eye has ended" (56). Telotte comments that "instead of taking over where the police have failed and sorting out the mystery they are unable to unravel, Hammer nearly botches the investigation and must have things sorted out for him" ("Fantastic" 12).

7. Carol Flinn argues that the woman's body becomes the meeting place for

"the fascination with film noir's femmes fatale" and "the fear of the A-bomb" (124).

8. Regarding the final scene, Palmer comments that "The flames intensify, and the film ends, apparently having recorded only the beginning of further nuclear destruction" (104). Telotte comments that "the film simply ends with this fantastic and apocalyptic imagery ... imagery which suggests the sort of destruction that could well be in store for our culture" ("Fantastic" 14).

10. Cold War Confessions and the FBI Plant

1. Post–Cold War declassification of documents has revealed that the countersubversive anti–Communists were at least partially correct. Comitern archives "have shown that the American Communists slavishly followed the directives from Moscow, that they from the very beginning to a large extent were financed by the Russians, and that the Communist Party maintained an underground apparatus for illegal activities" (Schmidt 361).

2. First-hand confessional accounts of experiences within the CP were popular in the 1950s, including those written by "reformed" Communists. Whittaker Chambers' *Witness* (1952) "became a national bestseller" (Halberstam 16). Elizabeth Bentley's memoirs *Out of Bondage* (1951) also met with popular success (Klingaman 24).

3. Joel Kovel's study of anti–Communist discourse argues that figures such as Hoover functioned rhetorically to protect the public from "the very breakdown of civilization" (88). Kovel links Hoover's anti–Communism to his sexual peculiarities, arguing that "as a result of [them] Hoover let an enormous amount of crime fester while he enthralled American with his mythic red hunting" (100).

4. One episode of the TV series *I Led Three Lives* directly addresses this issue. "The Secret Police" finds Philbrick stricken with conscience as he must give a negative report to the NKVD about a man whom he believes to be a misguided individual being duped by Communism. At the end of the episode, Philbrick discovers that the "misguided" man is really an NKVD plant who has been testing Philbrick's loyalty to the Party.

5. Leab points out that the firing of Cvetic did not come to light until 1991 (26).

6. The FBI disowned Cvetic, and refused to cooperate with the making of the film, surprising Warner Brothers: "The FBI — usually among the most cooperative of government agencies— made it clear that in regard to Cvetic and the movie 'it was too late to give any advice' and that the filmmakers 'could do what they wished'" (Leab 81). Further, Hoover sent memoirs to FBI branches making it clear that the FBI should deny any connection with the film (Leab 81).

7. Margot Henriksen argues that *I Was a Communist for the FBI* "leaves no room for the possibility that there may be real causes for protest in American society; in particular, it notes that there is no noncommunist motive for criticizing the workings of America's internal security bureaucracy" (70).

8. The duping of African-Americans by the Communist Party is a common feature of anti–Communist propaganda. See Chapter 3 of this book for further discussion of this issue.

9. As Leab relates, Cvetic's intense jealousy of Philbrick caused him to have several run-ins with the FBI, the result being that the FBI stopped Philbrick's editor from pursuing a book deal with Cvetic (116).

11. Anti-Communism and the Business World

1. The film was originally entitled *I Married a Communist*, but the title was changed when preview audiences reacted negatively to the sensational title.

2. *The Lonely Crowd* was a best-seller, selling more than a million copies by 1971 and 1.4 by 1995. That amount is twice the amount of any other sociology book written by an American or Canadian. Riesman's book was translated into fifteen languages, and he was the first sociologist to appear on the cover of *Time* magazine (Webster 66).

3. Granick was an economics professor who spent a month in the Soviet Union touring business and industry within the country.

4. In a similar book from 1957, *Inside Russia Today*, John Gunther blames the Soviet Union's lack of consumer goods on their own inefficiency: "Not enough consumer goods exist to go around partly at least because of waste, carelessness, and mismanagement" (373).

5. Granick recognizes that Soviets are limited in their ability to get good housing, a fact that causes him to remark that "In this respect, the Russian management family is somewhat in the position of the American upper-class Negro" (102).

12. The Bear and the Dragon: Representations of Communism in Early Sixties American Culture

1. The Doomsday Clock first appeared on the cover of the *Bulletin of the Atomic Scientists* in 1947. As Mike Moore notes, the clock "entered folklore as a symbol of nuclear peril and a constant warning that the leaders of the United States and Soviet Union had better sit up and fly right."

2. In the novel *Fail-Safe*, on which the film is based, fear of technological power gone awry is even more strongly emphasized. The malfunction that produces the error in recalling the troop cannot be detected by the men who constantly watch for technical error: "*It was a soundless event. There was a puff of smoke no larger than a walnut that was gone instantly*" (44).

3. The issue of abandoning manned bombers was paramount during the early Sixties. The Kennedy administration continued the trend of the Eisenhower period in eliminating manned bombers: "the primacy of the heavy manned bomber as the nation's main instrument of nuclear deterrence had come into question after the Korean war and finally ended in the Sixties" ("Global Pressures").

4. During the Cuban Missile Crisis, military leaders on both sides attempted to sabotage negotiations. Lemay in Washington and General Plyev, the Russian commander in Cuba, "affected indifference to the danger" ("Kennedy Tapes").

5. Margot A. Henriksen says of *Fail-Safe*, "Balanced against this nightmarish vision of the atomic age, however, is the limited scope of destruction and the unlimited prospect for change promised by the new sober and responsible leaders of America and the Soviet Union" (335). In the novel *Fail-Safe*, which was published in 1962, the authors make no attempt to disguise the leaders, clearly identifying them as Khrushchev and Kennedy.

6. Recently declassified documents have revealed Mao's ideological extremism. As Nigel Gould-Davis notes, "The Realist view is that Mao primarily sought the restoration of Chinese power and concluded an alliance with the Soviet Union only because the United States was hostile to Communism. It now emerges that Mao was in fact prepared to sacrifice Chinese state interests, which would surely have been furthered by U.S. recognition, in order to protect the latter. Security and ideology implied very different choices, and China chose the latter" (107). Whatever the reality of Chinese Communist ideology was, representations increasingly adopted Schwartz's view of an amoral, uncommitted China.

7. As Michael Rogin argues, popular culture of the Fifties frequently associated Communism "with secret, maternal influence" (9), a notion probably stemming from widespread awareness of Philip Wylie's concept of Momism. Rogin discusses how that concept influenced the character of Raymond's mother in *The Manchurian Candidate*.

Conclusion

1. Joel Kovel notes that in a 1988 survey of the American electorate the pollsters found that as "an identity, anti–Communism is virtually universal in America" (4). More people in this survey identified themselves as anti–Communist than as religious.

2. Haynes comments that "Communism aroused the hostility of people on the right, the center, and the left" (197).

3. Nearly two years in the making due to the maniacal tinkering by producer Howard Hughes, *Jet Pilot* was deemed unreleasable upon completion in 1951; only when Universal-International took over distribution of a handful of RKO Radio productions did it finally see the light of day in 1957.

Works Cited

"Address to the UN General Assembly, Sept. 23, 1960." *Modern History Sourcebook*. Online *http://www.fordham.edu* 25 Oct. 2001.

Albright, Joseph, and Marcia Kunstel. *Bombshell: The Secret Story of America's Unknown Atomic Spy Conspiracy*. New York: Times Books, 1997.

Alexandrov, Victor. *The Tukhachevsky Affair*. Trans. MacDonald and Co. Englewood Cliffs, NJ: Prentice-Hall, 1963.

Allen, Raymond B. "Communists Should Not Teach in American Colleges." *Educational Forum* 13.4 (May 1949): 1–7.

Almond, Gabriel A. *The Appeals of Communism*. Princeton: Princeton University Press, 1954.

"The Apes of Rath." *Get Smart*. Dir. Richard Benedict. Nov. 28, 1969.

"Atomic Attack." Dir. Ralph Nelson. *The Motorola TV Hour*. ABC, 1950.

The Atomic City. Dir. Jerry Hopper. Paramount, 1952.

Barson, Michael. *"Better Dead Than Red": A Nostalgic Look at the Golden Years of Russia Phobia, Red-Baiting, and Other Commie Madness*. New York: Hyperion, 1992.

The Beast of Yucca Flats. Dir. Coleman Francis. Crown International, 1961.

Benshoff, Harry M. *Monsters in the Closet: Homosexuality and the Horror Film*. Manchester: Manchester University Press, 1997.

Betheland, Faith, and Elisabeth Young-Bruehl. "Cherishment Culture." *American Imago* 55.4 (1998): 521–542.

"The Big Fear." *I Led Three Lives*. Dir. Henry S. Kesler. ZIV Productions, 1954.

Big Jim McClain. Dir. Edward Ludwig. Warner Bros., 1952.

Biskind, Peter. *Seeing Is Believing: How Hollywood Taught Us to Stop Worrying and Love the Fifties*. New York: Pantheon Books, 1983.

Bohr, Niels. "Forward: Science and Civilization." *One World or None*. Eds. Dexter Masters and Katherine Way. New York: McGraw-Hill, 1946. ix–x.

"Box Top Robbery." *Rocky and His Friends*. Dirs. Bill Hurz, et al. ABC, 1959.

Boyer, Paul. *By the Bomb's Early Light: American Thought and Culture at the Dawn of the Atomic Age*. New York: Pantheon, 1985.

Brians, Paul. "Red Holocaust: The Atomic Conquest of the West." *Extrapolation* 28.4 (1987): 319–29.

Bronfenbrenner, Urie. "The Mirror Image in Soviet-American Relations: A Social Psychologist's Report." *Journal of Social Issues* 17 (1961): 45–56.

Brooks, Peter. *Troubling Confessions: Speaking Guilt in Law and Literature.* Chicago: University of Chicago Press, 2000.

A Bullet for Joey. Dir. Lewis Allen. United Artists, 1955.

Burdick, Eugene, and Harvey Wheeler. *Fail-Safe.* 1962. Hopewell, NJ: Ecco Press, 1999.

Burke, James Wakefield. *The Big Rape.* New York: Popular Library, 1953.

Burnham, James. *The Web of Subversion: Underground Networks in the U.S. Government.* Boston: Americanist Library, 1954.

Byg, Barton. "Nazism as Femme Fatale: Recuperations of Cinematic Masculinity in Postwar Berlin." *Gender and Germanness: Cultural Productions of Nation.* Eds. Patricia Herminghouse and Magda Mueller. Providence: Berghahn Books, 1997. 176–188.

Cameron, N. "The Paranoid Pseudo-Community." *American Journal of Sociology* 49 (1943): 32–38

_____. "The Paranoid Pseudo-Community Revisited." *American Journal of Sociology* 64 (1959): 52–58.

"The Candidate." *I Led Three Lives.* Dir. Eddie Davis. ZIV Productions, 1953.

"Caviar." *I Led Three Lives.* Dir. Lambert Hillyer. ZIV Productions, 1953.

Chadwick, Peter K. *Borderline: A Psychological Study of Paranoia and Delusional Thinking.* New York: Routledge, 1992.

"Classification: Dead." *Get Smart.* Dir. Gary Nelson. December 23, 1967.

Collins, Max Allan, and James L. Traylor. *One Lonely Knight: Mickey Spillane's Mike Hammer.* Bowling Green, Ohio: Bowling Green State University Popular Press, 1984.

"Communist Camouflage and Deception." *Air University Quarterly Review* 6 (April 1953): 90–100.

Compton, Arthur. Introduction. *One World or None.* Eds. Dexter Masters and Katherine Way. New York: McGraw-Hill, 1946. v–vi.

Condon, Richard. *The Manchurian Candidate.* 1959. New York: Jove Books, 1988.

Conspirator. Dir. Victor Saville. MGM, 1949.

Corner, George M. *Attaining Manhood: A Doctor Talks to Boys About Sex.* 2nd ed. New York: Harper and Row, 1952.

Curtin, Michael. *Redeeming the Wasteland: Television Documentary and Cold War Politics.* New Brunswick, NJ: Rutgers University Press, 1995.

Cvetic, Matt. As Told to Pete Martin. "I Posed as a Communist for the FBI: Part One." *Saturday Evening Post* 15 July 1950: 17–19; 92–96.

_____. _____. "I Posed as a Communist for the FBI: Part Two." *Saturday Evening Post* 22 July 1950: 34–35; 50; 52–54.

_____. _____. "I Posed as a Communist for the FBI: Part Three." *Saturday Evening Post* 29 July 1950: 30; 99–100; 102.

Davis, Murray S. *What's So Funny? The Comic Conception of Culture and Society.* Chicago: University of Chicago Press, 1993.

"A Day Called 4 Jaguar." Dir. Richard C. Sarafian. *I Spy.* NBC. March 9, 1966.

"The Day They Raided Knights." *Get Smart.* Dir. Reza Badiyi. Jan. 11, 1968.

Dayton, Tim. "'The Annihilated Content of the Wish': Class and Gender in Mickey Spillane's *I, the Jury.*" *Clues* 14.1 (1993): 87–104.

Deane, Philip. *I Was a Captive in Korea.* New York: W.W. Norton, 1953.

De Oliveira, Prado. "Schreber, Ladies and Gentlemen." *Psychosis and Sexual Identity: Towards a Post-Analytic View of the Schreber Case*. Eds. David B. Allison, et al. Albany: State University of New York Press, 1988. 169–179.

"Die, Spy." *Get Smart*. Dir. Gary Nelson. March 30, 1968.

Dowling, D.H. "The Atomic Scientist: Machine or Moralist?" *Science-Fiction Studies* 13.2 (July 1986): 139–47.

Edelman, Murray. *Constructing the Political Spectacle*. Chicago: University of Chicago Press, 1988.

Ehrenreich, Barbara. *The Hearts of Men: American Dreams and the Flight from Commitment*. New York: Doubleday, 1983.

Fail-Safe. Dir. Sidney Lumet. Columbia, 1964.

Fautua, David T. "The 'Long Pull' Army: NSC 68, The Korean War, and the Creation of the Cold War U.S. Army." *The Journal of Military History* 61.1 (January 1997): 93–120.

The Fearmakers. Dir. Jacques Tourneur. United Artists, 1958.

Ferenczi, Sandor. *Sex in Psychoanalysis*. 1912. Trans. Ernest Jones. New York: Basic, 1950.

Feynman, Richard P. "Los Alamos from Below." *Reminiscences of Los Alamos*. Eds. Lawrence Badash, Joseph O. Hirshfelder, and Herbert P. Broida. Boston: Reidel, 1980. 105–32.

Flinn, Carol. "Sound, Woman and the Bomb: Dismembering the 'Great Whatsit' in *Kiss Me Deadly*." *Wide Angle* 8.3–4 (1986): 115–127.

Foreign Relations of the United States 1961–1963: Volume XI: Cuban Missile Crisis and Aftermath. General Editor David S. Patterson. Washington, DC: GPO, 1996. Online *http://www.state.gov* 5 Sept. 2000.

Foster, Dennis. *Confession and Complicity in Narrative*. Cambridge, England: Cambridge University Press, 1987.

Freedman, Carl. "Towards a Theory of Paranoia: The Science Fiction of Philip K. Dick." *Science-Fiction Studies* 11 (1984): 15–24.

Gianos, Phillip L. *Politics and Politicians in American Film*. Westport, CT: Praeger, 1998.

"Global Pressures and the Flexible Response." *American Military History*. General Editor Maurice Matlof. Washington: Center of Military History, 1985. Online. Electric Library. 3 Sept. 2000.

The God that Failed. Ed. Richard Crossman. New York: Harper and Row, 1949.

"Goof Gas Attack." *The Bullwinkle Show*. Dirs. Bill Hurtz, et al. NBC, 1961.

Gould-Davis, Nigel. "Rethinking the Role of Ideology in International Politics During the Cold War." *Journal of Cold War Studies* 1.1 (1999): 90–109.

Government Agents vs. Phantom Legion. Dir. Fred C. Brannon. Republic, 1951.

Granick, David. *The Red Executive: A Study of the Organization Man in Russian Industry*. New York: Doubleday, 1960.

"The Groovy Guru." *Get Smart*. Dir. James Komack. January 13, 1968.

Guilty of Treason. Dir. Felix Feist. Eagle-Lion, 1949.

Gunther, John. *Inside Russia Today*. New York: Harper and Brothers, 1957.

Halberstam, David. *The Fifties*. New York: Fawcett Columbine, 1993.

Haynes, John E. *Red Scare or Red Menace? American Communism and AntiCommunism in the Cold War Era*. Chicago: Ivan R. Dee, 1996

Hendershot, Cyndy. *Paranoia, the Bomb, and 1950s Science-Fiction Films*. Bowling Green, Ohio: Bowling Green State University Popular Press, 1999.

Henriksen, Margot A. *Dr. Strangelove's America: Society and Culture in the Atomic Age*. Berkeley: University of California Press, 1997.

Hilfer, Tony. *The Crime Novel: A Deviant Genre*. Austin: University of Texas Press, 1990.

Hirsch, Foster. *The Dark Side of the Screen: Film Noir*. New York: A.S. Barnes, 1981.

Hirshfelder, Joseph O. "The Scientific and Technological Miracle at Los Alamos." *Reminiscences of Los Alamos*. Eds. Lawrence Badash, Joseph O. Hirshfelder, and Herbert P. Broida. Boston: Reidel, 1980. 67–88.

Hoberman, J. "Paranoia and the Pod People." *Sight and Sound* 4.5 (May 1994): 28–31.

Hofstaedter, Richard. "The Paranoid Style in American Politics." *The Paranoid Style in American Politics and Other Essays*. New York: Knopf, 1966. 3–40.

Hook, Sidney. "Heresy, Yes—Conspiracy, No." *New York Times Magazine* 9 July 1950: 12; 38–39. Rpt. in *The Age of McCarthyism: A Brief History with Documents*. By Ellen Schrecker. New York: Bedford Books, 1994. 235–242.

Hoover, J. Edgar. *J. Edgar Hoover on Communism*. New York: Random House, 1969.

_____. *Masters of Deceit: The Story of Communism in America and How to Fight It*. New York: Pocket Books, 1958.

_____. "Testimony Before HUAC, March 26, 1947." *The Age of McCarthyism: A Brief History with Documents*. By Ellen Schrecker. Boston: Bedford Books, 1994. 114–120.

"The Hot Line." *Get Smart*. Dir. Gary Nelson. March 23, 1968.

"The Hundred Days of the Dragon." Dir. Byron Haskin. *The Outer Limits*. 1963.

Hutcheon, Linda. *A Theory of Parody: The Teachings of Twentieth-Century Art Forms*. New York: Methuen, 1985.

I Was a Communist for the FBI. Dir. Gordon Douglas. Warner Bros., 1951.

"The Impossible Mission." *Get Smart*. Dir. Bruce Bilson. Sept. 21, 1968.

Invasion USA. Dir. Alfred E. Green. American Pictures Company, 1952.

"It's All Done with Mirrors." Dir. Robert Butler. *I Spy*. NBC. 13 April 1966.

Jancovich, Mark. *Rational Fears: American Horror in the 1950s*. Manchester: Manchester University Press, 1996.

Jervis, Robert. "Was the Cold War a Security Dilemma?" *Journal of Cold War Studies* 3.1 (2001): 36–60.

Jet Pilot. Dir. Josef von Sternberg. RKO, 1957.

Jette, Eleanor. *Inside Box 1660*. Los Alamos, NM: Los Alamos Historical Society, 1977.

Johnson, Gary. "The Serials: An Introduction." *Images* 4 (July 1997): 1–5.

Kefauver, Estes. *Crime in America*. Garden City, NY: Doubleday, 1951.

_____. Foreword. *Barbarians in Our Midst: A History of Chicago Crime and Politics*. By Virgil W. Peterson. Boston: Little, Brown, 1952. ix–x.

Kennedy, John F. "Ich Bin ein Berliner." Debate Information Center. Online. Available: http://www.debateinfo.com/hall_of_fame/speeches.jfk.html 08/06/00.

"The Kennedy Tapes: Inside the White House During the Cuban Missile Crisis." *New Statesman* 24 Oct. 1996. Online. Electric Library 3 Sept. 2000.

Kinkead, Eugene. *In Every War but One*. New York: W.W. Norton, 1959.

Kiss Me Deadly. Dir. Robert Aldrich. United Artists, 1955.

Klingaman, William K. *Encyclopedia of the McCarthy Era.* New York: Facts on File, 1996.

Kovel, Joel. *Red Hunting in the Promised Land: AntiCommunism and the Making of America.* London: Cassell, 1997.

Landay, Lori. "Millions 'Love Lucy': Commodification and the Lucy Phenomenon." *National Women's Studies Association Journal* 11.2 (1999): 25–47.

Langmuir, Irving. "An Atomic Arms Race and Its Alternatives." *One World or None.* Eds. Dexter Masters and Katherine Way. New York: McGraw-Hill, 1946. 47–52.

Laplanche, J. and J.B. Pontalis. *The Language of Psychoanalysis.* Trans. Donald Nicholson-Smith. New York: Norton, 1973.

Latham, Rob. "Subterranean Suburbia: Underneath the Small Town Myth in the Two Versions of *Invaders from Mars.*" *Science-Fiction Studies* 22.2 (July 1995): 198–208.

Laura, Ernesto G. "Invasion of the Body Snatchers." *Focus on the Science Fiction Film.* 1957. Ed. William Johnson. Englewood Cliffs, NJ: Prentice-Hall, 1972. 71–73.

Leab, Dan. *I Was a Communist for the FBI: The Unhappy Life and Times of Matt Cvetic.* University Park: Pennsylvania State University Press, 2000.

"Leadside." *Get Smart.* Dir. Gary Nelson. March 9, 1969.

Lee, Kun Ho. "The Character of the Invader." Trans. Hugh Heung-We Cynn. *The Reds Take a City: The Communist Occupation of Seoul with Eyewitness Accounts.* By John W. Riley, Jr. and Wilber Schramm. New Brunswick, NJ: Rutgers University Press, 1951. 46–64.

Le Gacy, Arthur. "*Invasion of the Body Snatchers*: A Metaphor for the Fifties." *Literature/Film Quarterly* 1 (1978): 285–92.

Levine, Irving R. *Main Street, U.S.S.R.* New York: Signet, 1960.

Lifton, Robert Jay, and Greg Mitchell. *Hiroshima in America: Fifty Years of Denial.* New York: Putnam, 1995.

Maltby, Richard. "Made for Each Other: The Melodrama of Hollywood and the House Committee on Un-American Activities, 1947." *Cinema, Politics and Society in America.* Philip Davies and Brian Neve, eds. Manchester: Manchester University Press, 1981.

The Manchurian Candidate. Dir. John Frankenheimer. United Artists, 1962.

Mantley, John. *The 27th Day.* 1956. New York: Crest, 1958.

Mast, Gerald. *The Comic Mind: Comedy and the Movies.* 2nd ed. Chicago: University of Chicago Press, 1979.

May, Elaine Tyler. "Explosive Issues: Sex, Women, and the Bomb." *Recasting America: Culture and Politics in the Age of the Cold War.* Ed. Lary May. Chicago: University of Chicago Press, 1989. 154–70.

May, Lary. *The Big Tomorrow: Hollywood and the Politics of the American Way.* Chicago: University of Chicago Press, 2000.

McClay, Wilfred. "Fifty Years of the Lonely Crowd." *The Wilson Quarterly* 22.3 (Summer 1998): 34–42.

Meyerowitz, Joanne. "Beyond the Feminine Mystique: A Reassessment of Postwar Mass Culture, 1946–1958." *Journal of American History* 79.4 (March 1993): 1455–1482.

Moore, Mike. "Midnight Never Came (How the Clock on the Cover of the *Bulletin of the Atomic Scientists* Represented Nuclear Tensions)." *Bulletin of the Atomic Scientists* 21 Nov. 1995. Online. Electric Library. 3 Sept. 2000.

Moore, William Howard. *The Kefauver Committee and the Politics of Crime: 1950–1952.* Columbia: University of Missouri Press, 1974.

Mumford, Lewis. *In the Name of Sanity.* New York: Harcourt, Brace, 1954.

"The Mysterious Dr. T." *Get Smart.* Dir. Gary Nelson. December 30, 1967.

Noble, John. *I Was a Slave in Russia.* New York: Devin-Adair Company, 1958.

"The Not-So-Great Escape." *Get Smart.* Dir. Don Adams. March 15 and 22, 1969.

O'Brien, Chris. "It's a Bird. It's a Plane. It's a … Bomb? Commies, Crime, and Comics, 1945–1962." *Mid-Atlantic Almanak* 7 (1998): 89–100.

"One, Two, Three." *Variety.* 1 Jan 1961. Online. *http://www.variety.com.* 23 Oct. 2001.

One, Two, Three. Dir. Billy Wilder. United Artists, 1961.

Overstreet, Harry, and Bonaro Overstreet. *What We Must Know About Communism.* 1958. New York: Pocket Books, 1960.

Palmer, R. Barton. *Hollywood's Dark Cinema: The American Film Noir.* New York: Twayne, 1994.

Petrov, Vladimir. "Soviet Role in the Korean War Confirmed: Secret Documents Declassified." *Journal of Northeast Asian Studies* 13 (Fall 1994): 42–67.

"Pheasant Under Glass." *Get Smart.* Dir. Don Adams. Sept. 26, 1969.

Philbrick, Herbert A. *I Led Three Lives: Citizen, Communist, Counterspy.* 1952. Washington, DC: Capitol Hill Press, 1973.

Pickup on South Street. Dir. Samuel Fuller. 20th Century–Fox, 1953.

Pietz, William. "The 'Post-Colonialism' of Cold War Discourse." *Social Text* (1988): 55–75.

Powers, Richard Gid. *Not Without Honor: The History of American AntiCommunism.* New Haven: Yale University Press, 1995.

Quart, Leonard, and Albert Auster. *American Film and Society since 1945.* 2nd ed. New York: Praeger, 1991.

Rainey, Buck. *Those Fabulous Serial Heroines: Their Lives and Films.* Metuchen, NJ: Scarecrow Press, 1990.

"Red Chinese Battleplan." Department of Defense, 1964.

The Red Menace. Dir. R.G. Springsteen. Republic, 1949.

The Red Myth: A History of Communism from Marx to Khrushchev. Stanford University, 1962.

Red Nightmare. Dir. George Waggner. Warner Bros., 1962.

Red Planet Mars. Dir. Harry Horner. United Artists, 1952.

Reminiscences of Los Alamos. Ed. Lawrence Badash, et al. Boston: D. Reidel, 1980.

Riesman, David. *The Lonely Crowd: A Study of the Changing American Character.* New Haven: Yale University Press, 1950.

Riley, John W., Jr., and Wilber Schramm. "Surveillance and Penalties." *The Reds Take a City: The Communist Occupation of Seoul with Eyewitness Accounts.* New Brunswick, NJ: Rutgers University Press, 1951. 138–148.

Rogin, Michael. "Kiss Me Deadly: Communism, Motherhood, and Cold War Movies." *Representations* 6 (Spring 1984): 1–36.

"Run, Robot, Run." *Get Smart.* Dir. Bruce Bilson. March 16, 1968.

The Russians Are Coming! The Russians Are Coming! Dir. Norman Jewison. United Artists,1966.

Samuels, Stuart. "The Age of Conspiracy and Conformity: *Invasion of the Body Snatchers.*" *American History/American Film: Interpreting the Hollywood Image.* Eds. John E. O'Connor and Martin A. Jackson. New York: Frederick Ungar, 1979. 203–17.

Sandels, Robert L. "The Battle of the Sexes." *The Armchair Detective* 20.4 (1987): 350–358.

Sayre, Nora. *Running Time: Films of the Cold War*. New York: Dial Press, 1982.

Schmidt, Regin. *Red Scare: FBI and The Origins of AntiCommunism in The United States, 1919–1943*. Copenhagen: Museum Tusculanum Press, 2000.

Schrecker, Ellen. *The Age of McCarthyism: A Brief History with Documents*. Boston: Bedford Books, 1994.

_____. *Many Are the Crimes: McCarthyism in America*. Boston: Little, Brown, 1998.

Schwartz, Benjamin I. *Chinese Communism and the Rise of Mao*. Cambridge, MA: Harvard University Press, 1951.

Schwartz, Fred. *You Can Trust the Communists (...to Do Exactly As They Say!)*. Englewood Cliffs, NJ: Prentice-Hall, 1960.

"The Secret Police." *I Led Three Lives*. Dir. Eddie Davis. ZIV Productions, 1953.

Seed, David. *American Science Fiction and the Cold War*. Edinburgh: Edinburgh University Press, 1999.

Segal, Hanna M. "Paranoid Anxiety and Paranoia." *Paranoia: New Psychoanalytic Perspectives*. Eds. Stanley Oldham and Stanley Bone. Madison, CT: International University Press, 1994. 17–26.

de Seversky, Major Alexander P. "Atomic Bomb Hysteria." *Reader's Digest* January 1946: 121–26.

Shattuck, Roger. *Forbidden Knowledge: From Prometheus to Pornography*. New York: St. Martin's, 1996.

"Shock it To Me." *Get Smart*. Dir. Jay Sandrich. March 1, 1969.

Shokoff, James. "The Feminine Ideal in the Masculine Private Eye." *Clues* 14.2 (1993): 51–62.

Silet, Charles L.P. "The First Angry White Male: Mickey Spillane's Mike Hammer." *The Armchair Detective* 29.2 (1996): 195–99.

Skousen, W. Cleon. *The Naked Communist*. 1958. Salt Lake City, Utah: Ensign Publishing Company, 1961.

Smoodin, Eric. "Watching the Skies: Hollywood, the 1950s and the Soviet Threat." *Journal of American Culture* 11.2 (1988): 35–40.

Sontag, Susan. "The Imagination of Disaster." *Against Interpretation and Other Essays*. New York: Farrar, Straus, and Giroux, 1966. 209–225.

Spillane, Mickey. *One Lonely Night*. New York: Signet, 1951.

"Spy, Spy, Birdie." *Get Smart*. Dir. James Komack. March 9, 1968.

Stedman, Raymond William. *The Serials: Suspense and Drama by Installment*. Norman: University of Oklahoma Press, 1971.

The Steel Helmet. Dir. Samuel Fuller. Lippert Pictures, 1951.

Stevenson, Adlai E. *Friends and Enemies: What I Learned in Russia*. New York: Harper and Brothers Publishers, 1958.

Stone, I.F. *The Haunted Fifties*. Boston: Little, Brown, 1963.

Stouffer, Samuel A. *Communism, Conformity, and Civil Liberties: A Cross-Section of The Nation Speaks Its Mind*. New York: Garden City, 1955.

Sullivan, Harry Stack. *The Interpersonal Theory of Psychiatry*. Eds. Helen Swick Perry and Mary Ladd Gawel. New York: W.W. Norton, 1953.

"Ted Hall Speaks." Bombshell Atomic Espionage Website. Online. *http://www.bombshell-1.com/tedstm.htm* 7 March 2001.

Teglas, Csaba. *Budapest Exit*. College Station: Texas A&M University Press, 1998.

Telotte, J.P. "The Fantastic Realism of Film Noir: *Kiss Me Deadly.*" *Wide Angle* 13.1 (January 1992): 4–18.

_____. *Voices in the Dark: The Narrative Patterns of Film Noir.* Urbana: University of Illinois Press, 1989.

"Tequila Mockingbird." *Get Smart.* Dir. Jay Sandrich. January 18, 1969.

Terry, Jennifer. "'Momism' and the Making of Treasonous Homosexuals." *"Bad" Mothers: The Politics of Blame in Twentieth-Century America.* Eds. Molly Ladd-Taylor and Lauri Umansky. New York: New York University Press, 1998. 169–90.

"The Treasure of Monte Zoom." *The Bullwinkle Show.* Dir. Bill Hurtz, et al. NBC, 1961.

The 27th Day. Dir. William Asher. Columbia, 1957.

Volkogonov, Dmitri. *Stalin: Triumph and Tragedy.* Ed. And Trans. Harold Shukman. New York: Grove Weidenfeld, 1988.

Watson, Mary Ann. *The Expanding Vista: American Television in the Kennedy Years.* New York: Oxford University Press, 1990.

Webster, David S. "David Riesman: American Scholar." *Society* (May/June 1999): 62–66.

Weibel, Kay. "Mickey Spillane as Fifties Phenomenon." *Dimensions of Detective Fiction.* Eds. Larry N. Landrum, Pat Browne, and Ray B. Browne. Bowling Green, Ohio: Popular Press, 1976. 114–123.

The Whip Hand. Dir. William Cameron Menzies. RKO, 1951.

Whitfield, Stephen J. *The Culture of the Cold War,* 2nd ed. Baltimore: Johns Hopkins University Press, 1996.

Whyte, William, Jr. *The Organization Man.* New York: Simon and Schuster, 1956.

Wolfson, Adam. "Individualism: New and Old." *The Public Interest.* 15 January 1997.

The Woman on Pier 13. Dir. Robert Stevenson. RKO, 1949.

Wubben, H.H. "American Prisoners of War in Korea: A Second Look at the 'Something New in History' Theme." *American Quarterly* 22.1 (Spring 1970): 3–19.

Wylie, Philip. "The Crime of Mickey Spillane." *Good Housekeeping* Feb. 1955: 54–55, 207–209.

_____. *Generation of Vipers.* 1942. New York: Rinehart, 1955.

_____. *The Smuggled Atom Bomb.* 1951. New York: Lancer Books, 1965.

Zinn, Howard. *A People's History of the United States, 1492–Present.* New York: Harper-Collins, 1980.

Index

(1) countersubversive anti-communism

(2) popular culture "thrived on presentations of a paranoic view of the Communist threat."

(6) "Popular culture was instrumental in keeping Americans continually terrified by the Communist threat" — but also showed absurdity of the Cold War

(130) <u>Invasion USA</u> (1950s)

(4) <u>Red Nightmare</u> (1962)

(130) China dislodges Russia as most evil in early 1960s — and thaw is US-USSR relations